C

The
RESTLESS
JOURNEY
of
JAMES AGEE

Geneviève Moreau

The
RESTLESS
JOURNEY
of
JAMES AGEE

Translated from the French by Miriam Kleiger
with the assistance of Morty Schiff

WILLIAM MORROW AND COMPANY, INC.
New York   1977

Grateful acknowledgment is made for permission to quote from the following:

Lines from selected poems in COLLECTED POEMS (including "Permit Me Voyage") by James Agee. Copyright © 1962, 1968 by the James Agee Trust. Reprinted by permission of Houghton Mifflin Company and Calder and Boyars Ltd. Twenty-six lines from page 143 in "Now as Awareness," and fifteen lines from pp. 93-94 in "They That Sow Shall Reap," in COLLECTED SHORT PROSE by James Agee. Copyright © 1968, 1969 by the James Agee Trust. Copyright © 1968 by Robert Fitzgerald. Reprinted by permission of Houghton Mifflin Company and Calder and Boyars Ltd., London. Six lines from page 152 and sixty-five words from page 409 in LET US NOW PRAISE FAMOUS MEN by Walker Evans and James Agee. Copyright © 1960 by Walker Evans. Copyright © Renewed 1969 by Mia Fritsch Agee. Reprinted by permission of Houghton Mifflin Company and Peter Owen Ltd., London. Excerpts from LETTERS TO FATHER FLYE by James Agee. Copyright © 1971 by James Harold Flye. Copyright © 1962 by James Harold Flye and the James Agee Trust. Reprinted by permission of Houghton Mifflin Company and Peter Owen Ltd., London. Six lines from pp. 37-38 and six lines from pp. 296-297 in AGEE ON FILM, Volume I, by James Agee. Copyright © 1958 by the James Agee Trust. Reprinted by permission of Grosset & Dunlap, Inc. and Peter Owen Ltd., London. Three lines from page 3 of A DEATH IN THE FAMILY by James Agee. Copyright © 1957 by the James Agee Trust. Reprinted by permission of Grosset & Dunlap and Peter Owen Ltd., London.

Printed in the United States of America.

1   2   3   4   5   6   7   8   9   10

Library of Congress Cataloging in Publication Data

Moreau, Geneviève.
   The restless journey of James Agee.

   Bibliography: p.
   Includes index.
   1. Agee, James, 1909-1955. I. Title.
PS3501.G35Z786   813'.5'2 [B]   76-25832
ISBN 0-688-03141-2

BOOK DESIGN   CARL WEISS

CONTENTS

FOREWORD

I FIRST THOUGHT OF UNDERTAKING THIS PROJECT DURING A STAY
in the United States in 1963, following a conversation with the
head of the English Department at Wellesley College. At that time
I was aware of Agee only as the author of one book, *A Death in the
Family,* which had won him a certain posthumous reputation, and
an article, "Six Days at Sea," published in *Fortune.* But gradually
I came to discover his other works: his early writings, which appeared in university or other literary magazines; poems; articles;
a strange narrative born of his journalistic research in the South;
book and movie reviews; screenplays; his novels; his correspondence.

In order to judge the import of Agee's work I had to find out first
the extent of it. After much research, which led me from the libraries of Harvard and the Phillips Exeter Academy to the archives
of *Time* and *Fortune,* the bibliography was completed. Then I
reconstructed Agee's life, his writings serving as guideposts. Initially, the course I had to follow was geographic: Knoxville and
Saint Andrew's, Exeter, Cambridge, New York, New Jersey and

the West Coast. My research was made possible by the coopera-
tion of numerous correspondents—parents, friends or relatives of
Agee—who were willing to share their recollections with me or
to trust me with letters and documents. From all these accounts
arose a composite image whose elements were often contradictory
and included enthusiastic portraits as well as reserved, cautious or
even quite critical judgments. All my informants seemed to agree
on the exceptional qualities of Agee's personality; many disagreed
on his merits as a writer and an artist.

Was Agee a great writer? How can we explain the small success his work had during his lifetime, the disproportionate cult
that grew up around him after his death? Can we predict the place
he will occupy in American culture? This book does not claim to
give definitive answers. More time will have to elapse before the
man and his work can be judged objectively, before they can find
their rightful place in American literary history of the thirties and
forties. My goal has been rather to shed light on the life and work
of James Agee, to disengage his life from the legend surrounding
it and to make his works more accessible by introducing the reader
to writings that are too widely scattered, or have been long out
of print, or never published, as well as to Agee's more familiar
works.

Now the collections of Agee's prose and poems edited by Robert
Fitzgerald have made most of the unpublished material available.
The University of Texas Library, which holds some of Agee's unpublished manuscripts and had for many years granted access to
those papers only to students and staff from its faculty, is now extending permission to all Agee scholars.

I should like to express my gratitude to all those who, by their
advice, recollections or opinions, the letters and documents they
showed me, the sympathy and material aid they brought to my
research, made this study possible.

I am particularly grateful to Professor Asselineau, who agreed
to supervise this project, and to Robert Fitzgerald, one of Agee's

friends, who took a continuing interest in the progress of my research.

During two of my visits to the United States, in 1962 and 1964, I received a friendly welcome and unreserved assistance from those who had known Agee: Mrs. Laura Wright, his mother; Olivia Saunders (Mrs. Wood); Alma Usha; Mia Agee; Father Flye; John H. Stroop, who knew Saint Andrew's well; David McDowell, a former student at Saint Andrew's, who was both a friend and editor of Agee's; Professor W. M. Frohock; Dwight Macdonald; Robert Saudek; Howard Doughty; Lincoln Kirstein; Mrs. Ellery Sedgwick, who knew Agee at Harvard during the thirties and again in New York; Archibald MacLeish and Walker Evans, who were with him at *Fortune;* Harvey Breit, Alice S. Morris, James Stern, Nigel Dennis, T. S. Matthews, Mr. and Mrs. John K. Jessup, Wilder Hobson, who worked for *Time* at the same time Agee did; Selden Rodman, Helen Levitt, Gladys Lea, Manny Farber, Mary Newman, his friends; Paul Brooks, Lillian Hellman, Howard Taubman, Margaret Marshall, B. H. Haggin, Louis de Rochemont, who knew him or worked with him during the years 1930–1940; John Simon, friend and critic of Agee. Without their help this book would never have been written. I would also like to thank the librarians and archivists who went to considerable trouble to facilitate my work in the libraries of Wellesley College, Harvard (Widener Library, Houghton Library, Archives), Exeter (Phillips Exeter Academy Library), Yale, New York City (New York Public Library, Museum of Modern Art Film Library), and the University Library of Los Angeles, which gave me information about several screenplays. In addition, I am indebted to those who guided my researches in the offices of Houghton Mifflin (Boston) and Peter Owen (London) and in the archives of *Fortune* and *Time*.

I should also like to thank Helena Harap-Dodd, who supplied me with initial bibliographical material, Dr. and Mrs. Bryer, who considerably facilitated my work at Exeter, and Isabel Barzun, who agreed to supervise the preparation of the translation for the American publisher.

I wish to express my special indebtedness to Morty Schiff. This book has benefited much from the careful scrutiny he has brought to the manuscript, the various suggestions he has made for the final editing of the French version and his improvement of the translation. Without his help and encouragement, this study on Agee would probably never have been published.

INTRODUCTION

THE PURPOSE OF THE WORK THAT FOLLOWS IS TO PRESENT BOTH
a biographical study of James Agee and an examination of his
work, exploring the complex relationship between the man and
the writer. Agee's life and his work seem inseparable. They cast
light on each other not only because his writings are in part autobiographical—although the autobiography may be either straight-
forward or disguised—but because they were at the heart of their
author's existence.

One must not look for an actual biography in these pages: Such
a work cannot be written until more time has elapsed and distance
permits more perspective and objectivity. Nevertheless, I have
tried to recreate the atmosphere in which Agee lived his life, to
describe its important moments and to discover the factors that
determined his vocation and that kept him from fulfilling himself
completely. This study does not claim to reconstruct his entire personality or his daily life. Although I collected numerous documents
and personal reminiscences, it would be presumptuous of me to
hope to produce a complete portrait of Agee, one that would do
justice to the multifaceted image that remains in the minds of

those who knew him. Anecdotal material is introduced only when it illuminates an interesting or outstanding aspect of his personality. Accordingly, I was selective in my use of the many documents I had collected.

Agee's life had to be studied partly in a historical perspective. I tried to describe different milieus, to demonstrate certain decisive influences—readings, encounters, landscapes, art—and to define his relationship to the various realities with which he found himself involved: the South, the Depression, journalism and the movies. But if I linger over certain descriptions, it is not only to depict Agee's environment but also to rediscover the physical, intellectual or emotional material that constituted the artist's personal universe and from which he drew the major themes of his work.

Agee himself was often the principal source of information, and it was revealing to compare other people's opinions of him to the scrutiny he brought to bear on himself. Introspective by nature and by taste, almost unhealthily subjective, accustomed since childhood to the examination of conscience, Agee left behind numerous self-analyses—portraits or confessions that were both complacent and pitiless—thereby contributing to the creation of his own myth. Obsessed by the idea that each life is dominated by a destiny, he sought to discover which destiny characterized his own existence, and by doing so, he gave a pattern to it. These self-portraits should be used with caution. Agee, consciously or not, practiced self-deception and could not discipline himself to achieve the lucid analysis he sought. Therefore the image he gave us of himself and his life is sometimes distorted. But these personal confidences shed a good deal of light, probably in ways that Agee was unaware of, on some elements one also finds in his literary works. The same dilemmas and obsessions, the same necessities and conflicts permeate both his life and his work; the emotional, ideological, moral or artistic problems he speaks of in his correspondence appear again in his writings, which were, in a way, attempts to devise a solution for them.

With this approach, striving for an intimate knowledge of the writer, I sought to treat Agee not as an object but as a subject, and to recreate, from within, his experiences. In this way one becomes aware of the currents of his inner life, its oscillations between exaltation and apathy, faith and doubt, rebellion and resignation, joy and despair. I gave considerable attention to both the deeper structure of his personality and to the emotionality that sometimes nourished his creative imagination. My goal was to reconstruct his inner adventure, to rediscover his conscious personality and the dynamism of his unconscious mind. The creation of his work was considered in relation to the gradual development of his life.

Agee himself invites the critic to draw such a parallelism. Written events appear as though they were actually lived and reality sometimes very much as though it were fiction. Boundaries between life and work, which some writers manage to preserve, are thus very often blurred in a sort of fusion, or confusion. Dispersion, obsessions, nostalgic quest, failure, creativity command both Agee's writing and his lived existence, the one sometimes carrying toward completion what the other left unaccomplished.

In a study of Agee, who was haunted by works "in progress," projects take on a particular importance. Accordingly, each major work has been examined both at the moment of its inception and in its later stages. A work that has been followed in its earliest form and presented as a special subject because of its particular significance in the author's life is also examined as an object, as it appeared to the reader and the critic. It is thereby possible to compare the result with the original intention—sometimes they coincide, sometimes there is a disparity that calls for explanation. The work appears alternately as a failed or incomplete attempt, sometimes as an accomplishment in which the author's intentions and a multiplicity of influences unite.

My method varied; at times I simply described the work and its contents, and at times I undertook to offer a more critical analysis. In the latter case I uncovered the themes or the underlying structures in a single work, or in several works that seemed to be interrelated, and studied the orientation of the work with respect to the literary milieu and the relationship of literature to all that is separate from it, social life or other forms of art or means of communication that transform it or subject it to question, journalistic experience, music or film.

The analyses that are proposed are merely outlined, for they exceed the scope of this study. These varied inquiries into the work constantly turn one's attention back to the writer.

The intention of this book is to follow the progress of Agee's inner life and to retrace the intimate history of a vocation and an activity that sought—sincerely and obstinately—to be creative.

"Root clenches root, dust into hard earth blends."
—"EPITHALAMIUM," *Collected Poems,* 33

*"I know I am making the choice most dangerous
to an artist, in valuing life above art."*
—JAMES AGEE

The
RESTLESS
JOURNEY
of
JAMES AGEE

PART I

PROLOGUE

ROOTS

"I have been fashioned on a chain
of flesh." (*C.P.*, 38)

Those who have gone before, backward beyond remembrance and
beyond the beginning of imagination, backward among the emergent
beasts, and the blind, prescient ravenings of the youngest sea, those
children of the sun, I mean, who brought forth those, who wove,
spread the human net, and who brought forth me; they are fallen
backward into their graves like blown wheat and are folded under the
earth like babies in blankets, and they are all melted upon the mute
enduring world like leaves, like wet snow; they are faint in the
urgencies of my small being as stars at noon; they people the silence
in my soul like bats in a cave; they live in their time as I live now,
each a universe within which, for a while, to die was inconceivable,
and their living was as bright and brief as sparks on a chimney wall,
and now they lie dead as I soon shall die; my ancestors, my veterans.
I call upon you, I invoke your help, you cannot answer, you cannot
help; I desire to do you honor, you are beyond the last humiliation.
You are my fathers and my mothers but there is no way in which you
can help me, nor may I serve you soon; meanwhile may I bear you
ever in the piety of my heart.[1]

Such was the prayer that James Agee addressed to his fore-
bears, the family that generation after generation recreated the

eternal mystery of life and death, spreading out its net over diverse nations and civilizations. Agee resurrected his ancestors from their distant ages and lands in order to weave, from the epic of their lives, the family legend that became one of the myths of his own existence.

In himself Agee saw merged the disparate threads of his father's and mother's patrimonies:

> In France, in Germany, in England, in Scotland, in Ireland, and in Virginia, and in the territory which was to become West Virginia, in the mountains of an untamed land which became Tennessee, my paternal family.[2]

Matthieu Agee, the first of his family of Huguenots to emigrate to America, came to Virginia at the beginning of the colonial period. He had received as a dowry, upon his marriage to Secily Hall, 3,200 acres of land near Richmond. Later the Agees moved west to Tennessee, where they became one of the original farming families in that region. In the eastern part of the state a village was named after its schoolmaster, Henry Agee, a distant forebear of Agee's father. Many of the Agees, in fact, studied education, medicine or law, and since they were moderately well-to-do and by tradition Republicans, they often were involved in the government of the young country. But each generation of Agees also had its share of farmers who lived either in the backwoods near Knoxville or at La Follette, where Agee's grandparents had their farm.

> In the west of England, in Scotland, in Ireland, in Massachusetts, New Hampshire, Vermont, the state of New York, Michigan, Tennessee where my own life began: my maternal family.[3]

Laura Whitman Tyler, Agee's mother, came from a more varied background than her husband's. On her mother's side she was descended from a Margrave who had emigrated to America after the Hessian Revolution and whose family eventually split into two branches—the Farrands, who lived in Connecticut and New Jersey, and the Whitmans, who lived in Weymouth, Massachusetts. On her paternal side she included among her ancestors Edward Rawson, who had settled in New England during the seventeenth century and had served as secretary of the Massachusetts Bay Colony for more than thirty years. Both Rawson and his wife were descended from Elizabeth Grindal, sister of Edmond Grindal, Bishop of Canterbury during the reign of Elizabeth I. From the East Coast the family roots were transplanted to Michigan, where Agee's grandparents, Joel Tyler and his wife, settled. Both attended the University of Michigan, where Mrs. Tyler earned the distinction of being the first woman university graduate. But Joel Tyler, who suffered from frequent bouts of flu, was urged to try the milder climate of the South; counting on the impending construction of the railroad in that area to provide him with an income, he bought a piece of woodland in the Smoky Mountains of Tennessee. But since the railroad did not go through until many years later, the project failed, and he subsequently went into partnership with an Englishman, with whom he managed a factory for the production of millstones. It was in Tennessee that the two branches of Agee's family—the Agees and the Tylers—met.

Hugh James Agee, Agee's father, first met Laura Tyler in Knoxville, where he worked at the post office. They were eventually married in Panama after Hugh had been sent there for his work. The young couple lived in Central America for two years until an epidemic of malaria forced them to return home. Their son, James Rufus Agee, was born in the Knoxville hospital on November 27, 1909.

The historical and geographical crossroads at which Agee's life begins point to how much his existence would be, spiritually as well as physically, a continuation of the lives of his ancestors. They had come to America from distant parts of the globe and had lived out their lives in obscurity or fame. Chance and fate brought Agee's parents together in Knoxville. The dead had bequeathed Agee a rich past that he would later recreate in his imagination; the living offered him their lives as vividly articulated initiates of innocence and experience. Agee's personality was profoundly shaped by an early reverence for these people, and the memories he kept from those early years came later to dominate his artistic concerns.

Reflecting later on the history of these two families, Agee recognized the contradictions that permeated his personality and his life. He had become the focal point of his twofold heritage, and he learned to see himself in this double perspective, geographically, socially and spiritually. On the one hand, he belonged to a bourgeois, refined and sheltered world that was both academic and artistic. On the other, he descended from the proud hills people who led a harsh and isolated life in the mountains of Tennessee. These two poles, at once opposed and complementary, suspended between them all the innumerable facets of the single personality that was the product of two inherited, disparate cultures. And, whether Agee chose to be rebellious or acquiescent, he was only pledging his intellectual allegiance to one heritage rather than to the other. Even at an early age he began to develop a form of dialectic that would later govern the rhythm of his life and of his writing. During his early years, however, the two poles, which he later chose to emphasize, even exaggerate, blended into a fairly harmonious childhood universe.

CHAPTER ONE

KNOXVILLE 1915: LONGINGS AND
DECEPTIONS OF CHILDHOOD

"How far we all come. How far we all come away from ourselves. . . . You can never go home again." (*A Death in the Family,* 76)

KNOXVILLE, AGEE'S CHILDHOOD HOME AND THE CITY TO WHICH he remained romantically attached throughout his life, was founded at the end of the eighteenth century and enjoyed several years of glory as the first major settlement in eastern Tennessee. The city subsequently became the administrative center of the state and a strategic outpost in the continuing war against the Indians. By the beginning of the twentieth century, however, Knoxville no longer dominated any specific region. It had not developed with the passage of time but remained drowsing in its past, content to bask in the ephemeral glory it had known. In spite of the lack of modernization and a gradually dwindling population, it still attempted to sustain its university and to foster from its proud site on the hillside the pretensions of an administrative capital. All the same it never achieved the wealth or aristocratic refinement of Nashville and Memphis, both cities having long since usurped Knoxville's position of power. Thus, its rough physical appearance, reflecting on its surface the generations of workmen and mountain folk who had lived there, remained unchanged into the early twentieth century.

Knoxville had two faces, as Agee later described it: [1] the trivial facade of a "typically American" city, "the erstwhile 28th most murderous city . . . in the U.S.," juxtaposed with the more romantic, old-fashioned mode of life epitomized by "the fine soft slur of speech in the streets, the still goodly number of Model T Fords, and the few deciduous Southern mansions with their 'hitching posts' and the 'niggertowns' with their clay beaten down by bare heels, and the whitewashed clapboard shacks and the old predilection of the valley men for lawing." [2] There, from time to time, one might even run into a gentleman of the old school, who "quotes Horace, talks horses, and holds his part of the country to be the greatest battlefield next to Virginia." [3] Agee claimed proudly that Knoxville was situated in one of the most beautiful, somber, cruel and wild regions of the United States. The hills people, the hillbillies, lived not far away on isolated farms that clung to the steep mountain slopes; after more than a century, they still spoke an Elizabethan dialect, cherished the traditions of their ancestors and, singing their songs of England and the sea, remained sturdy individualists.

The middle-class neighborhood that Hugh and Laura Agee lived in bordered the undeveloped outskirts of the city. It was a nondescript quarter sprinkled with washed-out billboards and smoke-darkened taverns frequented by blacks or by a motley group of white vagabonds and workingmen. Beyond that sparsely settled area "a flea-bitten semi-rurality" extended, among "mean little homes, and others inexplicably new and substantial" (*D.F.*, 44). Further on, the road stretched its length out with nothing more than rubbish and ramshackle cabins on either side. Into this disquieting but fascinating neighborhood Rufus (as a child Agee was always called by his middle name) made incursions first with his father and later with his schoolfriends. These exploratory strolls are recreated on certain pages of *A Death in the Family*.

Highland Avenue, where the Agees made their home, was by contrast an almost elegant thoroughfare, lined with modest late-nineteenth-century houses that were enhanced by verandas and surrounded by trees and lawns. The unassuming but respectable middle-class inhabitants of this quiet street lived in neighborly fashion. Rufus' earliest memories go back to this peaceful setting. Within this circumscribed universe he gradually learned to perceive life through his senses—to know various sounds, to tell the time of the day by the brilliance or softness of the light, to recognize the "strong green-black smear of smell" that belonged to grass, to distinguish the strident whistling of the grasshopper from the regular chant of the cricket. These impressions—evoked in the prelude to *A Death in the Family*, "Knoxville: Summer, 1915"—were associated with moments of mysterious happiness. And on summer evenings, when at a certain hour everyone gathered on the porch or the lawn under the friendly stars, the atmosphere overflowed with a peace and contentment tinged with melancholy. Specific sounds were associated with these evenings: the lingering noises of the city that the child kept on hearing late into the night through the open window, the footsteps of passersby, the cartwheels and horseshoes on the pavement, the creak of a rocking chair or the soft and familiar murmurings "like the voices of sleeping birds" (*D.F.*, 7-8).

It was on the lawns where everyone lolled during the summer evenings that Agee claims he shaped one of the earliest images of his father—that of a strong, handsome man in the unusual light, wearing a white, open-necked shirt, watering the lawn with a hose, as were all the other fathers on neighboring lawns. It was a relatively nameless image but one that associated the power and virility of the father with the sound of the streaming water. On Highland Avenue life, following certain rituals, unfolded placidly within the confines of the house, the lawn and the porch. The spirit of domesticity was characterized by the repetition of unassuming and simple gestures; it was a sheltered, muted existence in whose softness the stars themselves seemed almost to participate. Cradled in this atmosphere of familiar voices and lulled by the steady hum of watering hoses and of crickets, Rufus had nevertheless begun to dream of a more rugged existence. He sensed the promise of adventure in the adjoining countryside beyond the railroad tracks, where he occasionally walked with his father to watch for an approaching train and breathe the acrid smoke of the engines. For both father and son the tracks disappearing in the distance conjured up a feeling of restlessness, an urge to escape. Highland Avenue ran along a chain of hills below which a large valley extended. The valley was crossed by the railroad and strewn with factories and train stations whose "stained glass . . . smoldered like an exhausted butterfly" (*D.F.,* 17). Farther north the first spurs of the Cumberland Mountains rose up and, since the locomotives made constant switches in the valley to change direction, they could often hear an engine "cough and browse," its empty cars sounding like "broken drums." [4] Riding on the train, Rufus caught his first sight of the mist-shrouded Smokies: "On the sky above the scrubby hill, there was a grand lift of graying blue that looked as though you could see the light through it, and then the train took a long curve and these liftings of gray blue opened out like a fan and filled the whole country ahead" (*D.F.,* 243). It was as though for Rufus all the world—of space and of time—was discoverable from a train, the window past which the landscape magically sped, foreshadowing the movie screen he would later love so much and write so well about. The train that connected Knoxville and the back country also provided the link between the city and the legendary mountains of his ancestors, between the places of his present, everyday existence and the places of the glorious past. The majestic and blue-tinged mountains too fleetingly glimpsed from the train were the far-off homeland that both he and his father had adopted. Agee later retained lingering memories of those "solemn deep scoops of shady blue," and he vaguely sensed deeper ties with the back country than its lavish beauty alone could have inspired. And the rugged hillbillies who lived there came to attract him more than the placid middle-class neighbors of Highland Avenue.

The urban, rustic and mountain landscapes that so shaped Agee's sensibility were peopled for him with the faces of those who looked after him in his childhood. Agee has provided only short portraits of his paternal grandparents in his writings, perhaps because, though he made frequent visits to La Follette, he did not know them well. Matthew Agee, tall, handsome and endowed with a splendid black moustache, was a weak-spirited man, but his dependable good nature allowed people to accept him and love him just as he was. He profited unconsciously from a charm that operated on everyone at all times, and perhaps only his daughter-in-law Laura, Rufus' mother, permitted herself to judge him and to hold him responsible for some of the weaknesses she found in her own husband. From his paternal grandfather Agee seems to have inherited, in addition to his strong love of the land and of the country people, both his physical charm and, like his father before him, a certain weakness of character.

Rufus spent most of his childhood not in La Follette but in the more sophisticated city of Knoxville, where his maternal grandparents lived. Since the Tyler home was not far from Highland Avenue, Rufus came to know his mother's family rather intimately. Joel Tyler was an intelligent and cultivated man, an "individualist by conviction," an independent soul who was unwilling to be beholden to anyone. He was deeply attached to his grandson, whose intelligence and open-mindedness he admired, and Rufus in turn listened attentively to his grandfather. If at first he did not fully understand the long conversations they had together, at least he was exposed at an early age to a broad vocabulary as well as to abstract and philosophical forms of thought. Agee liked to think that he had adopted his grandfather's skepticism, a feeling of anxiety together with a genuine desire to allay that anxiety with faith; although, like his grandfather, he too eventually discovered the impossibility of reconciling that faith with reason. In the eyes of both his deeply religious daughter and his wife Joel Tyler was an atheist, but judging from the words Agee later attributes to him in *A Death in the Family,* he was more of an agnostic. He remained nostalgic about a religion that could not satisfy him and only reluctantly placed his faith in reason. Annoyed by the piety that reigned in his home in spite of him, he gave in to irony and sarcasm and became an accomplished blasphemer.

His son Hugh—Agee's uncle, who also inspired one of the characters in *A Death in the Family*—shared this skepticism but was even more intransigent than his father. He was endowed with a subtle mind, an extremely sensitive nature and an artist's temperament. A poet in his youth, he later became a painter; Hugh Tyler offered his nephew the living example of an artist whose vocation was to transcribe the beauty he perceived around him.[5]

For Mrs. Tyler, Rufus had a special affection, a tender though sometimes amused respect for her qualities: her aristocratic manners, her discretion and self-effacement, her sustained calm, her consideration for other people and her artistic sense and musical talent. Perhaps the fondness she inspired in Rufus grew partly out of his sympathy for her suffering, for she was extremely hard of hearing. It was in her case an ironic twist of fate since she was an excellent pianist and a talented singer. In music, though, she continued to find spiritual compensation for the daily frustration of her life. As a young child Rufus spent a great deal of time with his grandmother. It was as though he wished to make up for her isolation with the joy he knew his presence provided her. Later he watched her infirmities increase as, growing old, she finally went blind as well as totally deaf. He witnessed her suffering, her hovering at the point of death; perhaps it was remembering the agony of this once gay and spirited woman that made him hope to die young rather than live on as an invalid.

Laura Tyler had married James Agee somewhat against her parents' wishes, his situation seeming too unstable to them and his family not of the same social background. And although they remained deeply in love throughout their lives, their marriage was beset with many unhappy moments. In *A Death in the Family,* Rufus' mother is portrayed as a tidy, prudish and very puritanical woman, easily upset by her husband's rough manners and love of drink and strongly disapproving of his tastes and pleasures. It is interesting to note in the novel how much of the parents' life as a couple Agee depicts in adversarial terms. In order to work out his own dialectical relation to each parent, Agee elected to emphasize his father's and mother's worlds as opposite and antagonistic. And he chose to epitomize their various conflicts by staging them on one particular battlefield, religion. Laura Agee was a devout Episcopalian whose faith meant much more to her than regular church attendance. She instituted certain household rituals—the saying of prayers and grace, the formal examination of conscience and the strict adherence to biblical law. Rufus, deeply marked by his mother's rigid principles, became early obsessed with a sense of sin. But, jealous of the invisible God who ruled his mother's life, he also rebelled against having to lead an existence governed by prohibitions and commandments. Religion, though, gradually became identified with the feminine sphere of activity: It seemed the privilege of women. Men were either sublimely indifferent to it, like his father, or fiercely hostile, like his uncle and grandfather. Rufus sensed that these men had united for self-preservation in the overly religious atmosphere of the women's parlor. He too, would later act to detach himself from his mother's world of softness and tenderness, of prayers and remorse, of reticence and resignation, and of cotton-soft voices and muffled steps.

In contrast to his mother's tame and restricted universe, his father's world appeared triumphantly free and boundless. H. James Agee belonged to the splendid, virile brotherhood who valued independence and freedom above all else, for whom laughter was never stifled, pleasure never sinful. For Rufus, his father's rugged, violent world was associated with the mountain folk of Tennessee: the direct sensuous connections were with the mingled odors of smoke, dry grass, salt and leather; the tastes of beer, tobacco and whiskey; the vertiginous sensations of speed and giddiness; but most of all the physical "appearance" of his father, the rough fabric of his clothing, the big powerful body with the large veined hands, the nape of the neck "dark tan with crisscross cracks all over the back of it" (*D.F.*, 81). To the child it was a world of energy and defiance, and it sometimes also radiated a sort of brutal humor, heavy with menace and risk.

Caught between two universes that often clashed with each other, Rufus was increasingly drawn toward the masculine universe. He became aware of a certain dissatisfaction within his father, a thirst for liberty and solitude. The same disenchantment was scarcely born in Rufus at the time, but later impelled him toward rebellion: child and father spontaneously became conspirators, and the occasions for finding themselves alone together multiplied.

The evolution of their complicity is symbolically evoked in *A Death in the Family* as the stages of a long walk through Knoxville. Jay, the father, takes his son to see a Charlie Chaplin film; during one of the high burlesque scenes that used to horrify his mother, Rufus for the first time joins in his father's laughter. Their alliance is thus sealed. Starting home on foot at an hour when pedestrians are rare and when, in the growing darkness, faces are more mysterious, Jay takes his son to a bar, a second stage in the initiation of the child into a forbidden world. They pause ritually on the viaduct in order to inhale the smoke of a locomotive and watch for the signal of the next train, and later near a rock under the "tranquil and transparent" leaves of Forest Avenue, where the child deeply senses his father's loneliness. But they are both uplifted by the immense well-being they feel in being together, in their mutual dependence—all wordlessly experienced. The pause by the road on the outskirts of the city consecrates the alliance between father and son. It also links their happiness to a particular place and to a set of shared sensations—the light wind in their hair, the silent boughs, the friendly darkness. The physical presence of his father fills Rufus with delicious overwhelming sensations, which for an instant cause him to experience the fullness and stability of the world.

Beneath this happiness, which to Rufus Agee seemed to have

been granted to him more abundantly than to most children, a latent anxiety was already perceptible. With a child's premonition he guessed that this state would not last. He also began to sense how fragile the relation between his parents was. He was disturbed now to see how his father rebelled against everything he seemed previously to have tacitly accepted. Finally, Rufus became aware of his own loneliness.

A growing anxiety about his own nature manifested itself in a primitive, instinctive and uncontrollable fear, which Agee repeatedly evokes in *A Death in the Family* (*D.F.*, 66-67). A trivial occurrence was enough to transform Rufus' familiar world into a nightmare. Darkness, at times an alluring though ominous friend whose every secret Rufus longed to know, could at other times terrify him to the core of his being. Out of the darkness one night death bends over the child smiling, with a fanged and jagged mouth. Unable to control his fear, the child screams for his father and the understanding he had with the darkness is abruptly betrayed.

Life thus presented two faces to the young Agee. Every image of joy had its twin image of anguish; every happiness seemed strangely fragile and transitory; sadness marred the most perfect joy; a vague foreboding of unknown tragedy permeated everything. Agee sensed the duality of experience before he was fully conscious of it. A pampered child, he already had an acute sense of solitude, and his childhood reflected the double nature that he later saw in life.

But duality also meant duplicity, illusion. The child is not only the one deceived but may himself be the playful or serious deceiver. The idea of deception was an early obsession with Agee—the reciprocal deceptions of the world as it offers itself to him and of himself as he presents himself to the world. In Agee's mind the child is sustained in his illusions by hiding from himself.[6] As a writer Agee later returned to the images of happiness that his childhood evoked, but as a child he aspired to a less confined and harsher world. Deceptions aside, he looked for experiences that would reveal him to himself, free him from his uncertainties, help him understand the contradictions he saw and unveil for him the secrets of the universe.

It was not within his family, with its promise of a self-congratulatory happiness, that Rufus found what he was seeking. His father had given him a first taste of a world of adventure and challenge; he later rediscovered this world with other children in the streets of Knoxville, in the outskirts of town and in school.

Having reached the age where he was allowed to play unsupervised with his fellows in the street, Rufus became part of a fascinating though bewildering universe. Envy, curiosity, fear and respect motivated his first overtures toward the "big boys" whose rejection of him only increased his desire to become one of them. Accustomed to gentle and affectionate words, he found himself for the first time the butt of teasing and cruel pranks. Agee liked to emphasize that Rufus was a "nigger name" and the fact inspired many jokes at his expense—("Uh-Rufus, Uh-Rastus, Uh-Johnson, Uh-Brown, Uh-What you gonna do when the rent comes roun'?")—which were not unlike the verbal games played on street corners by local black boys.

School was as well a long-awaited emancipation. When Agee entered the little school in Knoxville he believed that he was finally gaining access to the real world, but it was a world he had not fully anticipated. He realized immediately that he was different from the other children. He became aware of the emotional, intellectual and material privileges he had enjoyed. A charitable visit in a donkey cart to a settlement of mill workers with a friend of his mother's created the same kind of shock: For the first time the young Agee witnessed a degree of destitution that he never could have imagined. He immediately began to take his shoes off to give them to the children who surrounded him, without understanding that his gesture carried a measure of insult.[7] After meeting at school children from very modest backgrounds, he became indignant at their poverty and at the relative luxury in which he had lived. Guilt festered in him, and he began to detest the well-clothed and well-nourished child he was. Many years later, when he discovered the condition of the tenant farmers of Alabama, he again found himself powerless before the misery of others.

Thus, on the eve of the event that was to upset his life, Rufus Agee was both timid and daring, naively confident and easily troubled. Impulsively compassionate and indignant, he was in the process of rebelling against his sheltered childhood. He was intensely impatient to live and he eagerly awaited a new life that he could claim as his own. Astonished to discover so many ambiguities and contradictions around him, he suspected that he was himself living under false pretenses, a person as skillfully hidden from himself as others were from him.

CHAPTER TWO

BEREAVEMENT AND BETRAYAL

"Death never swoops us round with
sudden black . . ." (*C.P.,* 129)

RUFUS AGEE'S IMPATIENCE FOR NEW EXPERIENCES WAS MET
one day with unforeseeable brutality. His father, H. James Agee,
was killed in the prime of life in an automobile accident on the
sixteenth day of May, 1916. Thirty years later, in writing *A Death
in the Family,* Agee recreated most of the circumstances of his
father's death, describing them as they appear to the book's six-
year-old hero, Rufus. Behind the disguise "God let him go to sleep
and took him right away with Him to heaven," behind the detours
and euphemisms of the grownups' language, the little boy searches
for the truth, and the first idea of the meaning of death comes
through a multitude of sense impressions. The child investigates
the familiar objects that had belonged to his father and that might
hold a clue to death's secret. He examines the armchair where
there remains only "a cold smell of tobacco and . . . a faint smell
of hair" (*D.F.,* 212). He runs his finger along the inside of an
empty ashtray and licks it sensing only a taste of darkness.

Later at the mortuary Rufus sees the body of his father, to whom he is allowed to say good-bye: He observes the immobility, the stiffness and the air of complete indifference that cut the corpse off from all living creatures. For him the body becomes an image of strength, of self-completeness, immutable and indestructible. Rufus' last impression of his father, before the lid is placed on the coffin, disconcerts him, however. "His face looked more remote than before and much more ordinary and it was as if he were tired or bored. He did not look as big as he really was" (*D.F.*, 231-232). The child, overcome by the heavy odor of the masses of flowers, gives him the preoccupied attention one would give a picture. With the arrival of relatives and friends, the crowd of mourners, their "vitality . . . so many-souled and pervasive," no more intimacy is possible with the dead man. When the men lift the coffin the child feels a last stirring of pride noticing how heavy his father seems to be. Rufus thus experiences ambivalent feelings toward his father's death. It is impossible for him to admit that anything could extinguish his father's strength. On the other hand, this mysterious thing that had happened completes the glorious image he has of his father; it was possibly the most beautiful death one could imagine for such a man—he had met it with his customary boldness, refusing to retreat or compromise. Although his drinking and fast driving habits made him a likely victim to a tragic end, he was also a man who knew no fear, who doubled his intrepidity in the face of danger; to die was for him a gesture of defiance.

James Agee's death became a mystic event. His son would later regard all deaths in this light and would even foresee his own passing in these exalted terms, realizing with respect, as the young hero Rufus does, "that it was more creditable to get killed than just to die" (*D.F.*, 205). The images that Agee retained from this event pervade most of his writing, to be reworked in terms of a fall from innocence, of a first contact with a world of violence and tragedy, betraying the comfortable delusions of childhood.

Having lost his father, the child Agee would now have to assert and defend himself to prove that he was a fitting son. Death had made its entrance into his universe and his mythology, and he associated it with images of strength, courage and defiance that he now hoped to adopt as the laws of his existence. He longed to bury the slightly delicate and fearful child he had been. Burning to assert his manhood, he would accomplish the various stages of his liberation as though in homage to the memory of his father. He would henceforth see his own existence in the light of his father's, an existence made up of achievements and failures, of audacious confrontations alternating with flight. It remained to Agee the writer to reconstruct in poetic terms the myths revealed to him at this early stage of his life: those of an innocent condition of history and of humanity followed by a condition of exile and betrayal.

> Tears are the touchers of that secret earth
> No alien rains attend; be therefore tears;
> Grieve and your holy land accords you mirth
> Pity brings wrens of the most batflight fears.
> *(C.P., 63)*

The loss that had caused such upheaval in Rufus Agee's life was nevertheless soon partially forgotten. For a time the intensity of his grief gave way to a strange quietude. Agee found himself under the guardianship of his mother, drawn back in spite of himself into the feminine and religious web he had hoped to escape. In the meantime this second stage of his childhood took him from the luminous clarity of Knoxville nights to the shadows of the cloisters of Saint Andrew's, from the moist odor of recently mowed lawns to the smell of incense in an Episcopalian chapel.

CHAPTER THREE

THE EDUCATION OF THE PRINCE

"He must strike down his father's cedar shadow
Sever his mother's terrible and sorrowing mouth . . .
He must make the dark journey into the hollowing sea." (*C.P.*, 65)

UNTIL THEIR FATHER'S DEATH RUFUS AND HIS YOUNGER SISTER, Emma, had spent their vacations in Knoxville, making occasional trips to La Follette. When her father-in-law, Matthew Agee, died only a couple of months after her husband,[1] Laura Agee decided to rent a small house near Sewanee, at Saint Andrew's, Tennessee, for the summer of 1918. With its reputedly healthy climate, its isolation from the city and its proximity to an Episcopalian community, the town provided the perfect place for a religious retreat. The following year Mrs. Agee returned to Saint Andrew's and decided to make her home there permanently. She would pass her time doing some charity work, and light chores for income. Rufus began studies with the brothers, and Emma, still too young to go to school, lived with her mother in a house that was put at their disposal by the community. The family remained at Saint Andrew's until 1925.[2]

Saint Andrew's was located in the center of the Cumberland

Plateau in the southern portion of the Appalachians. The region had scarcely been touched by the westward march of civilization, and its isolation favored the establishment of a monastery. To get to Saint Andrew's, one had to get off the Nashville-Chattanooga train at Cowan, take the train for Sewanee and disembark at the request stop of "Gipson Switch." Situated on the main road from Memphis to Chattanooga, Sewanee was the nearest large settlement and, as it happened, the site of a university. Otherwise, Saint Andrew's was not accessible except by furrowed dirt roads that only tractors could travel safely.

The population of the mountains was very stable. The ancient races of the Anglo-Saxon pioneers who had settled there two centuries earlier were still recognizable in the men who lived there. They were austere, brave and loyal men with solid virtues and combative spirits. They also possessed the qualities of sensitivity and gentleness that Agee had already related to in the farmers of La Follette.

The school of Saint Andrew's had been founded in 1906 by the Order of the Holy Cross, an Anglican monastic order. Its purpose was to educate the children of poor farmers; fees for room, board and tuition were to be paid in produce. Even so, Saint Andrew's at the outset attracted only three students and had difficulty finding more. Whenever there was too much work to be done on the farm the children would be taken out of school for a few months. When there was insufficient work they were sent to the city to find a job to help support the family.

Saint Andrew's itself was established on the site of an old farm, and the quarters were rudimentary at first. Students and teachers alike took part in the construction. Certain tasks—cutting trees or clearing ground—were assigned to students as punishment or as healthy recreation. The children received an education appropriate to the agricultural or manual work they would return to after their stay at the school. The more gifted were offered a more extensive program, but it was above all a religious school. Although neither students nor teachers were required to belong to the Anglican

Church, the daily routine was monastic. After early rising came religious services. The hours of classes, meals, scholastic work, housekeeping and outdoor work were strictly scheduled according to a liturgical conception of the day as a succession of work rituals. The humblest gesture were assigned an ecclesiastical significance, and the moral import of every action was emphasized. Just as each hour was dedicated to an occupation, so each day was lived under a special sign according to the biblical week. Saturday, the day when the dormitories were cleaned and inspected, was set aside for confessions, penances and rewards (permission to go to the movies in Sewanee). Sunday was the day of prayer: religious services, performed with great solemnity in heavy odor of incense, involved a large number of officiants. Sunday was also the day of freedom. In the afternoon the children played in the nearby woods and mountains. When they returned, intoxicated with the fresh air, it was only for the evening benediction.

Nature had as much to do with the rhythm of life at Saint Andrew's as religion. The routine was simple and changed with the seasons. Life at the school was also intimately connected with the life of the country people. When, for example, Bill Henley, an old recluse who used to go to Saint Andrew's to find food for his pigs, disappeared, classes were suspended for three days while the school organized a general search. He was later found by two of the boys; he had been mysteriously killed and then thrown from the top of a cliff. With a mixture of curiosity and consternation, the entire school went to inspect the corpse.

A combination of discipline and liberalism reigned at the school. Religious observance, although strictly regulated, was not obligatory, and in spite of the supervision of the priests and instructors, the children were often left to their own devices. Outside of the strict surveillance exercised within the school, they often enjoyed hours of complete liberty. Left to themselves, they followed a code of mingled violence and honor. Their quarrels often turned into real battles, sometimes armed. As for corporal punishment meted out by the priests, Father Lorry, a Rabelaisian figure, was a famous practitioner. When he disciplined a student the child had to stand without pulling back his hand while the priest struck it a goodly number of blows with a ruler. Since violence conferred a kind of prestige on inflicter and victim alike, the ruthless father was one of the school's most popular priests.

Rufus Agee was ten years old when he entered Saint Andrew's; he did so by special permission since the institution was reserved for sons of farmers. Although his mother lived at the school, Rufus was admitted to the dormitory for younger boys, and participated totally in the life of the community. Mrs. Agee thought that her son needed to be subjected to rigorous discipline and to be directed and counseled by men. The brothers in fact could substitute for paternal authority.

At Saint Andrew's, Rufus received an exceptionally good education. The school had excellent teachers, some of whom had come there for reasons of health. The small classes allowed the teachers to know each student well. Because he was so precocious, Rufus attracted the attention of his instructors; he was granted certain special privileges, such as the use of the piano at certain hours, the use of the faculty library and the permission to borrow books. Very early in life Rufus showed an interest in writing, and the excitement language held for him is already evident in his first paper written on the theme of a verse from Keats's "The Eve of Saint Agnes." But it was between Agee and his history teacher that there grew a special bond. Father Flye, whom Mrs. Agee had met briefly during her first visit to Saint Andrew's in the summer of 1918, was an Episcopal priest who had come to the monastery from his parish in Georgia. Attracted from the start by Rufus' lively intelligence and curious mind, the father lent him books and engaged him in long discussions on history, religion and politics. The discussions between Father Flye and Agee continued for many years after Rufus' stay at the school, during the course of their long correspondence. Father Flye also decided to teach Rufus some French. With another student, Oliver Hodge, they read *Tartarin de Tarascon,* Alphonse Daudet's classic in the tall-tale tradition. Acting on this common interest in the French language, Father Flye and Agee started to plan a trip to France, which was eventually realized in 1925.

Father Flye also liked to invite students to his home, where his discreet and self-effacing wife would give them a warm welcome. Mrs. Flye was a painter and did a very interesting portrait of young Agee. Under her influence Rufus' taste for art and painting, originally awakened by Hugh Tyler, came to life again. The erudition of Father Flye, the artistic gifts of Mrs. Flye and their affectionate attention all made Rufus want to visit them more and more frequently. Their house became a haven for him within Saint Andrew's; he found there an atmosphere that might have reminded him of the Tyler household in Knoxville.

Although it has been suggested that Father Flye was a successful surrogate for Agee's father, the relationship between Father Flye and Agee differed greatly from the physical and emotional bond that had attached Rufus to his own father. Father Flye was a more spiritual father to him, and alternately a teacher, confidant, confessor and friend. The relationship with his actual father had a visceral as well as a mystical quality to it that Agee seems never to have found again in his life.

While Rufus came and went at liberty in the Flye household, he saw his mother only once a week. Laura Tyler's strong personality nevertheless had a great influence on him. Doubtless Rufus resented her for raising him with the authority of a father, according to strict rules, and he was often torn between the fear of displeasing her and the desire to rebel. He also reproached himself for being unable to fulfill his role as head of the family. In his adult life he frequently experienced this same fear of failing the women he loved. In his writing a mother figure often appears in situations similar to those he knew in his childhood: the mother in mourning in *A Death in the Family,* the initiator into the trials of life in "A Mother's Tale," [3] the stern educator compensating for the absence of a father in *The Morning Watch.*[4] While *A Death in the Family* explores the bereavement caused by death, the separation from the father, *The Morning Watch* is more concerned with the mother-son relationship—the feeling of estrangement and betrayal created by the enforced separation from the mother.

Paradoxically, the young Agee, who had so impatiently awaited his independence from the feminine world, experienced ambivalent feelings at the thought that his mother was at the same time so near and so inaccessible. The solitude he had dreamed of because his father made it seem desirable now terrified him. Forbidden to enter his mother's house except on visiting days, he often kept watches at a distance, secretly or openly. These solitary vigils must have been frequent, since Agee later used the "watch" metaphor to refer to this period of his life. One may surmise that he suffered deeply during his first few months at Saint Andrew's; though not always constant or even acknowledged, his pain was probably more acute than at the time of his father's death. And the state of separation from his mother strangely renewed the situation in which he had found himself two years earlier. In this fashion Agee approached adolescence on the defensive but also with a romantic self-complacency. He likened his states of mind to the changing seasons. True to prediction, winter brought on sadness and fits of masochism, increasing his isolation and his need for mortification. Far from trying to conquer his unhappiness, he delighted in it and nourished it with a thousand other real or imaginary pains.

Mrs. Agee had thought she was entrusting her son's education to men, to the brothers and laymen of Saint Andrew's, the pleasant ones like Father Flye and the awesome ones like Father Lorry. But in fact it was Rufus' schoolmates who mostly guided his emotional and physical education, and it was among them that he chose his models for emulation. There were several older students whose manly, independent and self-assured behavior inspired the envy and admiration of the younger boys. Agee was taken with one of them, Tautzenschein, whom he later portrayed as Willard Rivenburg in *The Morning Watch*. He came to attach a symbolic value to every aspect of Tautzenschein's masculine, self-sufficient universe, to his physical strength and his athletic ability. He was also impressed by his friend's language; his swearing and blasphemy were open signs of nonconformity. And the odor of coffee and cigarettes about him denoted the privileges of the adult. Tautzenschein even knew a few words of German, which seemed to Rufus more virile than the French he was trying to learn with Father Flye. Rufus' sense of his own intellectual superiority was not sufficient to compensate for what he felt was in himself a lack of the maturity and strength he admired in others. Comparing himself to his school-mates—as he had to his playmates several years earlier in the streets of Knoxville—he judged himself sensitive and effeminate and he felt some contempt for the child he still was, who occasionally still wet his bed.

Religious zeal was not rare at Saint Andrew's; it was a practice more or less imposed on the boys. Some gave themselves to it out of self-interest, others out of genuine feeling. It happened that Rufus, whose faith had already been shaken after the death of his father, now longed for serenity and conviction. In envying his comrades their piety, he decided to outdo them, to assert his superiority in the domain that counted most in school. He chose the most extreme course: He sought in the images of the saints and of Christ the possibility of an exalting identification. His excessive piety was in fact a form of rebellion and revenge against what he considered his own mediocrity. He felt the need to sublimate himself, to attract the attention that was denied him, to substitute admiration for the affection he sought from others. He would also show his mother how much superior his religion was to hers.

Religion offered him numerous compensations. With characteristic masochism and self-sacrifice, he deprived himself more and refused himself even the authorized visit to his mother. He identified with the martyrs and with Christ. His march toward sainthood would be secret; no one was to know of his self-imposed punishments and ordeals. And his imagination, nourished by pious readings and religious education, provided him with the image of his own crucifixion as a final apotheosis.

In spite of his diligence, Agee's religious strivings ended in failure. He gives an unrelenting account of this experience in *The Morning Watch,* denouncing the puerility of his hero's dreams and the role that vanity played in his piety. The attempts to transcend into the religious domain were effective primarily in Agee's own imagination. He had used religion to compensate for his own inadequacies, borrowing its words and images, its myths and mysteries without being completely faithful to them. His prayers lacked sincerity and conviction and reduced his religious aspirations to the level of his former dreams of knighthood. His only authentic emotion was shame. These ambivalent feelings toward religion remained with him throughout his life, and he constantly shifted between his desire to be utterly committed and his inability to accept certain religious precepts.

In fact, the religious education that Agee received at Saint Andrew's was essentially of an emotional and aesthetic nature. He was impressed by the external ceremony of religion, the rituals, the pomp, the orderliness, the richness of the robes worn during services, the beauty of the chants, the rhythm of the psalms and prayers, the odor of the incense. His artist's soul was sensitive to this variety and splendor. After he had ceased to believe, he remained attached to the beauty that had overwhelmed him. He sought to recreate it in his work by the accumulation of sensual images and by the solemn rhythms of his verse and prose.

Religion also played a role in determining the ethics of Agee's vocation. In it he discovered an elaborate Christian symbology. The entire school-year schedule at Saint Andrew's was in fact a rehearsal for the reenactment of the death and Resurrection of Christ. Lent and Holy Week evoked images of mourning, violence and luxuriance: the chapels draped in purple, then in black; the empty tabernacle that "gawped like a dead jaw" as one became intoxicated by the smell of incense and of perfumes mixed with wax; the altars tottering under the weight of flowers and candles; the devastation that made the church seem "as brutally secular as a boxcar" (*The Morning Watch,* 350-351). Easter was also death, the death of Christ, which Rufus, in his need to connect this mystery with his own existence, associated with the death of his own father. This memory, reawakened by the odor of the flowers and the smell of burning wax, brought back the feelings of emptiness and solitude and created a link between Rufus' first experience of death and his imagined mystical experience. Through the image of his father's waxen face and hands, he pictured the death of Christ. Death and suffering came to stand for the inexplicable meaning of life. And by observing a snake or a bird in its death throes, he hoped to fathom the mystery.

Life at Saint Andrew's was not always somber. The religious experiences were set within the regular rhythm of nature and community life. After the pious winter the spring and summer were largely spent in fostering a rugged, healthy life in communion with nature. The sudden and compelling revelations of a world of liberty and violence filled Rufus' imagination. And paradoxically, in the environment of Saint Andrew's, he once more resumed life under the sign of his absent father. In this new and exciting contact with untamed nature, he also rediscovered the solid mountain men who were his ancestors, and the kinship he had felt with the Tennessee country folk he had seen during his visits to La Follette was reawakened. He felt nostalgia for a past he had known mostly from legends and pictures. Thus the move from Knoxville to Saint Andrew's signaled a return to the archaic land of his ancestors.

During his free Sundays, Rufus ran with his comrades to play in the surrounding woods and streams. "Boys Will Be Brutes," a short story which appeared in the April, 1930, *Harvard Advocate,* derives its material from those early incursions into a world of violence. It tells how a boy, after having knocked some baby robins from their nest, puts them out of their misery by savagely stoning them to death. Despite the frantic cries of the mother bird, he carries the carnage through to the end, when, disgusted at the act he has just completed, he begins to vomit uncontrollably. The experience, however—the deliberate willfulness of his act—also fills him with pride. This acceptance of violence as a necessary reality marked for Rufus Agee his first victory, a kind of self-defeat, over himself. Initiated into violence by an experience he has neither sought nor refused, and which has left him intoxicated, he multiplied the occasions to prove to himself and to others that he was not a coward. He had no stomach for hurting anyone smaller than himself. If, however, his adversary was more powerful than he or his pride was involved, his need to assert his physical strength and thereby his masculinity often led him to battle. Feigning an uncharacteristic offhandedness, he one day told his mother, who was disturbed at seeing him come home covered with blood, "Don't keer, it ain't mine."

Violence was thus a crucial experience, a sort of emancipation through which he acquired self-esteem and the respect of others and reaffirmed his maturity and his identity. But if it was a means of knowing himself and the world, it also entailed the loss of a certain innocence. While moving toward the uneasiness of adolescence, he hesitated between the long-awaited call for violent experience and the nostalgic call for a world of sweetness and purity. Unwilling to sacrifice either, he was already dreaming of reconciling them. The reconciliation would become one of the dialectical pivots of his writing.

The years at Saint Andrew's were thus characterized by two encounters, one with the world of spirituality and the other with the physical world. Saint Andrew's also represented for Agee a break with his past and, through an inverse impulse, a return toward his past. Thus adolescence became for him both victory and retreat. He longed for an equilibrium and coherence between opposing forces in him, between the demands of the heart for tenderness and the imperatives of mind and body eager for knowledge. From this ambivalence stems the importance of imagination, which amplifies experience and reflection in Agee's mature philosophy. And henceforth he needed not merely to live, but to watch himself live, seeking out the pattern of his existence in an attempt to transcend and harmonize its various components.

CHAPTER FOUR

INTERLUDE: POPPYFIELDS IN FRANCE

IN 1924 AGEE WAS TAKEN OUT OF SAINT ANDREW'S AND FOR A year the family returned to Knoxville. Joel Tyler's health had taken a turn for the worse and, as his wife was no longer well enough to handle the situation alone, Mrs. Agee agreed to return to the city to help care for her father. During this year in Knoxville, James Agee studied the piano intensively, resumed his long talks with his grandfather and rediscovered the movie theaters he had been to as a small boy with his father. He also enrolled in Knoxville's public high school, an experience he later described in a short story entitled "Knoxton High." [1] The story presents an ironic and humorous picture of the power struggles within the school administration. ("Up to that time," the story notes, "when conflicting epidemics of patriotism and flatfootedness swept our land, the education of Knoxville's youth had been carried on in segregated and miserably cramped firetraps.") For Agee, the rules and regulations of the school constituted a great change from those at Saint Andrew's. Here the students were required to wear uniforms, and the discipline was of an almost military character. But if the tone of his story is any indication, this new regimen amused Agee more than it disturbed him. Meanwhile (to judge by his later writing) he was learning a great deal about the social comedy of life in a small Southern city.

Sometime that winter Mrs. Agee became engaged to the Reverend Erskine Wright, an Episcopal minister, and married him at Eastertime. It was a development that her adolescent son did not find easy to accept. He had no great affection for his stepfather, and in his mind the marriage only seemed to justify anew the suspicion he had felt at Saint Andrew's: that his mother did not really care for him and would abandon him at the right opportunity. But Agee had fortunately kept in touch with Father Flye during this year and, upset by the new betrayal, now thankfully agreed to accompany the priest on a trip to Europe.

The trip, during the summer of 1925, was Agee's first and last visit to Europe. He and Father Flye left in June on a Dutch liner and disembarked at Boulogne. At Amiens they rented bicycles and pedaled through the Loire Valley and the Ile de France. Agee was shocked to see how ravaged France had been by the war, but he was impressed that the French had attempted to carefully preserve the many ruins and artifacts of the war period, proud reminders of what they had so bravely endured. Some of the characters in his stories were no doubt inspired by the people he chanced to see on the byways of the French countryside. He was struck by the juxtaposition in the postwar landscape of majestic, pitiful ruins with brand-new buildings, the already visible promise of the future. Passing through Amiens and Beauvais en route to Paris, Agee saw "scars" that no amount of reconstruction could erase. The overly clean streets—a failed attempt, he thought, at rejuvenation—had a depressing effect on him. And finally, in spite of its apparent life and prosperity, the French countryside seemed desolate to him. Reminders of the war preyed on Agee's mind. The poppyfields, symbolizing bloodshed, seemed to his romantic imagination like a dagger that pierced a bloody sky.[2] And Agee sought refuge from the artificial optimism of the laboriously repaired cities and farms. He preferred the beauty and eloquence of the ruins that were forsaken by man and visited only by flocks of migratory birds.[3] The Gothic atmosphere sparked his imagination; he peopled the ruins with fantastic beings: gnarled sorcerers with predatory eyes whose fingers closed like talons about his wrists; mute, white-haired, stooped old men. He frequented the most quiet and secluded spots. He visited cathedrals in the evening when they were deserted, when the last rays of the sun shining through the stained-glass windows colored the clouds of incense that hovered round the pillars.[4] After the magnificent light had disappeared with the setting sun, the cathedrals would stand in solemn, icy splendor. Only a stray bird and the odor of incense still lingered, the last remaining signs of life.

Agee did not like to admit that France was losing the romantic beauty his imagination had bestowed upon it. He regretted the encroachments and blight of progress. And finally the admiration he had for the people also turned to disappointment. He now saw their patriotism as excessive and their pride in the war and in the heroism of their soldiers seemed just shameful docility. The trip to Europe was but a brief pause in Agee's life; nevertheless it was his first experience of a nation politically and socially different from his own. When he returned home he looked at America with fresh eyes. Meanwhile his friendship with Father Flye had grown even more important to him, as he felt his father's memory daily betrayed by his mother's remarriage.

In many ways the trip to France also signaled to Agee a farewell to childhood; it foreshadowed his eventual separation from his family and from a state that he was loath to leave. "Each child," he later wrote, "is a new and incommunicably tender life, wounded in every breath, and almost as hardly killed as easily wounded, sustaining for a while without defense the enormous assaults of the universe" (*Let Us Now Praise Famous Men*, 56). He always mourned the loss of childhood, remembering "the still inviolate lyric body of a child, very much of the earth, yet drawn into that short and seraphic phase of what seems unearthliness which it will so soon lose."

PART II

HILLBILLY IN THE ACADEMIC WORLD

CHAPTER ONE

EXETER: "THE SWELLINGS AND TREMBLINGS OF ADOLESCENCE"

"To . . . anatomists of truth and its revealers;
in scorn of their truth as truth; and in thanks-
giving for their truth in its residence in truth."
(*C.P.*, 11)

AGEE'S DEFINITIVE BREAK WITH HIS NATIVE SOUTH CAME IN
the autumn of 1925. His mother and her new husband moved first
to South Carolina, then to Florida and Tennessee before establishing their permanent residence in Rockland, Maine, in 1926. Leaving Knoxville, Jim, who had since ceased to be called Rufus in
favor of his more respectable Christian name, left behind the land
of his ancestors, his father's homeland, to take up life in the region
where his mother's family had first settled. At Phillips Exeter
Academy, the prestigious school he began to attend, he entered the
world of intellect of which the Tylers had given him a foretaste.
He relinquished his ties with the country for the refined atmosphere
of one of New England's best preparatory schools, an abandonment
he later considered a betrayal.

Exeter was justifiably famous for providing its students with an
excellent preparation for higher education. Its tradition, though con-

taining both liberal and puritan elements, demanded a great deal of exertion on their part; life there was very different from life at Saint Andrew's. Agee often compared the two schools, contrasting Exeter's sterile (in his opinion) intellectualism with the warm humanism of the monastery.

When Agee arrived at Exeter in 1925 he was, according to his teachers and friends, a tall, ungainly boy with brown hair and enormous hands and feet.[1] Myron Williams described his gait as "a swinging lope which earned him the nickname (he had several) of 'Springheel.' "[2] Well above average height, he was embarrassed by his body, and his low, soft, calm voice—he spoke almost in a whisper—was surprising in such a large person. "I remember Jim chiefly as a tall, angular young man with a tremendous passion for words, which came tumbling out of him like a waterfall," said Freeman Lewis, a nephew of Sinclair Lewis. Agee gestured energetically with his hands as he spoke, which lent a particular eloquence to his conversation. A son of Tennessee and proud of his rustic origins, he certainly did not look like a typical prep-school boy. He neglected his appearance to the point where he had to be reminded to have his hair cut, to take a bath and to brush his teeth. To many of his schoolmates his manners were clumsy and unrefined, but these were qualities that Agee often deliberately cultivated, less to distinguish himself from the other boys than to prove his loyalty to the only place he considered his home. For Maine, where his mother now lived, could never replace Knoxville in his affections. Indeed, Agee had no trouble making a choice between the cultural model Exeter offered him and the ideals he had learned in the South. After the rough but honest boys he had known at Saint Andrew's the "E man" seemed hypocritical to him. It was at this time that he began his long correspondence with Father Flye, thus ensuring himself a link with his former environment. It would be better for him, he disappointedly wrote Father Flye in his early letters, to retain the shy, unsocialized side of his personality than to identify with the Exeter man (*Letters to Father Flye*, 17-35). He criticized the insincerity and hypocritical docility of his schoolmates, and he often wondered whether he should not leave the Academy for a school better suited to his tastes and his temperament. Solitary by nature, he became even more of a lone wolf at Exeter, fleeing the company of his classmates. Refusing to adapt to the rigid routine and the multitude of regulations, he decided to organize his life on the periphery of the school.

Some of the escapades of the three years Agee spent at Exeter have become legendary. His nocturnal wanderings and his lateness in returning to the dormitory caused the hour of curfew to be moved up. The school's disciplinary council held special meetings to discuss his case. More seriously, he aroused the wrath of the administration and the censure of his teachers by his stormy relationship with Dorothy Carr, a girl who worked at the Exeter Public Library and who boarded just off campus with a Dr. Merrill, who was on the Exeter faculty. But Agee never deliberately tried to cause a scandal; he simply cared little about what people would say regarding his behavior. And although he was willing to listen patiently to the advice of his teachers, he never followed it.

His nonconformity was not a pose. More amoral than immoral, he would have preferred to live in peaceful coexistence with those who strenuously believed in conventions and customs. And he never rebelled overtly, nor did he try to reform the school. As an individualist he merely reserved the right to state his opinions openly. Around this time he wrote an imaginary journal, "Diary of a Disagreeable Young Man," [3] in which he made fun of his aspirations to manhood and independence, but it is not difficult to see that he took these aspirations seriously all the same. He repeatedly ridiculed Exeter's claim to offer to its students an initiation into life, and he advised his classmates not to scorn the school's ideals but not to expect either that upon graduation they would be able to solve the infinite complexities of life. In another article, whose tone foreshadows the ironic moralist he later became, he pretended to defend the "E book," Exeter's bible, and the ideal student, only in order to give more force to his concluding argument, an unremitting declaration of independence.[4]

Despite his reservations about the school, Agee did not remain a totally passive student. He in fact took full advantage of its many different activities and came to play quite an important role in campus life. He had an excellent record of participation in the swimming club, the music club, the Glee Club and the Lantern Club, the last a literary group that organized meetings and discussions with men of letters. Booth Tarkington and Sinclair Lewis came to speak there in 1926, Robert Frost in 1928. For the dramatics club Agee acted in *Katherine and Petruchio,* and played Baptista in *The Taming of the Shrew.* He was also active on the board of the school's literary periodical, the *Phillips Exeter Monthly Magazine.* Starting as an associate editor, he later became secretary, and in March, 1927, was chosen editor-in-chief. That same year, he was elected president of the Lantern Club.

It seems likely that Agee's uneven grades during those three years were owing as much to his numerous extracurricular activities as to his lack of self-discipline. Ever since he had entered Exeter in his lower middle year (tenth grade) he had been an unpredictable student, alternately mediocre and brilliant, and his inconsistency of performance often disconcerted his teachers. He studied history and English with a passion, music and art out of genuine fondness, chemistry more out of curiosity than true interest, and algebra (his poorest subject) with no interest at all. In his senior year he failed geometry and chemistry, and an attack of tonsillitis just before his final exam almost caused him to fail other subjects too. His only good grade that year was in English.[5]

Agee studied sporadically, concentrating on his work only when he needed the good grades in order to maintain the scholarship which had gotten him into Exeter. Extracurricularly, on the advice of his teachers, he entered several literary competitions. In September, 1927, he won the Merrill Prize in English composition. He won it again in 1928, when he also received the Lantern Club English Prize. And in 1927 he was selected to represent Exeter in a national essay contest in which he placed third.[6] By this time Agee had already developed into a fine prose stylist. "He was a tatterdemalion, but he wrote like an angel," recalled one of his teachers, who still remembered many years later a paper about superstitions that Agee had written for him.[7] He had a gift for words, and a sly humor. After Robert Frost spoke at the Academy, Agee observed that Frost "wrinkled up his face when he was going to have a whimsicality, like having a baby"; this kind of witticism of Agee's was repeated throughout the school.

Although he loved English more than any other subject, French also appealed to him. His interest in the language was further stimulated by Earl A. Barrett, who had been on the Exeter faculty for thirty-two years. Barrett tried to pass on to Agee a critical outlook for, although gifted with an extraordinary sensitivity, Agee was, according to his teachers, sometimes lacking in judgment. His English advisor, Myron Williams, remembered their conferences, during which Agee would discuss what he had read or written. "I know I don't have any taste," Agee would say in a tone that both acknowledged the fault and denied the responsibility for it. He was extremely modest and unsure of his talent and would always concede an argued point to his adversary. Once, when Williams criticized a passage in one of his stories, Agee answered simply, "That's all right, I am going to change all that."

Agee also loved Latin. He enjoyed reading Ovid and Virgil, and he even tried to translate and adapt works by Horace. He was fond of history but was very critical of the way it was taught at Exeter. His grandfather Joel Tyler and Father Flye had been his first teachers of the subject, and he had acquired a certain veneration for it. The dogmatism and the empty erudition of his new teachers disturbed Agee. "The history courses are *lousy*," he wrote Father Flye. "Everyone admits it" (*F.F.*, 28). For him the ideal history course was the record of man's cultural and artistic achievements, not the dry compilation of facts and events his Exeter instructors made it out to be. Of all his history teachers at Exeter, only Dr. Chadwick earned his admiration. Though he was unsparing in his criticism of his teachers, he later paid tribute in a long poem "to the leniency and wisdom of four men [one of them being Dr. Chadwick], to the scorn of another, who teach at Exeter Academy." [8]

But on the whole Agee seems to have taken little real interest in his studies. He confessed that, given the choice, he would have preferred to be self-taught like his father, or like Abraham Lincoln. His greatest pleasure at Exeter was derived from his involvement in extracurricular and cultural activities like reading, listening to and playing music and movie-going. Not content with ransacking the school library, he borrowed books from the public library. He read Whitman, Chaucer, Blake and Housman, whom he wanted to emulate, as well as contemporary American authors. He had a particular interest in Sinclair Lewis, whose nephew Freeman was a friend of his. Of Lewis' novels, Agee preferred *Babbitt* and *Mantrap,* because of their fresh style and the absence in them of the satirical tone that irritated him in the other books. Disappointed by *Elmer Gantry,* Agee wrote a review of it that was published in the May, 1927, issue of the *Exeter Monthly.* "One feels," he complained, "that Lewis wrote with his lips pulled flat against his teeth." He argued that *Elmer Gantry* contains too much uncontrolled spite and hatred of mankind, and that this bitterness dooms the satire to failure.[9] Disturbed by Lewis' ferocity, Agee came to prefer John Dos Passos, whose intentions seemed to him more honest. He felt that though Dos Passos also stressed the sordid aspects of existence, it was out of a genuine pessimistic persuasion. "He writes filth sincerely disbelieving in the existence of anything else. . . . He's not a cheap hack-writer, writing Pay Dirt" (*F.F.*, 29). Although Agee found Theodore Dreiser humorless, often tedious and a less accomplished artist than Lewis, he nevertheless appreciated his ability to avoid excessive sentimentality in spite of his evident tenderness for his characters. For Agee, these qualities redeemed the monotony of a mediocre prose.

Lewis, Dos Passos, Dreiser, those were the writers whom Agee first chose as his models; he made a thorough study of their work; he frequently recorded his thoughts about them, developing skills he later used as a literary critic. Of course, his judgments were not all equally sound. They could be pretentious and strewn with platitudes or hasty appreciations. All the same they plainly revealed his developing taste. He resented the numerous "literary hoaxes" who had become fashionable and he was thankful for the beautiful, tranquil and poetic books some authors found the courage to write (*F.F.*, 33). He also expressed a predilection for escape literature, such as the books of Robert Nathan and A. L. Benson, with their self-conscious poetic prose, but he liked tougher books, too, like Andy Tully's *Circus Parade,* which dealt with the brutalities and cruelties of existence. It was these two currents, the tender and the cruel, the sentimental and the macabre that ran through Agee's own work in the years to come. Agee was continually preoccupied by the relationship between reality and literary creation. He was amazed, for instance, that he was able to achieve the emotional detachment necessary to write coldly about death and murder, events which in real life he could not face with any such equanimity.

As for music, Agee's favorite composer was Mozart, though he considered Beethoven the "Master." He loved to play the piano for hours at a time and he often attended concerts in Boston. A performance presenting the Beethoven *Mass* and four of the symphonies that took place at Easter, 1927, impressed him deeply. Afterward he amused himself at his piano by playing from memory some of the pieces. He played fluently but with poor technique; he hit many wrong notes but always captured the spirit of the piece. He also could improvise with great facility. There were many who admired his exceptional gifts, and they tried to encourage him to study music. Agee felt himself incapable of the self-discipline necessary to become a good musician.

His love for the movies born during the excursions with his father into the dim moviehouses of Knoxville evolved while he was at Exeter. Agee began to study the cinema seriously and systematically. As president of the Lantern Club he arranged for films such as *Potemkin* and *The Last Laugh* to be shown at the school; he also tried to convince his teachers that film was an important art form and had been unjustly neglected at Exeter.

Agee saw infinite possibilities in the cinema and predicted its eventual predominance over the other arts. He wrote a long article, entitled "The Moving Picture," for the March, 1926, issue of the *Exeter Monthly*,[10] in which he expressed his hopes and his misgivings for the future. American movies, he felt, had become too commercial, and he preferred the achievements of the German cinema. He predicted the emergence of a new aesthetic in which Von Stroheim and Murnau would become as well respected as Mozart and Dickens. In 1927 he proposed in a letter to Dwight Macdonald, whom he had never met but had heard about (Macdonald had graduated from Exeter several years previously), that they exchange ideas and impressions about films: "the one interest I know we have positively in common—interest in moving pictures, especially from the director's point of view. We evidently write and think remarkably alike . . . I am not sure whether these common interests and similarities in style would palm out successfully into a correspondence acquaintanceship, but I'm most anxious to try it." This was the beginning of a friendship founded, among other things, on a sporadic but long-lasting correspondence. In one of his first letters to Macdonald, Agee discussed the technical aspects of film that fascinated him the most. Care in shooting and editing (Murnau's *The Last Laugh* was his idea of a great film) were paramount for him. "By regulating the speed of the camera's movement and the scope of its vision you can get indescribable effects—anything from long sweeping 'strokes' to short jabs and spurts. By thus manipulating the camera, you can achieve a marvellous pliance that no other art can hope to equal." [11] The motion picture was also capable of achieving a more complete and effective realism than the other arts; it could be made to convey poetry, it could even "photograph an idea." "The moving camera," he continued, "can catch the beauty of swaying, blinding lights and shadows, and by its own movement impart to it as definite a rhythm as poetry or music ever had."

In spite of his passion for music and the movies, Agee eventually turned toward literature for his vocation, that well-worn and, by his own admission, outdated art. In a letter to Macdonald he confessed: "I know I write imitatively, but I want to be as original as I can. My sneaking ambition is to be what's called a Pioneer." He chose his models among his favorite authors and found himself torn between the necessity of learning by imitation and the desire to find his own voice. He knew that writing was a demanding craft that required a long apprenticeship, but he was impatient to make progress. In his correspondence with Macdonald he explored at length the difficulties and paradoxes of literature. He exposed his uncertainties and deficiencies and questioned not only his own talent but the value of the proud, tormented and solitary vocation of writing. Agee worked with determination but without discipline. He did most of his writing during vacations, which he often spent in Rockland, but he never quite succeeded in settling down to work. He reproached himself for the same lack of discipline he showed in his studies. But he knew that, in his impatience to create a perfect work, he procrastinated. Agee suffered all the torments of creativity.[12] With touching naiveté he sought the approbation, encouragement and criticism of his friends as well as of some well-known writers. A friend of his, W. M. Frohock, whom he had met in Maine, introduced him into several literary groups, and when guest speakers came to Exeter—as did Robert Frost, who spoke at Aley Hall on April 22, 1928—Agee did not hesitate to give them one of his "works" to read. On the advice of S. Foster Damon, a Blake specialist whom he met at Exeter, he sent a verse play he had written to a number of writers and critics, including Edna St. Vincent Millay, Sara Teasdale, Robert Hillyer, Hilda Doolittle and Ezra Pound. Their impatiently awaited and near unanimous verdict was that Agee had the potential to become a good and perhaps great writer if he would be careful not to squander his talents. When Agee left Exeter in 1928 he was still dissatisfied with what he had accomplished but he felt encouraged by the criticism he had received.

During these years Agee published some of what he wrote in the *Exeter Monthly;* other works written at this time did not appear until later, and after much revising. Among the pieces in the *Exeter Monthly* were twelve short stories, nine poems and the only four plays Agee ever published. The only time he returned to a similar form was toward the end of his life when he wrote some dramatic adaptations for the screen.

Agee's plays are interesting less for their literary value than for the dramatic situations they portray. They contain the myths that appear obsessively in his later work. Whether he was writing about a Tennessee farmgirl (in *Catched*) [13] who is a prisoner of the hard life of the mountains or of Xanthippe (in *In Vindication*),[14] who dreams of leaving Athens to become the wife of a farmer, his imagination always explored the situations he had experienced, in reality or in dream, in his childhood. His separation from Tennessee continued to haunt him. The unsuccessful, dissatisfied characters he wrote about who dreamed of finding a better place were more or less conscious projections of himself. His caricature of Socrates —Agee himself had been nicknamed "Serkreetes" at Saint Andrew's —was only one of many self-portraits he embedded in a fictional character. And of course, he was still haunted by the death of his father. This obsession is often represented in his work by the inverted situation—the father surviving, even killing, the son. Both in *Any Seventh Son*,[15] which was based on popular superstitions, and in "Menalcas," [16] which was inspired by a discussion with W. M. Frohock about Eugene O'Neill, it is the father who kills and sacrifices his son. Menalcas' deed, an echo of Abraham's, seems like a gesture of defiance in the face of a malign destiny. The lines alternate between echoes of Shelley and accents of Swinburne, but in their variety of rhythms and images, they foreshadow an authentic poetry of Agee's own.

The poems that Agee wrote between 1925 and 1928 are only sporadically successful. With the exception of the long dramatic poem "Ann Garner," [17] these were generally very short pieces constructed around a single image. Echoing an image from Edna St. Vincent Millay, "Ebb Tide" [18] seems like a metaphor of Agee's life. In the poem, water symbolizes fertility; salt, the fruitless prolonging of life as its spirit ebbs away, the desiccation of the soul; the puddles left by the receding tide, the solitude of the human heart. The boundless sea and the starry sky embody indifference, emptiness and nothingness. The sometimes abrupt, sometimes full and expansive lines of the verse carry the message powerfully forward.

"Widow," published in the May, 1926, issue, is Agee's first poem directly inspired by his father's death. On Christmas Eve a young widow wonders which is the greater illusion, life or death. Now that her husband is gone she feels that his life was only an illusion and that her own life has been an absurd dream since his death. Agee portrays her entering the bedroom to seek strength and comfort only to find emptiness, a scene that he much later used again in *A Death in the Family.*

"Ann Garner," by far the most ambitious work Agee produced during these years, was published in the May, 1928, *Exeter Monthly,* the last issue before his graduation. It is a five-hundred-line narrative and dramatic poem elaborating on the themes of birth and death, sterility and fertility. It opens, like *Any Seventh Son,* with a scene depicting the mysterious rites of birth. On a narrow, crudely made bed, attended by a midwife who performs her enigmatic and disquieting rituals, Ann Garner brings a stillborn child into the world. The following morning the frozen earth receives the body of the infant, who is then reborn to preside at the birth of a new day. Henceforth Ann's life follows the rhythm of the seasons; the winter countryside, immobilized in snow, is the landscape of her soul. But, frozen as she is, she is mysteriously reborn in the spring when one night she slips off to the barn and in the dimness touches objects that reveal to her the mystery of life—a plow, symbol of fertility and of the labor of birth, and a bull, symbol of strength and virility. She becomes aware that life continues within her, just as it continues within the earth in wintertime. It is during the night, bearer of messages, that Ann sees nature reborn around her. The first sign is water, seeking to spring forth everywhere—a baptismal regenerating torrent threatening to break down walls. Then, with the day, heralded by the silver light of the stars, color appears. After silver comes brown and green, as though nature, like the poem, whose first verses evoked a picture in black and white, were finally liberating itself from night and snow. A violent wind envelops Ann, lashing her body and driving her into a frenzied dance. Only now does she discover her mission: Henceforth she will follow along the furrows, presiding like a pagan goddess over the labor of the fields. Just as winter is an endless night, summer is a long day of toil, when the earth adorns itself with a golden light. With the return of cold autumn Ann goes back to her spinning wheel, to the rhythm and mystery of her life:

> Life was in death:
> The world rolled back and barren in its mists,
> And life locked deep in the sheathing snows.

Silent and alien among the living, Ann Garner, the gardener, continues her solitary existence, presiding at births and deaths, announcing the arrival of the seasons until, with her own death, caused by the plow, she emulates the universal destiny. In the deep furrow that death, the new sower, had dug for Ann, the embrace of death is even more powerful than that of life.

In this long hymn to nature, which shows the antithetical aspects of earthly life and mingles mysticism and sensuality, Agee's talent was not always able to match his intuition. In spite of the grandeur of its inspiration, the poem contains many clichés, many trite conventions and much obvious symbolism. The influence of Robinson Jeffers and Robert Frost is sometimes too explicit. Yet there is originality in certain of the images, and in his skill with varying rhythms Agee reveals himself a true poet. Several years later he rewrote the poem, reworking the metaphors and curtailing the excesses.

Several of the short stories that Agee published in the *Exeter Monthly* were similar in inspiration to his poems. "Bound for the

Promised Land," [18] a comic treatment of death, deals with the theme that Agee later returned to many times with greater seriousness. With humor and irony, he describes the preparations for Mr. Rucler's funeral, the respectful silence of his friends and neighbors; and the awkwardness of the men "between [whose] knees dangled their hands; knotty fingers interlaced beneath puckered foreheads," who come to pay him a final tribute. While the members of the family and the preacher busy themselves around the corpse, the dead man's daughters watch a trickle of sweat running under the stays of their mother's corset. The undertaker's man with his coffin-shaped hands thinks with satisfaction of the handsome casket he has made for the occasion; the widow secretly basks in the knowledge that her past seven years of self-denial have enabled her to give her husband such a glorious ceremony. But when a medical student arrives offering to buy the corpse for Dr. Pickney, the dead man is suddenly deprived of any remaining heroic stature. And although *A Death in the Family* explores in a completely different vein how a father's death affects the family, Agee did make the point even in that work that life's most solemn moments are not devoid of comedy. In these early writings the theme of bereavement and departure often alternates with that of homecoming, which we find in "Widow" [19] or in "Chivalry" [20] with a medieval allegorical setting.

A common motif in the stories was failure: the ruined lives of Seigbert Pearson and Emerson Davis in "Jenkinsville," one a victim of his wife's religious hysteria, the other a victim of his in-laws and of his own weakness; the wasted efforts of "Minerva Farmer," who leaves her work in the fields for a life of study which, though successful, brings her no joy; and the futile existence in "The Circle" of Edward, an ambitious young man from La Follette whose life is sacrificed to a rich, old, miserly and capricious invalid aunt.[21] These are the stories of wasted lives of characters full of self-pity and unable to control their fate. Although some of them were probably inspired by real people they are also in many respects

literary projections of Agee. And strangely, the cruelly and real-
istically portrayed settings of these stories is Tennessee, the very
country he later idealized in *A Death in the Family;* La Follette
is his grandparents' town; Jenkinsville, Knoxville.

In contrast to the characters who spent their lives imprisoned
by a place, a person or a trade, Agee also portrayed his ideal of
the free man. John Ivy in "Between Trains" is a solitary wanderer,
a hobo character who reappears frequently in the short stories
Agee later wrote for the *Harvard Advocate.* His twenty-eight
years of wandering are evoked in a series of images that prefigure
the cinematographic technique Agee was later to adopt in his
major fiction:[22]

> Day-coach seats of mangy plush, the cinders jiggling on the cup-
> rimmed sill, and mile upon mile of sodden fields viewed through rain-
> scourged glass, swinging doors belching the grand hairy stench of
> beer . . . a large comely waitress, fingernails like fish-scales from
> dishwashing . . . his endless nights in day-coaches head hot on
> folded coat, body jack-knifed over the seat, his sleep a frayed thread
> in the labyrinth of sounds and stenches.

Agee's early works show the positive and negative traits of his
writing. His inquisitive mind was fascinated by all forms of speech,
from poetic diction to Tennessee dialect. He was equally at home
in several genres: the long lyric dramatic verse, comedy, dialogue,
and poetic prose. He was also skilled in producing images that
gave an unexpected turn to his style.

Psychologically, writing provided Agee with an opportunity to
master his excessive subjectivity and to free himself from his obsessions. It is interesting to note that few of his early poems and
stories are in the first person. "I can't write . . . subjective things,"
he wrote Father Flye. "I have to trump up a situation and story
and write them as of another character" (*F.F.*, 38). Ambitious
to become a writer, Agee deplored his inability to work as regularly
as he wished. But limited time and the absence of discipline were
not the only threats to serious concentration. Like any other young

man, he was often distracted by the demands of love and friendship.

Although he was known as a "lone wolf" at Exeter, Agee had a great need for love and friendship. He furthermore insisted that his friendships be more than superficial. The object of his first passion was a woman, several years older than he, Dorothy Carr, who boarded with a college professor. Agee's visits to her became widely known on campus and caused several scandals. In the process of pursuing his intense relationship with her, he broke all of Exeter's rules. When she fell seriously ill and was bedridden for months, he spent much of his time passionately reading poetry to her. Dorothy had none of the frivolity, "the affected squawks and squeals and shiverings," that ruined most of the girls he knew (*F. F.*, 24). At Rockland, Maine, where he spent his vacations, he met girls whom he found attractive but "pretentious." Dorothy, on the contrary, was surprisingly mature. His love for her was formed of a mixture of physical attraction and intellectual communion; she was his muse and also his first reader. When she fell ill, Agee decided to devote himself completely to her, and out of some chivalric impulse, even offered to marry her. Rumor had it that when Agee left Exeter he was engaged, even though by that time his relationship had gone through many stages of deterioration.

Dorothy Carr was not the only person for whom Agee felt first pangs of love. In 1927 he seems to have had a more painful experience, a failed love affair with an Exeter boy. In a letter addressed to Dwight Macdonald on June 16 of that year, Agee admits to having had an experience similar to one that Macdonald described in his short story, "Wall," published several years earlier in the *Exeter Monthly*. "Wall" tells of a young man who falls passionately in love with one of his schoolmates and who suffers terribly when his friend turns away from him. Agee wrote, "I was almost drowned in psychological meanderings too dreary and far too long for any story; quite frequently I've been on the verge of suicide. . . . Incidentally, what a hell of a tragedy friendship can become, can't it? Worst of all, apparently all but thickhead friendship must run that very course." Several months earlier he had written to Father Flye that he had just made a new friend and expressed high hopes for this "friendship between men" (*F.F.*, 30). But the relationship turned out totally different from the stable friendship he had anticipated, and his disappointment brought on a deep despair.

The heart's capriciousness led him to the bitter conclusion that the deepest friendships are subject to the hardest tests. At the end of the 1927 school year he found himself in a psychological and moral crisis. Agee felt the need to confide in someone who had been to Exeter, someone who shared his tastes in the arts, and in his quest, he was fortunate in being able to gain the friendship of Dwight Macdonald. A rational, intellectual and literary alliance would, he thought, be the antithesis of the purely emotional experience he had just suffered so passively.

By contrast with the emotional turmoil of 1927, 1928, Agee's last year at Exeter, was peaceful. School life settled into a pattern: He divided his time between his scholastic activities and his personal work. He felt no more than toleration for his classwork, but he compensated for it by reading a great deal and participating in various cultural activities. He also wrote more regularly than before. And it seemed to him that the trials of love and friendship he had been through had made him more mature.

By the time he left Exeter he was more favorably disposed to the school than when he had entered it. He even thought of his departure with a certain amount of regret and he was moved by the graduation ceremonies.

The years at Exeter and his first contacts with a university environment had marked a change in Agee's life. He would later come to view them as a time of betrayal. He had been transported from his native country into a world where he never ceased to feel to some degree out of place. During his school years he internalized the conflict between his mother's bourgeois, cultivated heritage and his father's rural traditions. He felt as though he were straddling two worlds, the one he had betrayed without having really known it and the one he had not yet adopted. These constantly oscillating feelings of allegiance and treason, inertia and enthusiasm, also characterized his years at Harvard.

CHAPTER TWO

HARVARD: AMBITION
AND ANARCHY

"That high-falutin flub-dubbery which is Harvard."

(Unsigned editorial, the *Harvard Advocate*)

EXETER'S REPUTATION AS ONE OF THE BEST PREPARATORY SCHOOLS
from which to seek entrance to the Ivy League colleges proved
true, and in September, 1928, Agee was admitted to Harvard.[1]
According to one of his professors, "He was made for Harvard,
and Harvard for him." But along with these enthusiastic comments
came a more perceptive prediction: "He will be the joy and despair
of his adviser." As for Agee, he was no more thrilled to have the
opportunity to go to Harvard than he had been to go to Exeter.
He feared he was becoming more and more deeply involved in
following a life course that, although flattering to his pride, seemed
to hold many pitfalls. He was afraid that he would be ensnared by
New England and lose his identity as a Tennessee son. All the
same, the change from Exeter to Harvard was not that significant
for him. Cambridge had been near enough for Agee to have made
frequent visits there on his trips from Exeter to Boston. (The trips

to Boston, he wrote, either to attend plays or concerts, or to visit the old port and the city morgue, left a taste in his mouth as if he had been "licking an old sardine can.") And when he got to Harvard he found several people there he already knew from Exeter, including Freeman Lewis.

As a freshman Agee lived in George Smith Hall; he took courses in English, history and Latin; he also studied geology, but he found it, as he confided to Father Flye, much less interesting at Harvard than it had been at Saint Andrew's. His reading of Plautus, Terence and Horace prompted him to work on various adaptations from their works.[2] These translation exercises provided him the means to acquire skill at his craft, and the influence of Latin, especially its syntax, on the poetry Agee wrote during that period is easily discernible.

As at Exeter, Agee also participated in many extracurricular activities. He became a member of the dramatics club, which was then going through a tense, lively period, as several of its plays had attracted the attention of the Boston censor. Though Agee was interested in the theater and in the club's courageous efforts to bring its outmoded repertory up to date, he was not very active in the company. The rehearsals sometimes went on until four in the morning, and this was more time than he was prepared to give to this one of many enterprises he was involved in.

Agee also became a member of the Harvard Glee Club, which was then directed by a Dr. Davison. Rehearsals took place two or three times a week, and the club gave regular concerts together with the Radcliffe Chorus and the Boston Symphony Orchestra throughout New England and also in New York City. Among the basses was J. S. Coleman, who became a friend of Agee's and whom he later saw often when they were both in New York.

From his earliest days at Harvard, Agee was an enigma to his fellow students. To them he led a somewhat mysterious life, disappearing on occasion for several days at a time and returning without offering any explanation to anyone for his absence. Sometimes he was the gayest and most entertaining person, but just as often he would close himself up in silence and become the "lone wolf" again. He showed, at the same time, a strong predilection for both liquor and prayer. He was known to frequent Saint Francis' House, an Episcopalian monastery in Cambridge. He regularly served Mass there and made no secret of his admiration for the monks of this community, who had in his opinion escaped the pitfalls and eccentricities of monastic life. In the evenings, however, he drank, often to excess. But he displayed an astonishing physical stamina, since he would always awaken early the following morning to serve Mass. Agee moved easily between the world of religion and the uninhibited life of the university, and he sought neither to hide nor to rationalize either activity in the face of the other. And in spite of his doubts, he was no more able to do without the religion of his childhood than he was able to stop drinking. He spoke of drinking as a well-established vice he had no intention of giving up, but which he would try not to overdo.

His love life, never an uncomplicated matter, was turbulent too at that time. Though he was still seeing Dorothy Carr, he no longer had the same feeling for her, and he reproached himself bitterly for his fickleness. The numerous frantic letters Dorothy wrote him no doubt contributed to his emotional ambivalence. At Harvard he had begun seeing another girl, a young photographer, which made his relationship with Dorothy even stormier.

Christmas vacation only deepened his depressed mood. He gave up his plans to go to New York in order to have his tonsils out and he almost died of hemorrhaging, as he chronically suffered from a mild form of hemophilia. His misery increased during the first months of 1929, when he described himself as living in a fog, a fog that only dispersed with the arrival of spring.

Agee was further depressed by the fact that he had written almost nothing since "Ann Garner," a work by which he now continually gauged his artistic achievement. He felt that any literature worthy of the name had to deal with the themes of life and death, and that automatically relegated the other stories and poems he had written to the category of literary diversions. The fear of failing to achieve greatness shut him up in a proud and painful silence, since for him at that time no compromise was possible between genius and mediocrity.

His paltry (so he felt) literary output nevertheless frightened him. He tallied up his work: a short story (perhaps "A Walk Before Mass," which he later published in the *Harvard Advocate,* one of the university's literary monthlies), a dozen short poems and translations of odes by Horace. In April of his freshman year he resolved to overcome his inertia. He decided to put the first idea that came into his head into the form of a short story or a poem and from that beginning to try to start publishing regularly in the *Harvard Advocate.*

Agee's interest had not initially been directed toward the *Advocate.* In a letter to Father Flye written in June, 1928, he expressed a desire to restore to its former splendor the *Harvard Monthly,* a more courageous magazine (in his opinion) than the present *Harvard Advocate,* but "which died of wounds rec'd in the Great War." Conrad Aiken, E. E. Cummings, Heywood Broun, S. Foster Damon and Robert Hillyer, among others, had been on its editorial board, and Agee, who later took a course given by Hillyer, clearly would have preferred to work for the *Monthly.* But he had to content himself with writing first for the *Lampoon,* a satirical and humorous magazine, for the newsweekly, *Crimson,* and then for the *Advocate.*

The *Harvard Advocate,* which was more conservative and exclusively literary, had been founded by two members of the class of 1867 one year after the demise of the *Harvard Magazine.* Known at first as *The Collegian,* it was suppressed by the faculty, but by subterfuge it was able to reappear soon under the name of the *Advocate.* Agee first joined the editorial board as an associate editor, and then served as secretary until March, 1931, when he became the editor-in-chief. In an article published in the 1932 *Class Album,* Otto Ernst Feuerbringer, past editor of *Crimson,* expressed the criticisms generally made of the *Advocate.* The magazine, he wrote, paid more attention to style than to thought, and it remained silent and inactive in the face of current issues. These criticisms were perhaps partly owing to fear of competition, since the *Advocate* was a popular campus publication (in 1933 it also counted among its contributors such now famous writers as James Laughlin, William Carlos Williams, Hillyer, and Ezra Pound), but they were also, to some extent, justified. While *Crimson* was involved with contemporary issues, the *Advocate* seemed to practice an art-for-art's-sake approach to literature. Agee was probably not much bothered by the *Advocate*'s deficiencies since at this time he was not very social-minded and was devoted to the cause of "art" to the virtual exclusion of any other. Writing was for him more a personal than a collective venture; he welcomed opportunities to discuss problems of inspiration and expression but only in conversation with one or two friends. At official meetings of the editorial board he remained silent, though conscientiously performing his secretarial and editorial functions.

During his freshman year Agee published two poems, one the Horace ode, "To Lydia," in April, 1929; and the other "Apotheosis," in June. Many of the other poems he wrote during this period—simple exercises he was dissatisfied with—were probably destroyed, but some were reworked and published the following year. It is not always possible to say what impelled him to publish one poem rather than another. He continued to read his works to his friends, and their opinions probably often determined his choices. Meanwhile Agee had reworked "Ann Garner" for publication in the Spring, 1929, issue of *Hound and Horn,* a triannual literary magazine published in Portland, Maine. *Hound and Horn,* since its creation in 1927, had provided a forum for the works of literary critics and poets such as R. P. Blackmur, Lincoln Kirstein and J. B. Wheelwright. Young poets were encouraged to publish, and T. S. Eliot and the metaphysical poets were the models emulated. The magazine succeeded in starting a movement centered at Harvard, and it is not surprising that Agee was attracted to it. The new version of "Ann Garner" retained the title and spirit of the original, but entire sections of the poem were eliminated. Although Agee published nothing else in *Hound and Horn,* he remained in contact with the group. His tastes leaned toward the metaphysical poets—Donne, Vaughan, Herbert—and also toward American poets such as Emily Dickinson, in whom he found prefigurations of his own work.

In his first year at Harvard, Agee's grades were average or below. He even failed in one subject and, since he had not earned enough credits, he was put on probation the following year and was temporarily classified as a freshman. It would not be until his last year at Harvard that he caught up with his own class of 1932.

About the only positive event that occurred during that first year was his meeting Theodore Spencer, his tutor in English and soon his friend and confidant. Otherwise, the year left Agee self-disgusted and deeply confused, with mixed feelings about whether or not to remain in college. He wondered whether he was doing himself an injustice by pursuing a life-style that did not correspond to his ideal. By remaining at Harvard in the company of the elite was not he lending support to a society-created myth he did not believe in? "Harvard, or any university, is an incredible mirror maze of fake self-perceptions; only a little fool who never questions nor examines can get out without embarrassment or injury," he wrote in an editorial.[3] Agee's fear of taking himself too seriously caused him to succumb to an opposite excess: he sought, through his uncouth behavior and careless dress, to express his disapproval of the conventions of the university. He was going to show the civilized world just how intransigent a student could be who had been so fortunate as to have been born a Tennessee hillbilly. And Agee alternately shocked and astonished and charmed his Harvard contemporaries by his various displays of humor, reverse snobbism, loyalty to his origins, rebellion, pride and bravado. In each of these attitudes, he revealed a true part of himself.

In September, 1929, after an active and studious vacation, he returned to Harvard—he was now living in Thayer Hall—only to sink back into the same frame of mind as the previous year. He had hoped, as he wrote to Father Flye, that his vacation "would effect a reasonably permanent cure for the irrational side of [his] unhappiness, but no such luck" (*F.F.,* 42). He did sense a change in himself, however, whose nature he went on to explain to Father Flye in what was at once a clinical analysis and a literary confession. Now that he had survived the throes of puberty and adolescence, he wrote, he had attained a new maturity, a rather abrupt change that struck him with as much force as had the onset of puberty. It seemed to him that his mind and his body were awakening, that his judgment was more acute and more reliable than before. He had the exciting sensation of finally emerging from a thick fog. He now experienced the sensual joy of moving toward a goal, but he was also worried to see his self-confidence developing at the expense of his spiritual awareness. This inner slackening was apparent not only in his indifference to and his rebellion against current morality and religion, but also in his attitude toward his friends and his family. His affection for them was as real as ever, he thought, but he could no longer express his feelings in the old manner. He was brutal and impatient now, because he was too tender and idealistic; and as a result, he was in a constant state of irritability and nervous tension.

He hoped he would be able to ride out this difficult stage of growth, just as he had largely outgrown the erotic daydreams of his adolescence. It seemed to him now that his troubles were intellectual. He continued to question the values according to which he had been raised. He still remained sentimentally and aesthetically attached to a religion his intellect could no longer accept, but he was not able to free himself from a notion of sin that engendered feelings of both fear and self-hatred.

A short poem entitled "The Storm" [4] describes his inner turbulence during this period (only by becoming a storm could he conquer the chaos of his life), while in a short story written at the same time, "A Walk Before Mass," [5] rain symbolizes the atmosphere of imprisoning obsessions in which the hero lives. The story deals in a fairly recognizable manner with many of the problems that were troubling Agee in 1929 although the situations and plot are imaginary: A man, obsessed by a murderous impulse—to kill his son in order to break the ties that hold him to his wife—decides to confess his compulsion to his son. In the morning the father awakens his son and takes him to the place the thought had come to him. But, as he speaks about his obsessions, he pushes the child into the water. The resolution to confess the imagined crime had created the circumstances that lead to the actual tragedy. In this horror story Agee projected and thereby exorcised his familiar demons. He may have identified in part with the father, endowing him with some of his own recognizable and self-confessed character traits, notably his weakness, his difficulty in facing his problems, his confusion in organizing his thoughts and his habit of calling on religion to deal with his own superstitions. The father, passionately hating his wife and passionately ambivalent toward his son, is not unlike the person Agee saw himself to be in his relationships with other people. The story may also be seen as a meditation on his own father's premature death, which he once more represented inversely by the untimely death of a child. "A Walk Before Mass" thus repeats the situation of *Any Seventh Son* and of "Menalcas" though the respective themes of these stories are somewhat different. "A Walk Before Mass" deals with new problems concerning the impulse to murder and the extent to which the mind can be controlled by obsessions—Agee was at the time reading books on witchcraft and on violence. In addition two other favorite motifs emerge, one treating the family—husband and wife riddled with hatred for each other, and the child victimized by his parents' weakness and cowardice—the other exploring Agee's drive toward suicide. For the son is also Agee, the projection of a precious undesirable self. The story has biblical overtones and can also be read as a mystery play—evil triumphs over and crushes innocence—or as an allegory on the destruction of creative impulse.

In the fall of 1929 as Agee began his second year at Harvard he remained troubled but determined not to kill the talent he might possess. He divided his time between his studies, his various activities and his friends, especially Theodore Spencer and Robert Fitzgerald, whom he had recently met in a course given by Professor Hillyer. He read a great deal. After Horace he discovered Catullus, whom he found amusing and easier to translate. He read novels and expressed his enthusiasm for Richard Hughes's *The Innocent Voyage*. He concerned himself particularly with form and restated his conviction that the Bible was the ideal work he should strive to emulate. Meanwhile, in order to earn a sufficient number of credits, he increased his workload. He took Professor Lake's course on the Old Testament and an introductory course in philosophy. He became particularly interested in a course on English literature from 1603 to the Restoration. At the same time he continued to participate in the Glee Club and he also joined the Liberal Club. In November that year he was elected to the editorial committee of the *Harvard Advocate* and in March, 1930, chosen secretary. His grades were slightly better than the previous year, so that in May he received, with the support of Theodore Spencer and Professor Hillyer, a special recommendation for a Harvard scholarship.

Between February and June he published regularly, poetry primarily, in the *Advocate*. In all, the poems indicated his growing concern for technical perfection. He also wrote a number of short stories: "Boys Will Be Brutes," published in April, 1930, and "Near the Tracks," in June of the same year, revealed both his desire to use the materials of his own childhood with the greatest possible explicitness and his continuing inability to write well subjectively.

"Boys Will Be Brutes" is set on Highland Avenue in Knoxville; Agee did not even bother to change its name. A story of the impulsive cruelty of childhood and of the remorse that follows unconscious ferocity, it introduces one of the earliest versions of the hero who later appears as Richard in *The Morning Watch* and as Rufus in *A Death in the Family*. For the first time, Agee wrote openly about the child he had been, analyzing his excessive sensitivity, his attraction and repulsion for cruel games. The Rufus of the story experiments with violence with a mixture of enthusiasm, pride and disgust and finds out too late that in spite of himself he has become a killer of birds. But violence also becomes an element of redemption. By thoughtlessly killing the fledglings, the children preserve the innocence of the baby birds and liberate them from the cruelty of life. The child who in "A Walk Before Mass" is the innocent victim, becomes here—accidentally—the murderer of still more innocent creatures, the birds. Agee also identifies the child with the slaughtered bird: every child, he felt, is destined sooner or later to be thrown from its nest, ensnared and betrayed. He later returned to this same incident, transposed and stylized it in *The Morning Watch,* where the teenage protagonist kills a snake. (In fact the same motif recurs frequently throughout Agee's work.) The idea is almost certainly derived from that unpleasant experience of his childhood when he looked at the bird he had just killed and vomited from his intense emotional reaction. The theme of the dead bird is also connected with the memory of his father's death and also, symbolically, with the theme of the fall; the fall of the bird from the nest becomes a metaphorical representation of death.

The many implications of the theme of "Boys Will Be Brutes" are related to the system of aesthetics and ethics that the young writer was seeking to establish. He looked at each event he experienced as though it were an allegorical drama. The bird hunt and the child's reaction to it fit into a dramatic form: The child's fear of doing evil is slowly displaced by anticipation; the capture of the birds and the sight of their death agonies cause him to feel a mixture of guilt and pride; after the deed—a personal triumph over fear at the expense of innocence—come repentance and a need to confess. In *The Morning Watch* the dramatic structure will be almost identical, with much more complex implications.

"Near the Tracks" consists of a series of scenes dealing with cowardice, a trait once again embodied in a male character. Ed, who has escaped from prison, flees to the girl he loves. He agrees to marry her and to mend his ways, but, afraid of being confined by family life, he runs away again. The girl, who tries to follow him as he climbs into a moving train, falls and is killed. The train carries Ed away, relieved all the same to have regained his freedom. The plot provides Agee a way to examine the all too familiar personal temptation to escape, to leave on the first train, but he did take care to show contrary interpretations of Ed's action. Escape is a desertion, and it is also a liberation. Agee openly admired the unscrupulous scoundrel who is brave enough to act on impulse and has the ability to put the suffering he causes others out of his mind. "Near the Tracks" takes on added significance with the knowledge that Agee finally broke with Dorothy Carr that year. One may suggest that Agee probably contrived that rather melodramatic situation and flight in order to pass judgment on himself. In his protagonist he was depicting his inability to love, his resentment of ties. By portraying a more reprehensible but also a more courageous character than himself, he may have freed himself of regret and quieted his own uncertainties.

The poetry written during this period moves beyond the preoccupations with his own life to the exploration of mythological and religious subjects. "Good Friday" is an incantation that draws on both pagan and Christian sources. While it is a celebration of Pan and his mysterious and exalting rites, there appears among the prophecies murmured by the oaks and laurels of Dodona the tale of Christ's crucifixion on Golgotha.[6] The poem also conveys the spirit of Lent, and elements of the Christian liturgy are transposed into a pagan context: Pan in fact envisions himself crucified. The vision prophesies the death of the gods, all of whom are soon to be replaced by Christ. The poem blends two moods, a delirious pagan joy and a Christian temper of asceticism. The mystery of Easter continued to inspire Agee in other stories, notably *The Morning Watch.* "Good Friday" is thus the first manifestation of a lifelong literary preoccupation.

"Death Never Swoops Us Round," published in the 1930 commencement issue of the *Advocate,* won the Garrison Prize for poetry. The contest established by the class of 1888 was open to all Harvard undergraduates. This first official encouragement further strengthened Agee's determination to be a poet.

Around Easter, 1930, Agee began to think seriously of leaving Harvard and looking for a teaching job. Theodore Spencer, his friend and tutor, persuaded Agee to meet one of his friends, a Professor Saunders who taught history at Hamilton College, before he made a final decision. During the Easter vacation Agee and Spencer went to Clinton, New York, where the Saunderses lived, and his new friends quickly dissuaded Agee from leaving Harvard. The Saunderses were, furthermore, instantly charmed by Agee, and they adopted him into their circle. Agee, in turn, was taken with the Saunderses. Though they exemplified a way of life he sought to avoid—an orderly, tradition-bound, middle-class existence—he nevertheless found himself strongly attracted to them. His mother's remarriage, the death of Joel Tyler and the increasing infirmities of his grandmother, who would die that year, led him to think more nostalgically than was his custom about family life. Mr. Saunders reminded him most of all not of his father but of his grandfather. Mr. Saunders was, in Agee's estimation, the kind of man his grandfather could have been had his life been less turbulent. The two men were alike in their serenity, good looks and courage, but whereas Joel Tyler had always been in search of the impossible ideal, Mr. Saunders had contentedly settled for a calm, industrious life harmoniously divided among his profession, his family and his music and painting. Rarely happy, feeling himself lacking the inner peace he found in Joel Tyler and Mr. Saunders, Agee aspired to identify with both of them. He admired Mr. Saunders' moral qualities, his balance between introversion and extroversion. He thought he saw in him an incarnation of the Greek ideal of the golden mean. The only disharmony he detected was Mr. Saunders' attitude toward religion; here Agee's strong feelings on the subject made agreement between them impossible (*F.F.*, 51). Mrs. Saunders had a more nervous, more "electric" and less balanced personality than her husband. In all they had three children: two daughters, Sylvia and Olivia—nicknamed Via—and a son. Another exceptionally gifted son had died at the age of fifteen. The family owned a flower industry in Clinton and ran it lovingly, as if it were an object demonstration of their worship of beauty. Everything in their lives, it seemed to Agee, their work and their play, their careers and their pastimes, produced beauty, and they remained for him a perpetual source of wonder.[7]

Although Mr. Saunders persuaded him to remain at Harvard, Agee did not entirely give up his dreams of escape. He wavered continually between his attraction to an orderly life that would favor the disciplined development of his talents and his desire for a more marginal existence. It is at this time that he began to look toward California and the world of movie making. He devoted the summer of 1930 to bumming around the country. He felt a strong need to get away from the intellectual and academic environment of the East and also from his family and from all emotional entanglements. Attracted by the mystique of the hobo, he yearned to live for a while outside of society, to travel the country roads and to reestablish contact with the land and country people. He did just this for over seven weeks; he roamed from state to state, never bothering to send his mother any news of himself. (He did write to her once, but found the letter still in his pocket upon his return home.) Beginning in Kansas, he traveled through the entire Midwest. He found much everywhere to intrigue and fascinate him, especially the local dialect and accents. In Iowa he did occasional odd jobs.[8]

He later worked some of the events of that summer into two short stories. "Death in the Desert"[9] is a transcription of Agee's thoughts and sensations during one of his hitchhiking trips. The story, vividly evoking an atmosphere of torpor and indifference, analyzed the reactions of the young protagonist and those of the driver to a Negro walking along the road who, exhausted by the heat, tries to flag down their car. Under the unbearable summer sky reality is transfigured; the silhouette of the Negro beckoning on the road as they pass is as haunting as a nightmare. The moment of abandoning him announces the epiphany to come. To occupy his mind while crossing the desert, the narrator selects an arbitrary (or so he thinks) incident from his memory and tries to recreate it fully and accurately for himself, with all its original intensity. He remembers a day when, at the age of eleven while walking in the Tennessee woods, he saw a battle between a rattlesnake and a king snake. Only a silvery glint, a noise in the leaves, indicated the scene of combat. Then, incredibly, he saw the defeated rattlesnake begin to disappear slowly down the gullet of the king, the swallowed rattle sounding muffled in the jaws of the victor. The memory causes the narrator to feel the same profound horror he experienced at the actual event. As the memory experiment continues, details become more precise; he recalls an abandoned mine in the gully. At the bottom of the mine he sees ferns growing, unaware that they too will soon die and impress their patterns on the rock. As the memory vanishes it leaves only disappointment in its wake. The narrator denounces the fake character of the experience he has had. "I tried, I knew I would fail and failed to feel about it as I had when I was eleven. But the feeling now was so flat, so anaemic, that once had smoked with reality . . . all things were categorized and filed away with their proper metaphors." Thus memory divides a person from himself by allowing him a view of a past from which he is irremediably cut off. Dispossessed, the mind can only painstakingly reconstruct what it has lost.

This story appears to be a fundamental reflection on literary creation. The disenchanted conclusion to which Agee came— stating the artificiality of all re-creation and the ultimate distortion of past experience through language—would not, however, prevent him from conceiving the project of reconstructing his own lost past with the aid of words and metaphors.

"They That Sow in Sorrow Shall Reap," [10] with its biblical title, reveals another aspect of Agee's preoccupations. The story describes a rural Midwest boardinghouse where people of all origins and conditions find themselves together after work, at the hour when fatigue drains the being of all emotions. The other boarders take the young Harvard student for "the scion of a wealthy house," brought to their part of the country as much by curiosity as by the need to build up his strength by working in the open air. The student himself realizes that his presence is disturbing or at least suspicious to the other boarders. But he finds he particularly likes several of them: a quiet young woman, a workman whose "linked hands resemble scrubbed roots" and their host, a handsome elderly homosexual who eventually propositions him. The student discovers that an abyss of solitude and perplexity exists beneath the old man's Olympian calm. Unhappy at what he has brought about, he decides to leave the boardinghouse, but the feeling remains that he has worsened the difficulties and problems of his host and his fellow guests. The experience anticipates the scruples Agee felt several years later in Alabama toward the people among whom he lived, he thought, as a stranger, an intruder. But the story is mainly an inquiry into the relation between emotion and reality and into the challenge that the "sharp irrelevancies" of experience may present to the mind. "As a rule, experience is broken upon innumerable sharp irrelevancies; emotion and reality, obscurely fused and inexplicably tarnished, are irreducible, and the tarnish is irradicable. Their rhythms are so subtly involved, so misgoverned by chance, as to be beyond analysis and the living mind that must endure and take part is soon fugitive before or else, however brave, falls to pieces beneath this broad unbeautiful pour of chaos" (*Collected Short Prose*, 93-94). Yet at times the mind may become aware "of a definite form and rhythm and melody of existence . . . ; out of long contrapuntal passages of tantalizing and irreconcilable elements there emerges sometimes an enormous clear chord . . . and at that moment, the whole commonplaceness of existence is transfigured—becomes monstrously powerful and beautiful and significant—assuming these qualities validly but unanswerably— and descends through tangled discords, once more into commonplaceness, with nothing answered, nothing gained, and heaven undisturbed."

This is one of the earliest fully expressed statements of Agee's perplexity in front of reality. The fluctuation from utter confusion to sudden but fleeting revelations becomes the very pattern to which his (and all) existence seems to be set. Only perhaps through artistic activity can the mind hope to grasp the melody and the significance that are so briefly perceived, prolong the transfiguration and save reality from commonplaceness or chaos. In the face of the incongruities of experience the artist's task, as Agee saw it, is at the same time exhilarating and despairing.

Returning to Thayer Hall in September, 1930, Agee resumed his routine at Harvard. In spite of his horror of figures and finances, he was named treasurer of the Signet Society, but he resigned the following year. He remained secretary of the *Advocate* until March, when he was made president, and he continued to be a member of the Glee Club and the Liberal Club. Meanwhile his desire to write had become almost an unhealthy obsession, as he wrote to Father Flye, sometimes causing him headaches and fatigue from overexertion. Having decided to do everything he could possibly do to become a great writer, he was nonetheless aware, he wrote, that he only had the resources of a minor poet. "My intellectual pelvic girdle is not Miltonically wide" (*F.F.,* 46). He was ready to do anything to further develop what he considered was his inadequate mind. Material to write about, he felt, would then abound. Only the problem of adequate expression and form would remain. Treating his vocation with utmost seriousness, the twenty-one-year-old Agee set a huge and demanding task for himself. He began to read more and to write more regularly. He hoped eventually to write works inspired by music—literary symphonies, in which the characters, like musical themes, would be introduced only to reappear as so many variations. The verbal orchestration he was after would enable him to imitate not only the sonorities of music but also its structure. He felt from the first that his project could only be accomplished in the genre of narrative poetry and that he would have to devise for the purpose a diction so supple as to cover all possible events "as perfectly . . . as skin covers every organ vital as well as trivial of the human body" (*F.F.*, 48). He dreamed of a composite art, of a more flexible and complex mode of expression, which would also unite the qualities of the cinema with those of music. He thought he detected in the works of the new young poets an increased sense of organic movement and color, a characteristic rhythm of images.

During the fall of 1930 Agee led an ascetic existence, shutting himself up in the offices of the *Advocate* to write day and night, but his life did not yield any of the order and the beauty he was seeking. His relationships with his friends were still a constant torment to him; he knew that he hurt them, and he could not help blaming himself. Further, his fits of melancholy and his propensity for daydreaming and introspection made him unsociable. But he found a certain relief in his favorite distractions; nighttime walks, piano playing, browsing in record shops, Friday symphony concerts and, of course, the movies. He in fact detailed the pleasures Boston had to offer a young Harvard undergraduate in an editorial for the *Harvard Advocate*.[11]

By January solitude began to weigh heavily upon Agee, and he gradually resumed contact with some friends: Franklin Miner; Mary-Louise White, with whom he thereafter sustained a long friendship; and mostly Via Saunders. Whereas Dorothy Carr had been the object of an ambivalent passion, Via Saunders inspired in him less turbulent, more stable feelings. Several years older than Agee, intelligent and cultivated, and sharing his taste for books and music, she brought him a new equilibrium. Perhaps he also treasured the memory of her family and was grateful to her for the tranquil times he had known at Clinton. He began to write poetry again. The Christmas, 1930, issue of the *Harvard Advocate* had published his second sonnet, "I Have Been Fashioned on a Chain of Flesh," composed of elliptical and inverse phrases that appear in the middle of the lines and that finally transform the end of the poem into a biblical chant.[12] In the poem Agee pays homage to the dead. The poet sees that his mission is to continue the fight the dead have bequeathed to him and thereby to give them a kind of immortality. But he also realizes that, dying in his turn, he too will be defeated and rejoin those whom he has betrayed.

"Resolution" [13] shows Agee's skill in creating two levels of meaning at the same time, the strictly personal level, dealing with his own passions and uncertainties, and the more general level, dealing with the fate of humanity. "The Truce," a longer poem, describes a love that ends up having nothing but pity left to sustain itself.[14] The lovers, face to face, look into each other's eyes, which are like mirrors repeating to infinity the emptiness of their hearts. Their multiplied pity is thus a double hell. Agee was disturbed to see how quickly pity, which benumbs passion, destructively enters into love and how readily the heart accepts it. The poem, in its refined analysis, in its metaphysical explorations and in its careful elaboration of scientific images, contains echoes of Donne. There is also in the imagery a reminiscence of Brahms's Requiem "Behold All Flesh Is as the Grass," which was at the time part of the Glee Club repertory. The poem already was doubtless composed under the influence of I. A. Richards. Agee was familiar with the experiments described in *Practical Criticism* that Richards continued when, upon his return from Peking, he came to Harvard in the second semester of 1931.

"You, Andrew Volstead," a story published in the *Advocate* (March, 1931), is a comic portrayal of the point to which passion can deteriorate when it is no longer even capable of pity. Young Andrew takes to drink in order to escape from his girlfriend's reproaches. The dialogue between the two lovers, as the young man becomes increasingly drunk and the girl increasingly bitter, reflects Agee's concern for an accurate transcription of dialect. In a brief summary of T. S. Matthews' novel *To the Gallows I Must Go,* Agee mentioned his admiration for H. L. Mencken, whose treatise on the American language would help American writers to achieve a deeper sense of the possibilities of their language. At Easter, 1931, Agee actually met I. A. Richards, and thus began an acquaintanceship that had a decisive influence on his life. Agee saw Richards as the incarnation of an intellectual ideal, much as he saw the Saunderses as the incarnation of an aesthetic ideal. Richards' teaching, devoted to the study of beauty and to the perfection of his students' perception of it, had a great effect on Agee, who became one of the master's enthusiastic disciples. To him, Richards was a cross between Hamlet and a character from a Dostoevski novel, because of the way Richards seemed to understand evil, suffering and death without causing himself much personal torment.

Richards' teaching bore fruit that summer as Agee, who had finally caught up with his own class before embarking upon his senior year, devoted his vacation to reading and writing poetry. Before leaving Cambridge, he had already written a lyric poem and three sonnets and he wrote four more pieces in three days at the home of Theodore Spencer. He felt he had now succeeded in his verse (following Richards' prescription), in establishing the applicability of the English poetic tradition to poetry about contemporary American reality. At his mother's house, where he spent his vacation, he began to read Dostoevski, whom Richards had helped him appreciate. He first read *The Possessed,* and he found it completely different from anything he had read up till that time. It seemed to him to be a perfect, powerful realization of a poor short story he had written several weeks earlier.

He shared impressions of the books he was reading with Father Flye and Via Saunders. Enlightened by Dostoevski's example, he analyzed his own failings. He chastised himself for seeking verbal or formal beauty at the expense of the force of an idea.[15] He compared *The Possessed* and *The Sound and the Fury* and found the Faulkner novel not entirely successful. Though it represented an attempt to reconcile strength and beauty, it did not achieve a balance between them. (The book made you feel, Agee wrote, like someone climbing into a boat that was always floating away.) On the other hand, Dostoevski was able to achieve his powerful effects by his almost total disregard of beauty.

That summer Agee set up for himself a severe writing schedule

—nine hours a day with one hour of relaxation around noon—but he rarely kept to it. In a room nearby a piano awaited him and often, when he left his work intending to relax for fifteen or twenty minutes, he would end up playing for over two hours. Aside from his reading and his work there were few distractions at Rockland. The movie theater showed poor films, and parties bored him. There remained the excursions with a young lady (whom Agee never names), who was "petrified" by small-town life and who entertained herself with the thought that one day she might kill herself, the hours spent in trying to distract his grandmother, whose illness had made her very demanding, and the drives with his family and with his friend, "Brick" Frohock. Toward the end of the vacation he spent three weeks in Clinton. I. A. Richards, who happened to be visiting the Saunderses also at the time, read his poetry and encouraged him to continue writing. It was during this stay that he realized what an important place Via had begun to occupy in his life, and he was thrilled to learn that she had decided to come and live in Cambridge.

Agee began his last year of college full of firm resolutions. For the first time the thought of final examinations plunged him into a frenzy of work. He studied until late each day and slept barely four hours a night. "It is the most extraordinary three months of my life. . . . Everything going continuously at top speed, mind, body, nerves, and with an intensity I've never known before: with powers, pain and joy, all humming at once; with everything terrifically actual, yet abstracted and clear. as glass" (*F.F.*, 54-55). He enjoyed long nocturnal talks with Via and with another friend, Irving Upham. At Eliot House, where he now lived, his acquaintances hardly ever saw him. His roommate, Robert Saudek, marveled at his strange habits. At the same time Agee was even more actively involved with the *Advocate,* of which he was now president. With Otto Shoen-René, he began working on a parody of *Time* Magazine, which they intended to finish by Christmas. And finally, he was writing poems, crafting them with a discipline as strict as if he were composing music.

He spent Christmas vacation in Maine, where he finished the parody of *Time*. But when he returned to Eliot House in January, 1932, he had another fit of depression; the enthusiasm of the last three months was gone. He had the feeling that his four years at Harvard were a waste; and he also found serious fault with himself. Again he wanted to leave college. And once again Father Flye and his other friends dissuaded him from taking any rash action. He then thought of seeking a scholarship to Oxford or Cambridge, but the letter of application he prepared for the Guggenheim Committee was so tactless that it all but guaranteed his being turned down. He made it clear to the Committee that he would, if he could, have preferred to do without its help since he felt that philanthropic institutions provided no solution for the problem of the artist living in a basically hostile society.

Agee remained at Harvard until graduation, having finally decided to accept the necessities of the moment. One course that did interest him that spring was Professor Kittredge's on Shakespeare. Meanwhile, as exams were fast approaching, he found his administrative duties as president of the *Advocate* too burdensome, and in April, 1932, he resigned. According to Julian Bach, who was a board member at the time, the editorial meetings had been boring Agee to death. When he spoke at all it was in a barely audible murmur. Taciturn bohemian that he was, with his sloppy appearance, heavy turtleneck sweaters and rounded shoulders, he was irritating to the regular Harvard, prep-school types, who never appeared anywhere without a suit and tie. Agee's indifference to personal appearance was interpreted by certain people as disrespect for others, but those who knew him accepted him as he was. Robert Fitzgerald, himself the "respectable" type, never thought to criticize his friend for what others found scandalous. Disconcerting for some, fascinating for others, but in any case with little concern for the effect he was producing, Agee, everyone agreed, had an exceptional personality and an undeniable impact on the *Advocate* and its members during his term as president.[16] When, in March, 1932, his parody of *Time* appeared, using *Time*'s format, headings and manner of presentation, it was acclaimed as a high point in the history of the *Advocate*. Agee of course was satirizing not only *Time* but also that aspect of American civilization that the magazine represented. Otto Ernst Feuerbringer, president of *Crimson,* congratulated the editors of the *Advocate* who for once, he said, had come out of their torpor and were daring to express themselves on serious, social issues.[17]

By the time the issue appeared, however, Agee had already forgotten the months of work that had gone into it and was busily occupied with other projects. He began revising a number of poems that he planned to submit to the next Garrison Prize competition. He read and reread his poems to his friends, listened to their criticisms and welcomed their suggestions. In April the Garrison Prize was awarded jointly to him and to S. P. Franckot. Agee won for a group of poems, all implicitly dealing with the process of creativity:[18] "I Have Been Fashioned on a Chain of Flesh," which had been published in the December, 1930, *Advocate;* "Strengthless They Stand Assembled"; "Poem of Poets," which had been published in October, 1931; and two longer poems, "Poet's Valediction," composed the previous summer, and "Epithalamium," which dated from 1930. Curiously, in submitting his poems to competition, Agee used his uncle Hugh Tyler's name as a pseudonym. In June, 1932, Agee bade farewell to Harvard and to the *Advocate* with an ode, written for the members of his class, which he read that June as part of the graduation ceremonies at Saunders Theater. He expressed in three verses of serene melancholy his vision of the world and of its inevitable demise.[19] He also wrote at this time a very long satirical poem, "Don Juan," unconventional, brilliant and disconcerting in its technique and composition.[20] A parody of all poetry Agee had admired—the Elizabethans, Donne and the metaphysical poets, Byron and Eliot—it is also a confession of the disenchantment and confusion of its author and ultimately a self-parody, interspersed with accusations against the reader be he "priest, pimp, matron, child, or spinster" and the critics. "Don Juan," however, was extremely ambitious in scope. Conceived as an "anatomy of evil," it would later expand into a much longer poem humorously surveying the evils of civilization through the tribulations of its hero, John Carter, a childish, extroverted personality endowed with diabolic powers. Believing strongly that every poem should be read aloud since language is best understood when heard, Agee had given a complete reading of "Don Juan" at the Eagle Hotel in Concord, Massachusetts, where he had gathered a small number of his friends, among them Frohock, Christopher Gerould and Via Saunders. "Don Juan. The Opening of a Long Poem" appeared in a heavily censored version in the *Advocate*.[21] Not only words but entire lines were omitted. But its author would no doubt have been offended not to have received the oblique compliment of censorship.

When Agee left Harvard he had a certain reputation, though it did not extend outside the university and his circle of friends. He was known not only as a poet and a writer but as a brilliant student as well, for he had graduated with excellent grades in English. Thus, whether he cared to admit it or not, he was leaving the university in a fairly conventional manner, with all the kudos accorded to a Harvard graduate. Now twenty-three, his personality was still a mystery to him about which he endlessly tortured himself. He dreamed of being whole and was himself divided. The anxiety he had felt during his childhood had only become more intense, and it sometimes created an inner vertigo pushing him toward suicide. Upon graduation in the middle of America's Great Depression, Agee also saw the irony of the vocation he had chosen. Preoccupied until then with personal and literary problems, he suddenly became aware of his social responsibility as a poet. He felt he could no longer ignore the world around him. He would now confront reality directly. In the America of the thirties, what else could be the hope, the justification and the mission of a writer starting out?

PART III

RESOLUTIONS

CHAPTER ONE

FORTUNE AND NEW YORK:
TRIALS AND DILEMMAS

"The shattered world groans its anguished last against our ear." (*C.P.,* 157)

AGEE'S FINANCIAL STATUS HARDLY FAVORED HIS CHOSEN CAREER. He had been a scholarship student at both Exeter and Harvard, and that situation probably contributed to his inability to feel at ease among his affluent fellow students at either place. Since he had no outside source of income that would allow him the freedom to write as he chose, he had begun looking for a job long before graduation. An unexpected opportunity appeared at once, solving his material difficulties but placing him in another dilemma.

Henry Luce, who ran *Fortune* and *Time* magazines, learned of Agee's *Time* parody and was taken by its skill and audacity. It was then easy for Dwight Macdonald, who himself worked at *Fortune,* to convince Luce to put Agee on his staff. For all his personal control over his publications, Luce appreciated literary excellence. He wanted brilliant and ingenious minds to be on the assembly line of his "great factory." And as a successful publisher he could offer aspiring writers not only an opportunity to write, but the material security they could not find elsewhere. In return, he was insuring the high literary quality of the articles in his magazines. Luce was nevertheless aware of the potential danger of taking independent intellectuals into an organization that had a predetermined editorial policy, and as a result, he set about deintellectualizing his staff. He had no use for original or radical thinkers; he wanted his writers simply to take the information gathered with the help of a researcher and work it into a sparklingly readable essay.

Of his two magazines, *Time* had been founded first, in 1923. In 1929 Luce conceived the idea of a new magazine more exclusively devoted to business and industry. When the first issue of *Fortune* appeared in October of that year, the economic circumstances seemed most inopportune, to say the least, yet the magazine turned out to be a huge success. And the crisis itself had a notable effect on the subject matter and the tone of the articles. During the next four years *Fortune* opened its eyes to the new reality: the New Deal and the continuing Depression.

The change in orientation was largely the work of the magazine's team of writers, who had undertaken to reveal the underside of American capitalism. There was in fact constant conflict between the writers, who demanded freedom of expression, and their editors, who were careful to see that the magazine's editorial position was respected. An editor would vigilantly rework each article submitted—softening the tone, cutting out an undesirable passage, removing an undesirable fact. Writers, however, were in short supply, in spite of the high salaries then being offered by *Fortune,* and the success of the magazine was too dependent on them for the management not to seek a compromise on controversial issues.[1]

Agee was nevertheless surprised to be asked to work for the very enterprise he had recently so publicly attacked. He also feared that for obvious reasons he would find the work distasteful. On the other hand, he reflected, Archibald MacLeish and Dwight Macdonald, who were both at *Fortune,* seemed to have survived. Macdonald encouraged him with the information that a writer could earn up to $12,000 a year after a probationary period; and the example of MacLeish convinced him that an artist could live in the world of Henry Luce without necessarily being destroyed. Nor did the political tendencies that were emerging at *Fortune* at the time totally displease Agee. He found it attractive to count himself among the liberal writers on one of the most conservative publications in the country; fond as he was of paradoxes and outrages, it stimulated his combative wit. He, too, would slip things past the vigilance of the editors, and so play—and win—the game. But Agee was nonetheless aware of the danger of his undertaking. Poets, in the America of 1932, had little chance for survival, whether they chose to compromise or not. The suicides of Vachel Lindsay and Hart Crane had tragically demonstrated that. And Hart Crane's own experience at *Fortune* under the sponsorship of MacLeish had ended in failure.

When Agee finally accepted *Fortune*'s offer, it was not without serious reservations. He left Cambridge immediately after graduation, hoping his career as a journalist would be brief. He could not anticipate that it would last for more than fifteen years.

Plunged abruptly into the New York City world, Agee reacted indifferently at first. And in the first weeks in his new job he found his life strangely empty, empty as the huge skyscraper he worked in, where he often took refuge during the night when all the offices were deserted. "I have taken very little advantage of what the Big City offers in way of ruination," he wrote Via Saunders on August 1, "—much less in fact than I did in Cambridge." His indifference puzzled him. He was alarmed at the thought that perhaps he was becoming a stoic, one of those admirable men whom he so scorned. He hoped, he humorously wrote Via, he wasn't prematurely turning into ice. His fears to the contrary, Agee questioned and studied himself more than ever during those first lonely weeks. The responsibilities of a new profession and the overwhelming presence of the city lent a more final quality to his actions and his decisions as well as to his despair and his defeats.

Again he was unsure whether his talent justified his ambitions and past hopes. There was nothing truly creative in him, he wrote to Via, not even any talent worth mentioning. Everything he had written seemed like a repetition of someone else's ideas or an imitation of someone else's style. He had mistaken for inspiration, he whined, the natural emotion aroused by beauty. He would, for instance, listen to Brahms and, driven by the emotion, write a short story, adding to Brahms's inspiration the mixed influences of Sherwood Anderson, Ernest Hemingway and John Donne: "Of course, I know that every man of talent or genius since the first incredible people who really began things, have depended upon such external excitements and handed down ideas and have written in them. I have nothing on earth against the several dozen lands of plagiarism that travel through any artist's head, except the sad fact that when they don't work, they don't work, and it's clear to me that mine don't." [2] In the absence of confidence that he was capable of truly original work, might it not be necessary, he asked, for him to cultivate a positive illusion about his talent? "In some cases," he continued, "I am not sure of the value of never fooling yourself, and writing is one of the cases; I think, as a rule, you are as small a writer as you feel, and if by any combination of fool circumstances you manage to feel like a great one, you have then at worst a fighting chance which you'd otherwise lack." [3]

He began to feel that he had lost his ambition and imagination, and that some of his faculties were dying. The feelings that music and poetry had once awakened in him had faded into memories. He admitted to Via that he was living in a comatose state and that only a thin membrane was separating him from pure madness. Lethargy alternated with moments of lucidity, and he seriously considered committing suicide. He expressed the same fears in his letters to Father Flye: "I have been used to bad spells of despondency always, but this is something else again: it seems to be a rapid settling into despair of everything I want and everything about myself. If I am . . . dying on my feet mentally and spiritually and can do nothing about it, I'd prefer not to know I am dying. I've felt like suicide for weeks now and not just fooling with the idea, but feeling seriously on the edge of it" (*F.F.*, 56). He saw only one other solution: taking refuge, "like diving into icy water," in an ironic detachment. But he found, of course, he was incapable of such control.

The letters to Flye and Via further show that in his emotional life Agee feared that he was weak and effeminate, a "sissy." He longed for an invulnerability that would give him a measure of indifference to people and events. Although during these summer months he was separated from the two people he most cared for —his friend Irving Upham, who was then in Europe, and Via Saunders, who was in Santa Fe—Agee felt more than ever dependent upon them. His relationship with Via, in fact, had become capricious and turbulent. Both he and Via had decided to test themselves by a separation. Via refused to return from Santa Fe when Agee asked her to. When she sent him a letter signed, "Sincerely, your friend," he grew angry at her coldness. In reply he sent two letters, one formal and distant, as from a casual acquaintance, the other in the form of a passionate hillbilly love poem: "I take this off moment in hand to axe after y'r health." Both letters were in Tennessee dialect, with characteristically imaginative style and spelling. This double disguise clearly revealed how uncertain his own feelings were as he vacillated between a detached friendship that was unfulfilling and a slightly naive confession of love. He was angry at Via's indifference, which he believed was not real, but he was, of course, ambivalent himself.

Marriage could perhaps bring some of the serenity he hoped one day to find, but Agee knew that his moods were changeable and his affections inconstant. Marriage demanded a certain permanence from which he fled at the same time that he sought it. New York had intensified his loneliness and created the need for a deep and stable attachment, but it seemed cowardly to him to ask another person for a support he could not find in himself.

These sometimes contrary states of mind Agee explored in a number of sonnets [4] that drew upon Elizabethan, metaphysical,

Christian and chivalric models. Whether dialogues with the loved one or meditations on the nature of love, they all dramatized his worries and disappointments and partially exorcised his demons.

Regarding New York, Agee's indifference grew into hostility. He saw it as an enormous trap, a monstrous city that threatened him with spiritual death. New York had two very different effects on him: on the one hand, it paralyzed and depressed him; on the other, it pulled him along in its own frenzied vitality.

During this time Agee lived in Brooklyn but felt no curiosity about a neighborhood that only a few months later came to fascinate him. He became friendly with Archibald MacLeish, whose poetry he admired. In August he met Selden Rodman, an anthologist well known in New York literary and artistic circles. He also was thankful for the friendship of Robert Goldwater and Eleanor Tracy. At night he would bring his friends to his office to listen to records he had bought or borrowed. Monday and Wednesday evenings, when all the offices were closed, the Chrysler Building, where *Fortune*'s offices were located, belonged to him. He had bought himself a phonograph, which he could not use in his apartment because the voltage was inadequate, and had brought it to the office to inaugurate it with Beethoven's Ninth Symphony, played at ear-splitting volume. "An empty skyscraper is just about an ideal place for it—with the volume it has" (*F.F.*, 60). And with New York at his feet, it was an exhilarating experience that could make him forget his loneliness and his problems.[5] He worked at night with whiskey and music. At dawn he would reluctantly leave the building, oblivious to the astonished looks of the workers who arrived to prepare the offices for the daywork teams. At this time Agee's letters to Father Flye contained many bitter reflections on friendship. "There is something sad and crazy about passing year after year of fairly short life in such poor communication with people you care for," he wrote (*F.F.*, 59). He found that separation pushed one toward new friendships that endangered the old ones without adequately replacing them. But life was not without its pleasant surprises. Irving Upham cut short his stay in Europe, Via returned from her "exile" and Agee renewed his friendship with a fellow Harvard student, Christopher Gerould. He began to feel that the crisis he had gone through in the summer months was reaching an end and announced to Via that perhaps one "would soon see a glimpse of goodness in his cold gray eyes." [6] His difficulties were gradually being resolved. He found a better located and more comfortable apartment, where he could finally use his phonograph, and he started to go out more, to concerts and especially to films.[7] But most important, he resumed his long late-night discussions with his friends. He reveled again in his marvelous gift of conversation, and in fact he preferred talking to the solitary experience of writing. Conversation freed him, allowing ideas to be born and to develop while his mind confronted other people's. Sometimes he drank heavily, too, but drinking brought him only discomfort and apathy.

His mind was again teeming with projects. He continued to work on "Don Juan" and rewrote almost 1,200 lines. Inspired by his rereading of Swift and by his admiration for his matchless understanding of the cruelties of human nature, he had begun working on a short story, which he described in a letter to Howard Doughty dated July of that summer: "I have lately been at work on a would-be-Swift-like story about two civilized virgins seducing each other, putting physical and mental action into as cold terms as possible. The idea is not without humor and, as it proceeds through repetitions of action and development of a code of ownership over certain areas not without its quota of nausea. But if I make it as anatomically explicit as I've started out, God knows who would publish it." The Swiftian lessons bore early fruit in lines Agee wrote on the Depression. Around him he saw nothing but disgust, egotism and cruelty, a total blindness to goodness and beauty. But even as he predicted the spiritual and moral ruin of America, he also sensed the dawning of the new order elsewhere: [8]

> The wide black breadth of Russia's but begun
> to rear its green illimitable power:

Our western zero shrewdly shakes our sun
　Yet in this brief and steeply shadowed hour
Ere flesh deserts and earth adopts the bone
　There's more to do but sit and make sweet moan.

Like so many intellectuals of his time, Agee turned with mixed feelings of hope toward Communism and the example of the Soviet Union. The suffering he had seen as a child among the people of Tennessee, his instinctive sympathy for the poor, his hatred of the rich and the philistine, led him to share with certain of his contemporaries the dream of a great militant Socialist brotherhood that would liberate the world. In 1932 he felt himself ready to leave his aesthetic preoccupations behind and take part in the struggle that had enlisted so many artists of his time. He looked forward to converting belief into some concrete form of action.

CHAPTER TWO

PITFALLS AND ATTRACTIONS
OF JOURNALISM

AT THE BEGINNING AGEE'S JOB AT FORTUNE HELD LITTLE IN-
terest for him. He was unused to writing articles to order, to meet
a deadline. He began by spending hours sitting in front of his desk
chewing on his pencil. In a neighboring office, Archibald MacLeish
worried that Agee would soon be fired if he were not more productive. He tried to encourage Agee and to get him to reconcile
himself to being a salaried writer. Patiently, he spurred him on and
gently lectured him on some of the advantages of the job. It would
provide a sensitive and intelligent writer with a singular opportunity
to learn firsthand a great deal about the current economic and
political situation in the country. Since Luce allowed his writers
some degree of freedom, Agee would surely be able to find a
subject to write about close to his own interests. MacLeish further
pointed out that the job could help him become interested in
things outside of his own moods and fantasies and perhaps thus
give him more confidence.

Agee, won by some of his friend's arguments, grimly knuckled
down. He soon learned the tricks of the trade. Since most of his

opinions were unlikely to be well received by his editors, he would dot his text with traps designed to distract the editors' attention from the short, apparently innocuous phrases that would carry the weight of his message. In addition, he devised another trick, which he used throughout his years in journalism. Because the texts he submitted were always much too long, his articles were heavily cut, and sometimes the passages he felt were most important were eliminated. He therefore decided to repeat each important point he had to make in three or more different sentences, in the hopes that at least one of the three sentences would remain in the final version. When his article finally appeared he would pounce on the magazine to read it and would feel triumphant when, in spite of all the changes in his text, he found unaltered one of the sentences he had painstakingly hidden. Like many of the other writers, he waged a guerrilla war against the editors and, by extension, against the system of capitalist ethics. These little victories, he felt, repaid him for the humiliations of his situation. He was constantly aware of the contradictions he was forced to accept as a combination poet and *Fortune* writer. He continued to fear that he was prostituting himself, that he was neglecting his talent and that he was devoting his energy to an enterprise whose spirit was repugnant to him. In spite of these strong misgivings, he eventually came to like the atmosphere of the office, to admire the team spirit that united author and researcher and to welcome the friendship that existed among some of the writers.[1]

He worked with MacLeish on his first assignments—an article on housing and another on aerodynamics. In the following three weeks he wrote reports on unemployment and on radical politics. His job was bringing him into contact with social classes and professions he would not otherwise have known.

At the end of the probationary period at *Fortune*, Agee still entertained thoughts of quitting. Once more he considered applying for a Guggenheim fellowship in order to be able to spend a year writing in France. With his usual mixture of desultory humor and vindictive earnestness, he began to fill out the necessary application forms. He outlined his projects, citing "Don Juan" as his major writing achievement. He now described it as a satiric-epic, comic, moral and metaphysical poem that attempted to depict the American scene.[2] By this time the poem was already over one thousand lines long and would, when finished, make a volume in itself. Agee also referred in his application to a short story, "Let Us Now Praise Famous Men," which he later did write but which seems unfortunately to have been lost. To support his application he submitted recommendations from Myron Williams, Conrad Aiken, I. A. Richards for all of his works, and from Stephen Vincent Benét, Archibald MacLeish, Robert Hillyer, Ted Spencer, Bernard De Voto and Robert Phelps. Toward the end of his application he mentioned the possibility that "Don Juan" might never be completed. Whether or not they felt irritated by the tone in which the application was drawn up, the Guggenheim Committee refused Agee the award. Back at *Fortune,* however, the management preferred to accept Agee's caprices rather than to lose him entirely, for he was beginning to be recognized as a considerable talent. Favorably impressed by an article he had written about the loom, the editors renewed his contract.

It was perhaps this guaranteed income that led Agee to begin seriously considering marriage with Via. "Seriousness means gloom to me," he wrote to Father Flye (*F.F.,* 64), and he made no secret of his lack of enthusiasm for the decision he was about to make. He was angry with himself for accepting, in his private as well as his professional life, a stability that he dreaded as much as desired. Little by little, however, he began to feel more relaxed, and propose he did and accepted he was. He found an apartment with two rooms and a tiny garden, in the basement of a brownstone on Percy Street, not far from where his uncle Hugh Tyler now lived. Via moved in first, alone, and their marriage took place in Utica, New York, on Saturday, January 28, 1933. The ceremony was nondenominational as Agee did not want Via to convert to his religion unless she did so of her own free will.

At *Fortune* there was little leisure for Agee. He was assigned a great variety of subjects, fascinating or trivial. He did all kinds of reporting; he became familiar with the world of business and learned how to juggle statistics in order to make a point. But in spite of the harassments of his editors, he retained, in Luce's world, his own individual style. And a piece he wrote at this time on baldness is saved from banality and dry exposition by his wonderful sardonic wit.[3]

Sometimes he would begin an article as though it were a fable: "On the Tibetan upland a shepherd whose name we shall not invent . . ." thus seducing the reader by using stylistic devices that had no relation with the content of the article, the technical description of a weaving loom.[4] Writing of the "Cincinnati Terminal," he allowed himself all sorts of humorous digressions on the meaning of the word *terminus*.[5] He also spoke with respect of man's labor, of his discoveries and inventions, which he saw as the stages of a vast epic. Trades and handicrafts were as fascinating to him as the stupendous accomplishments of gigantic modern enterprises.

During the summer of 1933 Agee took a leave of absence, and he and Via divided their time between Clinton, at the Saunders', and Santa Fe, where Via had been the previous year. From these distances his work seemed to him even more hateful. He saw it, he wrote to Robert Fitzgerald, as a gesture of semisuicide. On returning to *Fortune,* however, he wrote one of his very best pieces, a long article on the Tennessee Valley Authority. To prepare the article he had traveled to Tennessee, a trip that also inspired a very fine poem called "Night Piece," later retitled "Theme with Variations" (*C.P.,* 53), which describes an unaltered nature at the hour when night gradually silences the day: "the tongue is furled and the fair dust not flawed and the wings shut high." But the article for *Fortune* was supposed to be technical; Agee, for the first time, had to assess his native region in terms of statistics. The article examined how the Tennessee farmers, hillbillies isolated from the rest of the world, would react to the intrusion into their lives of the TVA and its landscape-altering projects. Agee expressed his fervent belief that the Tennessee farmers would never change—in spite of the presence of the TVA.[6] The article, predictably, was written with a lyricism that stood out in a magazine devoted to the interests of business. Though it was not the economic study the editors had had in mind, it nevertheless attracted attention. It was praised as one of the best pieces the magazine had ever published; Luce called Agee into his office to congratulate him personally and even offered him a permanent job provided he would agree to get further training in the world of business. Should he be willing to go back to Harvard for a year to study at the Business School, the magazine would cover all his expenses. No proposal could have been more ironic for Agee. He had little desire to become an economist and would have preferred to tell Luce that he wanted no part of a career in his offices, but he refrained. "I'd much rather succeed than fail this job before I quit it," he wrote to Father Flye (*F.F.*, 66). He came to consider each article as an opportunity to practice his craft. In his inability to do a job carelessly, and as a means of appeasing his literary conscience, he spent hours revising the pieces he wrote. And indeed the very conditions of his work imposed on him an exemplary discipline.

But there were incidents. When Luce asked him to write an article on railroads, Agee refused, claiming that it held no interest for him. This was, in fact, the first time Agee had dared to protest so intransigently, and he held his ground until finally the assignment was given to another writer. Winning the issue was sufficient to assure him a certain autonomy in future assignments.

In 1934 Agee wrote a series of articles for *Fortune* on diverse and innocuous subjects—few of which had any relevance to the crisis that was threatening the nation: quinine, butlers, cockfights, American ambassadors, arbitration, Roman high society, ministerial cabinets in Italy, the roadside landscape of the United States, the drought in the South and illuminated manuscripts. Once the facts had been gathered, Agee worked them into a story that, though it contained the necessary figures and statistics, was always leavened by a note of fantasy, humor or irony. His article on butlers began: "A sprinkling of elderly, leancheeked, perfectly appointed gentlemen who spoke with good dry accents and who bore themselves with all the effortless aplomb of cabinet ministers . . . They were products of a lifelong training in bearing and manner and poise and tact, gentlemen who spoke pridefully of their life's work as a profession: they were butlers." [7] In many pieces he found an opportunity to extol the dignity of poor people or the beauty of the humblest trades. In "Cock Fighting" [8] he insisted upon the "rooster worshippers'" unspoken code of honor as they practiced their ancient though prohibited sport. Cockfighting, he noted, was not merely an entertainment, it was a sacrament, the cock itself the symbol of a mortal though triumphant individualism. A report on the stock market and "arbitrage" plunged him into the dizzying world of finance,[9] while an article on the "American Roadside" [10] sent him back to his days of bumming; he likened the American continent to "an open palm spread frank before the sky against the bulk of the world," and he skillfully adapted the rhythm of his sentences to the countryside he depicted, from the rugged coast of Maine to the vast central plains. Agee describes the American roadside in the early morning in all its variety as being as fascinating for the driver—for all its ugliness—as for him who dares travel it on foot. He also vented his rage against the automobile, which was by then (1934) beginning to jam up the open road.

That year Agee wrote an article on the great drought, which made 1934 one of the poorest years of the decade.[11] Accompanying the eloquent photographs of Margaret Bourke-White—"the clear dispassionate eye of the camera," Agee's text described "the piteous meagre sweat on the air, the earth baked stiff and steaming." Where the corpses of starved cattle being devoured by vultures now littered the landscape, there used to be, Agee poignantly remembered, abundant life. "When the wind woke you up at night with its hustling on the heavy grain . . . the blades chattered and choked on the fat wheat . . . beneath the temperate air the rooted sea poured the sheen of its proud plain wealth." Two years later *Fortune* was to send Agee to the South with another photographer,

Walker Evans, with the same sort of assignment. Only this time Agee's subject was no longer the sins of nature against man, but those of man against himself. The result was Agee's and Evans' most powerful book, *Let Us Now Praise Famous Men.*

In spite of his prolific activities, Agee remained deeply dissatisfied. Disturbed by his growing involvement in professional obligations, he continued to dream of being free to concentrate on his own work. He might have sought aid from the Works Project Administration, through which writers obtained a regular subsidy from the state, but he remained suspicious of such organizations. He steadfastly believed that the writer should live on the fringe of society. Once again he toyed with the idea of becoming a teacher. He told Father Flye that he was considering returning to Saint Andrew's, but he did not know if Via would be able to adjust to the calm, rural life of Tennessee. Father Flye succeeded in convincing him that he was made neither for teaching nor for a secluded existence in the South—at least, not yet. Agee also considered taking a leave of absence in 1936 to withdraw to Yaddo, the artists' colony near Saratoga. He secretly hoped that if he could change the conditions of his life, he would be cured of the melancholy that had seized him again. He knew it to be an inner disorder, although he would have preferred to blame it on external causes. His despair caused him anew to contemplate suicide. He began to speculate obsessively on what the very instant before death could be like. He thus proceeded, one October day in 1934, to coolly tempt himself. In his office, high up in the Chrysler Building, he tested his attraction to death, "balancing over suicide as you might lean out over the edge of a high building as far as you could keep from falling but with no special desire to fall" (*F.F.*, 68). The "edge of a high building" was not a figure of speech. One of his friends, entering Agee's office, saw only his hands clinging to the outside window sill and was an unexpected witness to the terrifying scene: Agee hovering over the Manhattan void. Dumbstruck, the friend quietly waited behind the door until he heard the reassuring sounds of Agee climbing back into the room. Afterward he found Agee to be strangely calm and he took care not to reveal his own fright.[12]

Agee's depressions were often manic. Sometimes he was morose and silent, other times he was overexcited and talked incessantly. When speaking to a friend in the street he often walked backward, apologizing profusely to passersby he bumped into without seeing. Whatever his mood, he seemed constantly preoccupied; he confessed that he felt as though he was inhabited by "freely roaming animals or crossed by a high wire tension." The sudden news that a collection of his poems had been accepted for publication by the Yale Press lifted him abruptly from his intense melancholy and forced him to reconsider his vocation as poet.

CHAPTER THREE

POETIC VOYAGE

"Take these who will as may be: I
Am careless now of what they fail:
My heart and mind discharted lie . . ."

—"Permit Me Voyage" (*C.P.*, 49)

WHEN AGEE LEARNED THAT THE YALE PRESS HAD SENT A COPY
of his collection to John Livingston Lowes, who had been one of
his professors at Harvard, he wrote him an apologetic letter: "I had
thought of it and then thought it best not to bother you (you would
scarcely or never have heard of me); but when I heard from the
Yale Press this morning that they were sending you a copy of
Permit Me Voyage, a first book of my poems, I was very glad and
I am writing to say so. . . . I am glad a copy is coming to you
not because I think you'll like them, but because I'm reasonably
sure you won't." [1]

It was MacLeish who had finally convinced Agee to submit his
manuscript to the Yale Press. Stephen Vincent Benét, the editor
of the Yale Series of Younger Poets, had already published writers
as diverse as Norman Foster, Muriel Rukeyser and Margaret
Walker. From the forty-two manuscripts submitted to him in 1934,

he chose Agee's. On June 22, 1934, Benét sent it on to Eugene Davidson, his colleague at the Yale University Press, with a letter of recommendation. "I think the long poems show extraordinary promise, especially the 'Dedication' one." [2] Benét was concerned with getting publicity for the collection. Since he wanted a good preface, he thought of MacLeish, who accepted without hesitation.

In the preface MacLeish presents Agee as one of the most promising and interesting poets of the new generation; literary generations, he said, don't succeed each other as rapidly in the United States as they do in France, for example, where a new movement appears every three years. Only the work is able to signal a revival, not the techniques and the themes that inspired it. The advent of Communism, the enthusiasm it arouses, the Marxist theories—none of these things suffices to create a new art. Agee's poems will scarcely excite those who seek new ideas: Agee takes no stand. However, the emotions and ideas are all there— love of the land, scorn for his country's civilization. The emotion is controlled. Everything is said with moderation and the equilibrium is never broken; the labor, the care brought to each poem, the "craft"—*that,* said MacLeish, is what's important. MacLeish praised the modesty of "a serious artist, conscientious and humble," stressing that the work exists independently of the author's opinions and intentions. "It is not enough to assert in verse the merits of Marxism . . . a vigorous belief in the beauty of existence. What is necessary in either case is to make the thing *happen* in the poem as it has never happened before." [3] MacLeish was actually criticized for this preface for having used Agee, of whom he speaks only in the final lines, as a pretext to expound his own ideas on poetry.

The book is divided into seven parts:[4] it opens with nine short lyrics, then "Dedication," "Ann Garner," "A Chorale," "Epithalamium," twenty-five sonnets and finally the title poem. From the first, the lyric poems were intended to open the collection, each in fact a brief introduction to one of the book's recurring themes: love and disillusionment, innocence, untimely death, the contrast between dream and reality. Agee's original conception was that "Ann Garner" should follow (he conceived of the entire collection as a musical structure divided into ordered movements), but Benét persuaded him to place "Dedication" before. Benét, in fact, had wanted to put "Dedication" at the very beginning, but Agee had doubtless opposed this. He would have felt it clumsy to introduce the book with a long prose poem so personal in tone. Instead, the lyrics are short, classical and rapid in rhythm:

> Child, should any pleasant boy
> Find you lovely . . .
>
> Spread all your beauty in his sight
> And do him kindness every way
> Since soon, too soon the wolfer night
> Climbs in between and ends fair play. (*C.P.*, 3)

So the collection begins. A second lyric evokes the despair of a love that cowardice alone preserves, and a third, "The Happy Hen," humorously deals with quick, uncomplicated passion. "His hottest love and most delight/The rooster knows for speed of fear . . ." (*C.P.*, 7). Still another evokes the austerity of winter in a series of brief, elliptical notations:

> Still thorn bone bare
> Iron in the silenced gully
> Rattling only of the air
> Through hornleaved holly. (*C.P.*, 7)

The poetry is by turns simple and sophisticated. At times it draws on the language of popular songs; elsewhere it borrows the "concetti" and mannerisms of the Elizabethan poets. In all cases the poems are skillfully constructed. And the imagery could be as striking as that of the phantom who puts an end to the poet's dream:

> The shade o'erswam me like a sheet
> Of draughty disappointed vans
> And lobbered beak, and drawling feet. (*C.P.*, 3)

In "Dedication" Agee lists everything that, in his eyes, could give meaning to his imperious vocation and pays homage to those who have served the truth he himself is impatiently seeking. The poem attempts to present all the contradictory aspects of the "culture" that man has built up over the centuries: societies created by necessity or the illusion of necessity, laws that "make a whore of justice," work whatever its goals—utility, decoration, distraction. In the hierarchy established by Agee it is noteworthy that science is ranged well below religion, a preference that associates him with T. S. Eliot and the "Agrarian" poets. Like them, he glorified science only insofar as it was founded on religious tradition. Otherwise he felt toward it a mixture of gratitude and mistrust, colored by a scorn coming very close to total condemnation as he declares, "in the right end of their busyness, we would all be healthful and undesiring as animate stones" (C.P., 11).

In a series of maledictions against war, conveyed through prophetic and apocalyptic imagery, Agee calls down vengeance on those men who "of all nations unhindered . . . make it their business to destroy concord and to incite war and to prolong it . . ." (C.P., 11). He skillfully and ironically alternates the tone of a public proclamation ("by public arrangement") and biblical echoes ("pain very eternal") to emphasize this violent diatribe. The poet's malediction is also extended to his nation and his era. He is scornful of scientific or socialistic utopians who delude themselves that they can make fundamental changes. The victim, whether blinded by the passion of others or by his own bad faith and credulity, is the common man represented in the poem by Leopold Bloom. After honoring pedants, agnostics, and skeptics alike, the poem concludes with a celebration of the beauty of the earth and a confession of faith in the permanence of spiritual values. The list of names and the endless enumerations correspond to Agee's initial desire to include all opposites in a vast cosmogeny. His goal as an artist was not simply to imitate the rhythm and incantatory effects of biblical verse; he strove to encompass reality in all its multiple aspects, correcting, modifying or extending his statements without fear of contradiction or paradox.

Section III of *Permit Me Voyage* consists exclusively of "Ann Garner." Compared to its earlier versions, the poem here is considerably shortened. Agee deleted parts that were obvious or explanatory. But in spite of the care with which he reworked it, "Ann Garner" still fails by reason of its original faults. The symbolism, still too explicit and wordy, is not capable of unifying the themes it seeks to illustrate. "Chorale" (*C.P.*, 27) returns to one of the major themes of "Dedication," the desacralization and secularization of the world, in a purely Christian context, whereas "Epithalamium" (*C.P.*, 29) more closely resembles "Ann Garner" as it evokes the rites of the wedding night and the cycle from day to night and from flesh to dust.

The twenty-five sonnets suggest an epic of the human condition (*C.P.*, 37-49). The first ones evoke the mystery of love, faith and knowledge while the final sonnets return to the theme of the poet and his mission.

The octosyllabic lines of the last poem, "Permit Me Voyage" (*C.P.*, 49), better suit Agee's purpose: the emphatic statement of the poet's prophetic mission. The homeland he has chosen, unlike that of Hart Crane, is a sort of mystical paradise at the farthest reaches of Love. (*Love,* which was more effectively written with a small "l" in Crane's poem "The Third Voyage," is significantly enough capitalized by Agee.)

The critical responses to *Permit Me Voyage* were varied.[5] Most critics praised the poet's social conscience, although some criticized Agee's manner of expression as lacking conciseness and clarity. Others saw an uncommon subtlety in his effort to understand reality in its various and contradictory aspects. They acknowledged the courage of a young mind that sought to be honest and free and rejected all systems. They praised his accurate ear, musical sense and mastery of the language. On the other hand, they criticized his overly visible and self-conscious technique but they also looked forward to the time when his obvious promise would be fulfilled.

To the modern reader Agee's poetic voyage may appear as a partial failure, devising an experimental poetry whose force is sometimes lost in its labored technique. It reflects the preoccupations of that generation of poets (ingenious in their sophisticated research) [6] who wrote their first verses during the Depression and rose up against the reign of materialism and science that had destroyed myths only to replace them with misleading allegories.

In spite of the audacious stand Agee took on certain issues, neither the left nor the right recognized itself in his poetry. Classifying him among the Catholic poets, side by side with Thomas Norton or Robert Fitzgerald, the radicals found him suspect and were offended by the fervor of his religious beliefs, while the traditionalist, disquieted by his basic skepticism and ambivalences, were too lazy to seek the meaning of his Christian radicalism.

CHAPTER FOUR

FLIGHT

"A low pit and sink of shade
And funneled dark I find we made . . ." (*C.P.*, 56)

IN A LETTER TO FATHER FLYE, AGEE REFERS TO A SYSTEM OF
human classification he found in the work of a nineteenth-century
French author. The four categories were: *Fils-du-Roi, Imbécile,
Drôle* and *Brute* (*F.F.*, 73). He amused himself by using them in
his own way: "Roosevelt a Drole, so possessed by circumstances
as to be almost Imbecile and to appear a Fils by few wide removes;
Beethoven, a Fils by bootstraps; by nature a Brute-Imbecile, therefore a Drole." One is tempted to say that by virtue of his complex,
still unresolved personality, Agee himself fitted all these types: he
had the egotism of the *Fils-du-Roi,* the naiveté of the *Imbécile,* the
wit of the *Drôle* and the bitterness of the *Brute.* Such was the stuff
poets were made of, perhaps, although these traits did render his
life difficult.

In the year following the publication of *Permit Me Voyage,*
Agee returned to work on a number of poems he had begun in
1932, as well as on the second section of "Don Juan," and on
"Day-Night Poem," a long poem that he had started in 1933. He

circulated his work among his friends, sometimes carelessly allowing his manuscripts to go astray. Occasionally a friend would rescue a page that in a rage Agee had threatened to destroy. The title he chose for his day-night poem, "Themes and Variations," suggests his continued reference in his verse to musical structure [1] (*C.P.*, 53-55). Also, Agee wrote still another poem on the death and Resurrection of Christ, "Him we killed and laid alone," and a sequel, "When Eve first saw the glittering day." Lastly, he composed "A Poem for Brahms' Death Bed," in praise not only of Brahms but also of other musicians—Bach, Mozart, Handel and Beethoven—each successively evoked in one line:

> One grandly gay, serenely strong:
> One who walks shining in his grace
> One gross-cheeked in huge natural song
> And one with stunned translated face. (*C.P.*, 144)

"Don Juan," retitled "John Carter, a poem in Byronics," resumed the project of the earlier poem: It was now to be a tableau of contemporary America as well as an examination of the relationship of evil to human history and civilization (*C.P.*, 81-122). As Robert Fitzgerald points out in his introductory essay to the *Collected Short Prose,* the protagonist's nihilism is in many ways reminiscent of Stavrogin's in *The Possessed.* John Carter is a new pilgrim, wandering across America, destroying his victims according to their peculiarities of thought and conduct. The second version has dramatic and narrative strength that traditionally belong to prose. It was Agee's purpose to infuse the verse with a variety and a vitality "it had lacked since the Elizabethans."

Agee was also busy with other projects. He thought of writing a life of Jesus and also an impersonal impressionistic history of the United States—a pastiche of lyrical passages, quotations, statistics, satire, composed of variations on themes drawn from historical facts (*F.F.*, 75). These projects confronted him once more with the problem of language. In a letter to Father Flye he wondered whether realism, the "consciousness of 'anthropological' correctness," which demanded that each character must speak only the language of his occupation and his environment, did not in fact limit the power of words. How much better it would be, he thought, if a single sentence were allowed to contain sailors' jargon, miners' slang and some liturgical vocabulary as well. Although he does not mention Joyce, it was probably his type of experimentation that Agee had in mind (*F.F.*, 75).

Unfortunately, his work for *Fortune* left him little time to delve into the problems he had raised. He now wrote articles on the manufacture of glass, gunpowder, American art, modernism, the history of Williamsburg, and though time-consuming, he found some of these assignments interesting. For "Williamsburg" [2] he researched the history of the old Virginia town; he later wrote a screenplay on the same subject. In "U.S. Art, 1935" [3] he voices his opinions on modern art; he wrote that the eye of the American painter, no longer a personal, purely physical organ that perceived and then recorded its perceptions, had become a social organ that operated selectively, according to norms learned in a long process of education. In "What Do You Mean, Modern?" [4] he recalled that the cradle of modernism was Europe, not America, and he exposed certain current misconceptions about what was called "modern art" in the United States.[5] His second article on the TVA gave an account of the disturbances civilization had brought to the Tennessee Valley.[6] Although he found the technological innovations of the TVA fascinating and was amazed at the ingenuity used in the construction of the dams, his major concern was the human aspect. The stubborn mountain folk in whom poverty and habit had created a force of inertia could offer the TVA much greater resistance than nature itself. Without doubt, the most difficult task of all would be to win the support of the white and black sharecroppers of the valley. Agee thus directed the reader's attention toward the difficulties that might otherwise have been forgotten in the enthusiasm aroused by technological achievements. His Southern background had sensitized him to problems that the creators of the TVA had not seemed to anticipate.

Two other assignments, both of which dealt with well-known forms of snobbism, especially interested him: horse races at Saratoga, and orchids. In the first he described in beautiful prose the atmosphere at Saratoga in August, the tranquil beauty of the last day of the season, when men and horses alike withdrew like an army, leaving the strange little town to resume its own character in the deathlike cold of winter.[7]

He was in a completely different state of mind when he wrote his article on orchids. He had come to believe that nothing was more useless, more detestable than the orchid. "The flower itself isn't responsible: but people's reactions to it have been and are so vile that I hate its very guts along with theirs," he explained to Father Flye (*F.F.*, 77, 81). As the biggest, flashiest, most expensive flower, the one with the greatest eroticism, glamour and prestige, the orchid derived all of its value from the snobbism that had grown up about it. That was already sufficient reason, he felt, to resent its undeserved popularity, without the fact that the anatomy of the flower itself was repulsive to him. Certainly all flowers were created so as to reproduce themselves, but the orchid seemed to take advantage of the privilege.

Indignant that Agee should turn a piece on orchids into a diatribe against snobbism and ultimately against capitalism, the *Fortune* editors refused to accept the article. What they had asked for was a history of the flower and of its commercial success; but to bear a grudge against it, stripping it of its glamour by slyly putting erudition in the service of a vast joke, was proof of extremely bad taste. When asked to rewrite the article, Agee agreed to eliminate the passages in which he had reduced the flower to a disquieting sexual symbol. But the incident shows his growing impatience with the values of the magazine. By 1935 he was defying the editors with an article calculated to shock them and he prided himself on his audacious insolence, delighting in its repercussions.

By this time he was also thinking of leaving *Fortune* for a few months, if not permanently, and, after a tiring summer, he did take a leave of absence from November, 1935, to May, 1936. He considered for a while getting a job at *Newsweek,* but this was super-seded by other plans. One thing, though, emerged with certainty: He had to get away from the constant tension and agitation of New York. A friend offered Via and him a house in northern Connecticut, but they found it still too close to the city. New England, they argued, had been inhabited for so long that the very soil was exhausted. They were more attracted to the South or the Midwest. Their main requirement was that the place be sufficiently far from all distractions. Even friends were to be kept at a distance, since conversation often took up time and energy that could have been spent in real work. Agee was giving himself a last chance. After having undertaken so many projects without ever finishing them and having written primarily in a satirical or moralizing vein, he wanted to devote himself at last to what he thought should be the goal of all art: an effort to express things as they are, apart from all personal opinion or emotional involve-ment (*F.F.,* 77).

The Agees finally decided on Anna Maria, Florida, a town they had learned about from a colleague at *Fortune.* They rented a house for only twenty dollars a month and otherwise lived cheaply dur-ing their stay. The warm climate afforded Agee immediate physical relaxation and the solace of being alone. He read a great deal: Malraux's *La Condition Humaine,* from which he adapted a scene several years later; Céline and Silone. He found Céline's *Voyage au bout de la Nuit* to be a mixture of Swift, Rabelais and Mon-taigne. He reread Chekhov's plays, Van Gogh's letters to his brother, Blake's *Songs of Innocence* and a biography of Beethoven by J. W. N. Sullivan. Finally and most significantly, he read Freud and he promptly thereafter began to write down and analyze all of his dreams. He also wrote several poems. One was published the following year in *transition,* and others were included in one of Louis Untermeyer's anthologies of American poetry, published the following year. Inspired by some remarks on the Ethiopian war made by the British Minister, Sir Samuel Hoare, Agee wrote the last verses that were ever to be written of "John Carter." It was doubtless also at this time that he began work on "Knoxville: Summer 1915," a short lyrical evocation of his childhood in Tennessee, and on "The House," a script written as an allegory of the contemporary scene. Nevertheless, having a great deal of time at his disposal hardly seemed to have liberated his muse. All considered, he was doing relatively little writing, having once again fallen into inertia, a state of spiritual and intellectual torpor that dissolved his creative enthusiasm and encouraged him to be complacent and lazy. He now had come to face the fact that he had only himself to blame. He mercilessly described his weaknesses to Father Flye. He blamed himself for too much self-pity, for too intense and destructive a form of ambition and for preferring death to failure. He longed to rid himself of his troublesome ego and to discipline himself. He would have to moderate his cynicism, which he saw more as a mental trick than a genuine philosophy. It had first manifested itself, he thought, during his trip to Europe, though he felt that at one point it had been "chemically" necessary to his evolution. He also feared that he had made a serious error by becoming a journalist, though he admitted that owing in large part to the three years he had spent at *Fortune,* a greater social and political conscience had awakened in him. He now felt even more strongly attracted to Communism, which seemed to provide the most satisfactory solutions to the world's problems. Yet he remained sufficiently detached to see Communism's failings and to condemn the fanaticism of certain militants.

Altogether Agee's stay in Florida did afford him the chance to find his bearings as he searched for an equilibrium between what he was and what he hoped to be.

Agee returned to New York by way of New Orleans and Tennessee, where he arranged a visit to Father Flye in time to be at Saint Andrew's for Easter. Several days at the school were enough to reawaken warm memories of the past. He was now curious about the child he had once been, and it is likely that his visit was the origin of the project, realized years later in *The Morn-*

ing Watch, of evoking the period of his life spent in the Episcopalian community. Easter had been the time of year that had had
the most meaning for him as a child, and he was astonished to
rediscover the emotions he had felt then. He no longer dared to
believe in religion, but he retained a deep attachment to its rituals.
If his intellect held dogma in doubt, his whole being clung to religious mysteries and feelings. Thus, at the same time that Agee
was moving toward Communism, he discovered that he had remained a Christian and what he was seeking in Communism were
the very Christian virtues sometimes betrayed by religion itself.

When he returned to New York he set to work revising the things
he had written during the winter months, and it now seemed more
satisfying to him than he had expected. He was considering writing
an English version of the libretto of Gluck's *Orpheus and Euridice,*
when *Fortune* asked him to do an article on the tenant farmers of
the South. His task would be to describe their daily life and its
seasonal cycles, to report on the farm economy, on the efforts of
the federal and state governments to improve the situation, on the
theories held by Southern liberals and on the history of the two
farm associations that had been established. With the exception of
the TVA articles, this was the first time that his work overlapped
his interests. Sharecropping was a problem he was deeply concerned
with, and he already knew he would be unable to take a purely
economic approach to the situation. His ties with the South and
his sympathy for the tenant farmers caused him to feel a great
responsibility for this new job. He left for the South immediately,
expecting to spend one month on research. Traveling with him was
his friend Walker Evans, who had been assigned by the U. S.
Government to do the photographic report.

CHAPTER FIVE

HOMELAND REGAINED AND LOST

EVANS AND AGEE LEFT NEW YORK ONE SATURDAY IN JUNE OF
1936. A change in plans switched their original destination of
Tennessee to Alabama where, during the weeks that followed, unforeseen events left them stunned and amazed. Their disturbing
though gratifying adventures jolted their consciences as well as
their emotions.

Upon arrival, their first task was to find a family to stay with.
To share and observe the life of a family for four weeks had
originally seemed a clear-cut, easy assignment. Circumstances soon
proved that the first step would be the hardest and most disquieting.
To the poor Southern farmer, Agee and Evans, the reporter-pho-
tographer team, were joint representatives of a society that had
ignored the sharecroppers' problems. Their presence might truly
arouse legitimate suspicions about the nature and goal of the inquiry they were engaged in. Agee suffered pangs of conscience and
felt both hostile to the men who had sent him and traitorous to
the people he had come to observe. His article would put them on
display for a prurient audience. The " 'honest' piece of work" he
was expected to produce (although "honest journalism" was itself

a paradox) might meet with general sympathy but it could not satisfy his conscience.

Agee's and Evans' feelings of responsibility toward the tenant farmers increased in proportion to their sense of estrangement from the magazine—to the point where soon after they arrived they decided to forget that they were journalists and to trust their personal rather than their professional judgment. Evans performed his job with his characteristic simplicity and integrity. Agee, convinced of his own unworthiness, judged himself severely. He hated his official mission. He lamented his inexperience and worried about how the farmers would react to Walker Evans' camera, "a weapon, a stealer of images and souls . . . an evil eye."

The stay in Alabama was broken into two different periods.[1] At first Agee and Evans researched and traveled through the unfamiliar territory they had come to explore. They made their first tentative efforts at communicating with a people who were often closed and hostile. The second period was more satisfying, since they carried out their original intention of living with a family. They established some genuine and fruitful contacts and got to know the Southern farmer from up close. The method of research they adopted during the first weeks was partly of their own choosing and partly imposed by circumstances. They were constantly in motion, traveling to all corners of the state by train and automobile, together and separately, trying to make the necessary contacts. But the ones they first made were few and generally disconcerting. Sometimes they were introduced to the local authorities, who provided them with an escort to take them to the nearest village. But Agee would refrain from asking questions; it made him unhappy to find the man's face revealing either distrust or shame at his own misery.

Like the faces of the people, the countryside seemed inaccessible, too. It played tricks on the eye, misled the intruder and delighted in making him lose his way. Should he set out in search of farms, it spread before him an infinite expanse of woods or cottonfields. It hid its villages so well that a stranger needed a guide to find them. Vast and desolate, it was to Agee's eyes the perfect setting for the obscure lives of the people. They too were exposed to the full force of the elements, their skin deeply furrowed from over-exposure; the same fate seemed to await them both. In fact, the vocabulary Agee uses in his descriptions of the land and its inhabitants tends to identify them completely with each other.[2]

As they wandered Agee and Evans gradually absorbed the atmosphere of the region. At first it was as though they were conquerors in an enemy country that was still ready to fight back. The people offered them a nervous courtesy. Sometimes their eagerness to talk seemed to be used as a defense against indiscreet questions, and any such show of hospitality made the reporters uneasy. At other times they were met with silence and pretended deafness that they could find no way to circumvent. Sunday was the day Agee dreaded most. Their visits that day took on a more official character; conversations became awkward and left them with the impression of being intruders who interrupted family gatherings and forced people to expose themselves. A characteristic scene in *Famous Men* describes such a Sunday when three black singers are summoned to perform for the two strangers, do so unwillingly but without protest (*F.M.*, 30). During such encounters, Agee and Evans had nothing to give in return but a few coins slipped into the hand. They could only exchange trivial phrases. To admit what they were really feeling—respect, pity, tenderness—would have been more offending than polite superficialities.

There were other more spontaneous but equally disturbing meetings: chance encounters that took place on the roads, in the fields where massive sunflowers grew or in the silence of an archaic valley, where gracious and melancholy women still wore sunbonnets (*F.M.*, 37). Such was a meeting with a young couple sitting on a porch, whom Agee approached to ask directions. As he came closer he admired their statuesque qualities, the beauty of their veined hands. He felt their gaze come to rest on him. Although their eyes betrayed some hatred and anger, they themselves remained beatifically detached. Near them sat an older man, who was unable to hide his nervousness. "A broken felt hat struck through with grass hair was banged on flat above his furious leaky eyes and from beneath its rascally grin as if from ambush, he pored at me walleyed" (*F.M.*, 34). His strange behavior offered an awesome contrast to the calm serenity of his companions. As he tried to talk only inarticulate sounds came from his mouth, and a thick stream of saliva trickled the length of his beard. By his side the young couple spoke calmly to Agee about the conditions of their existence, uncomplainingly and without resentment, as though their hatred of the world was something above pride and shame.

In yet another part of the state they came upon a young Negro couple walking along the road in the sunshine. The travelers could not help but admire their gentle, mysterious faces, the sober vitality of their bodies and the sureness of their gait. Suddenly the girl noticed that Agee was following them. At once the dignity and harmony of their motions vanished, to be replaced by the tense gestures of tracked beasts (*F.M.*, 41). At this early stage in their explorations Agee's eye, like Evans' camera, had already begun to seize upon striking images that he would hastily set down in his notes.

The meeting through which they finally established contact with the tenant farmers seemed no different from the others, but circumstances made it decisive. One day, as they were standing outside the municipal hall of a small town, they began talking to a man waiting in line in front of the welfare office. Evans asked permission to take a few pictures, and a friendly conversation ensued between Agee and this man, whom he later wrote of as Fred Ricketts. Two of Ricketts' friends joined them, timidly at first, then with increasing confidence. When Agee and Evans drove them home they agreed to pose with their families on the porch for more pictures. There was nothing in this encounter to make the reporters suspect they had found the family they had been so anxious to meet. A few words and glances were exchanged, expressing trust as well as hostility, amusement as well as reproach. Agee and Evans left the Ricketts' not knowing whether they had made friends or enemies. But Agee felt guilty that he had gotten their hopes up for help he could not give them. To clear up any misunderstanding, Agee and Evans returned to the remote farms where the three families lived. They let drop in the ensuing conversation their desire to board with a sharecropper family. Surprised by a positive response, they were soon confronted by a new obstacle. It seemed impossible for them to single out one of these families without hurting the others. Meanwhile the summer was almost over, little had been accomplished and they were expected back in New York. Fortunately, an unhoped-for incident brought an end to this period of equivocation. One night a violent storm forced Agee to stay with one of the families he was visiting. He suddenly realized that his presence among them created no tension. Without any further hesitation he accepted for the rest of his stay in Alabama the hospitality that was offered that evening.

It is significant to contrast Agee's self-evaluation in these situations with Walker Evans' descriptions of his friend as he was at that time.[3] Whereas Agee keeps harping on his guilt and embarrassment and the hostility he met with, Evans emphasizes his friend's charm, openness and ability to allay the suspicions of the people he wished to know better, while the image he presented in his cheap clothing inspired confidence. Even physically he resembled the men he was dealing with. His height, his broad shoulders, which gave a deceptive impression of strength, even his large hands gesturing exuberantly as he talked, identified him with the local people. But mostly it was an "ingrained courtesy, an uncourtly courtesy that emanated from him towards everyone . . . ," his diffidence that won people to him.

Agee also seems to have felt a sudden liberation in this new environment. The memories of his childhood, of the frequent visits to his grandparents, and his continuing nostalgia explain the persistence of his attachment to this back country, although he had felt increasingly cut off from it as the years went by. The lives he had been coincidentally assigned to observe and to share could have been his own. This was an aspect of him that had been slumbering for years and that he had only partially seen and experienced through the imprecise and innocent consciousness of the child he had been. He now hoped to regain it. He had, in fact, stumbled on the very circumstances he had unknowingly been seeking in Florida: a great deal of stimulation, and a job that had meaning for him. He had had too much leisure in Anna Maria, and it had been of no use to him. In Alabama, pressured by an overwhelming subject, there was no time for idle thinking. He was happy to leave behind the refined intellectual atmosphere of Greenwich Village and New York offices, a world, as Evans describes it, "of high-minded, well-bred, money-hued culture, whether authoritarian or libertarian."[4]

As soon as Evans and Agee finally agreed to move in with the Gudgers, one of the three families, Agee set to work with a vengeance. He felt a kind of vertigo when he considered the depth of his task. From *Fortune* he had obtained permission to stay four more weeks, and each day had to be put to good use. He scarcely slept. He shared the farmers' lives completely, even the lice, bedbugs, the odors of excrement and of rancid grease that impregnated everything, including the Bible that had been placed at his bedside.

Agee did not miss a single moment of the family's existence. He woke up early and watched the breakfast preparations, admiring the gestures of the woman who busied herself in front of him. During the day he followed one or another of the family members through their occupations. On certain occasions he took advantage of their absence to examine the house from top to bottom like a thief but with a "quietly triumphant vigilance" (*F.M.*, 137). He worked at night when "there was no longer any sound of the sinking and settling . . . of the bodies and brains . . . through the late stages of fatigue unharnessed" (*F.M.*, 19). Tirelessly, he recorded his impressions and his observations.

The reflections that this stay had inspired went far beyond the scope of an article, but he was now writing mostly for himself and for the tenant farmers. Already skilled in his profession, he made use of journalism's methods of investigation and research. But his concern was now more that of the ethnologist. He recorded the

location of each house, how it had been built, board by board, how
the rooms were arranged and how each room looked, the arrangement of the furniture and the appearance of each item. He even
listed the contents of drawers. He inventoried the farmers' living
conditions, their lands, their animals, their position with respect to
the landowners. He collected the largest possible number of specific
facts that might help to define the ambiguous word *tenant,* gathered
observations, data and testimony that could situate the tenant farmer
in a social context. He was like a sociologist: there was no fact so
minor, no statistic so humble that it did not merit his consideration.
He tried to estimate the total income of each of the people he was
writing about. Patiently counting their livestock and the tools they
had at their disposal, he compared the situations of the three families. He took down information in notebooks and on scraps of
paper without regard to how he would ultimately organize it, although he was beginning to reach some conclusions. Since these
conclusions were not at all those which *Fortune* could anticipate,
Agee could not help foreseeing with delight the storm that was to
come. His observations did not permit him to remain for very long
in the coldly objective climate essential to "honest journalism." His
indignation at American society and at the self-styled "reformers"
who claimed to have all the answers was quickly aroused. The cause
of the evil went deeper than anyone suspected, and no improvement
could result from reforms that were designed primarily to take the
immediate pressure off people's easily satisfied consciences. Carried
away by his anger, Agee began to denounce all forms of corruption
and blindness. In this general indictment he did not spare himself,
a young intellectual, raised in traditional bourgeois security and
leisure, and sheltered from the problems that were now cruelly
apparent to him. He did not believe there would be any material
improvement in the tenant farmers' lives in the near future, and
paradoxically, he did not truly hope for it, since it might in turn
spell their own doom and corruption. His task would consist mainly
in helping them survive in a hostile world. To do so he would propose no program but would proceed to make a savage examina-

tion of the causes of their present situation. He was not a social scientist, an economist or a politician. He was just an angry young poet who would shout in the face of the world his indignation but also sing his "praise" of the sharecropper and strive to make "famous" the reality of their existence.

After four weeks at the Gudgers', Agee and Evans left the South for New York. The photos Evans brought back with him were of classical purity—austere, objective, perfect. Agee wrote three articles in which he expressed many of the things he felt needed to be said immediately. That still left three-quarters of his notes unshaped. By that time *Fortune*'s subscribers had grown uneasy about the progressive tendencies of the magazine, and the new editor had issued stricter guidelines for future articles. As a result, Agee's three pieces were promptly rejected. He was asked to rewrite them, to moderate their tone. Angered by *Fortune*'s insensitivity, Agee began to envision a much larger project. But he decided that before sitting down to write a full-length study he would step back from his experience in the South and let his discoveries sort themselves out in his mind.

In spite of the uproar caused by his articles, Agee stayed at the magazine. And soon he found himself reclaimed by his regular work, by the city itself and by his personal affairs.

He was immersing himself again in the further pleasures and obligations of friendship. Among the friends Agee saw at this time were Franklin Miner, a brilliant intellectual and indefatigable reader who had quit his father's business in the suburbs of Boston to come to make his life in New York—he never did make a place for himself in the city and eventually went insane; his old friends from Cambridge, Mary-Louise White (then editor at *Harper's Bazaar*), Christopher Gerould, Theodore Spencer and his wife, who were frequent visitors to New York; the Robert Fitzgeralds; Hugh and Paula Tyler; and of course, Walker Evans.[5]

Agee was always a brilliant conversationalist. Talking among friends, he would spontaneously generate an idea and, making a dazzling sketch of it, he would write it, so to speak, as he talked.

This, in fact, was the most remarkable feature about him. He continually tossed out long, rhythmic sentences embellished with images and metaphors, which in a book would appear to have been carefully constructed. It was not only Agee's thoughts that captured his listeners' attention, but the language through which he explored first one idea, then another. And the gesturing of his long hands seemed to complement his voice in the most engaging way. When he became involved in a subject Agee could speak almost inexhaustibly, late into the night. Preoccupied with tomorrow's schedule and tired from lack of sleep, his friends would leave reluctantly. But given a single listener, Agee would continue heatedly, as though the discussion had just begun. Even more relaxed in such a tête-à-tête, he was oblivious to the lateness of the hour or the next day's responsibilities. His friends often wished at such times that they could slip a pencil into his hands so that his words would be recorded and the projects he spoke of would be immediately realized. They would have liked to tell him that he should not waste his talents on brilliant discussions of which they were the only audience and whose phrasing would soon slip from their poor memories. However, they could not help being thankful for the hours he spent with them, and had he followed their advice, they would have been the first to complain.

Agee naturally found these evenings stimulating. Instead of trying to gauge the response of hypothetical readers, he was dealing with a live audience whose reaction he could watch and immediately respond to. These gatherings served as a change from the solitary experience of writing. Agee did write, though. Afflicted as he was with insomnia, he often wrote tirelessly through the night, discarding, rewriting; sometimes yielding to the urge to write a poem, sometimes concentrating on a page of the book he was preparing on the South and sometimes working on an assignment— an article for *New Masses,* a questionnaire sent to him by *Partisan Review.*

If one compares the number of projects Agee planned with those he finally completed, one would think that he accomplished very little, but the years that followed his memorable summer in Alabama were very productive for Agee. And although his name is not directly associated with the decade, it was during the latter part of the thirties that, truly possessed by the will to write, he brilliantly overcame his career ambivalences and made his first major contributions to contemporary American literature.

CHAPTER SIX

THE PUBLICATION OF PERMIT ME VOYAGE IN 1934 HAD MARKED
a promising debut for Agee as a poet. In June, 1936, his poem
"Vertigral: Lyric" [1] was published in *transition,* the international
magazine founded by Eugene Jolas in 1927 that concentrated on
publishing experimental writings that explored the unconscious or
returned to the origins of literature, to mythology or even to magic.[2]
The word *vertigral,* coined by Jolas, aptly describes a poetry that
aspired to be visionary. Agee was thus joining the avant-garde, but
by no fickle change of aesthetic. Certain poems and many lines in
Permit Me Voyage foreshadowed his venture into experimental
writing. In "Vertigral" (*C.P.,* 153) the tendency to use novel means
of expression as an end in itself appears in an extreme degree; the
poem uses a compressed, elliptical syntax reminiscent of Gerard
Manley Hopkins and is austerely stripped of all superfluous elements: "Demure morning morning margin glows flows foaled /
Fouled is flown float float easily earth before demurely . . ."
Juxtaposed terms end up having several functions, lines remain
unresolved, intentionally vague or ambiguous. The goal of this
poetry, so the theoreticians claimed, was to return language to its

source, to rediscover the "plasticity" of words and thus to achieve a kind of "verticality" through which the poem becomes a vision.

"Vertigral: Lyric" caused an immediate controversy. A letter to the editor, entitled "Spook Writing," appeared in the August 15, 1936, issue of the *Saturday Review*. The letter singled out Agee's poem for special condemnation. And a response from Mary M. Glum, published September 5, defended the poem with equal passion. During the same year Agee's work was anthologized for the first time in *Modern American Poetry*.[3] The editor, Louis Untermeyer, speaks of Agee as a poet who affirms his originality and his independence from the Southern "Vanderbilt School" with which it would be tempting to associate him because of his Tennessee origins. In the February, 1937, issue of *Forum*,[4] in a section devoted to fifteen new poets—a group that included Robert Fitzgerald, Elizabeth Bishop and Wallace Stevens—two other Agee poems appeared: "Rapid Transit," an indictment of the inhuman life of the cities, and "Sun Our Father," a celebration of the Communist dream and a hymn to human labor. The latter poem contains a striking combination of biblical images and specific allusions to Russia, thus merging the Christian and Communist ideals.

Agee's articles in *Fortune* written during the same period testify to preoccupations similar to those of the poems. Thus, "Smoke," published in June, exhorted against the evils of modern civilization. Examining the scourge of the industrial era, Agee found it to be a curse sent by a dark and nameless god, the symbol of our time and of man's destiny, doomed as he is to fall victim to his own deeds. In a particularly striking image, he sees the earth as a garden planted with poisonous mushrooms, clouds of smoke rising above each city like the breath of a monster.[5]

The poem "In Memory of My Father" appeared in the winter issue of *transition* (*C.P.*, 59).[6] It is similar in technique to "Lyric," and nostalgically evokes the familiar atmosphere of summer nights in the poet's native South. "Sunday: Outskirts of Knoxville, Tennessee" appeared several months later in *New Masses* and deals with the obligations of love and the inexhaustible tenderness that, for Agee, seemed to triumph in the blue Southern nights (*C.P.*, 65).[7] After chronicling love's growth and its subsequent degradation before the coming of death, the supreme treason, the poem ends with an ambiguous prayer. "Now, on the winsome crumbling shelves of the horror / God show, God blind these children!" The poem is a skillful expression of the poet's double vision: A serene and idyllic scene communicated in soft sounding rhymes precedes the sudden unleashing of a stream of pitiless images.

In December of 1937 the *Partisan Review* published a series of eleven poems of Agee's entitled simply "Lyrics" (*C.P.*, 60-65).[8] The first poem deals with the terror of war and probably evokes the horror of Guernica:

> Remember limber thunder in the deaf: the metal tasting air:
> Cities like silly medals lay: wind:
>> Flashed the whole forest pale:
> Spasm and blindness blenched and the bunched cloud
>> Delivered his blue columns
> Remembering thunder: deliberating in the shadow cold: the fuse air

As image follows upon image, the poem echoes the incessant noise of the cannonade, whose steady rumbling can be heard in the very sonority of the line, "remembering unlimbering thunder."

The subsequent poems continue the first poem's images of catastrophe and war, but after the ordeal hope is reborn and the wounded recover. After the fall of the broken-voiced bird, "and falling, wing find air," comes death, which only undecaying straw, "bones, and their bran," will survive. As in "Ann Garner" and "Epithalamium," the dead are an ever-present fertilizing and beneficent power. They rejoice to see that others are carrying on the struggle they had begun.

The last poems of the series deal with revolution and change. Progress is compared to a dandelion whose seeds, flying in the wind, represent the foreseeable changes that will take place in the world.

The readers of the thirties found in these poems one continued meditation, reflecting by turns the necessity and the uselessness of struggle, the joy and anguish it brings. One finds, in addition to a rather bitter irony, echoes of Whitman's poetry in the invitation to join the fight and in the sense of solidarity and of a common destiny uniting all men. Yet the message of these poems remains deliberately ambiguous: Struggle, while necessary and inescapable, will not bring the expected relief, but leaves men's hearts in a new state of disorder and anguish. At the same time Agee also manages to express the hope that man is not altogether doomed.

Three further poems published in the early months of 1938 close this vast lyrical meditation. "Millions Are Learning How" and "Summer Evening" celebrate the rebirth of hope after the "spended day," whereas "Dixie Doodle" makes an ironic comment on the nation's racial problems.[9]

Thus, over the course of several months, Agee's poetry underwent a remarkable evolution. Almost exclusively literary at first, it rapidly became politically involved and combative. Whereas it had been concerned primarily with the intimate feelings of love and betrayal and the joy and pain of living, it now moved toward a greater social awareness. Agee felt he had a deep obligation to speak out. His life in New York, his job at *Fortune,* his friendship with MacLeish and Macdonald, his admiration for W. H. Auden, and especially his stay in Alabama, had opened his eyes to the true social reality. He now took his place among ideological poets of the age who, though formed by the experiences and emotions of the Lost Generation, were still further shaken by the revelations of the thirties. At that time, Agee made no secret of the fact that he was sympathetic to Marxism and Communism; he admired the Russian people, who had dared to do what other peoples had only timidly attempted, but he deplored the infiltration of Communist doctrine into literature. Although he was a leftist by sympathy and by conviction, he did not belong to any party (just as he refused to be part of a literary school), not only out of a desire for independence, but out of distrust of all sects and systems and above all because total and unconditional belief threatened to restrict and enslave his talent, to stifle the imagination. For him, as for the generation of progressive writers at the end of that decade, the writer's first obligation was not to propagandize for the doctrines he believed in, but to be true to his art.

In "Art for What's Sake," an article he published in *New Masses*,[10] Agee rehabilitated experimental literature, which the generation of the thirties had rejected, and demonstrated that it need not be antithetical to a Marxist point of view. Marxism and experimentalism could well be united in a single work to the benefit of both, and the resulting work would be revolutionary. The Surrealist revolution was, to art, comparable in importance to the revolution Marxism had created in the realm of ideas. By studying dreams, the subconscious and the irrational, it had opened up new fields for exploration and experimentation. Agee hoped that an alliance could grow up between Surrealism and Marxism. It seemed to him that their reconciliation was foreshadowed both in the poetry of W. H. Auden and in the films of the Russian directors Eisenstein and Dovzhenko. The two latter had, in fact, replaced the logic of thought with the more powerful and primitive logic of movement, time, space and light and introduced undeniably Surrealistic elements into a fundamentally Marxist context. Poetry and the cinema were thus the art forms in which Agee envisaged this fusion of commitment and experiment.

At the time Agee wrote the article the leftist press was also expressing a desire for coexistence between experimental and Marxist literature. When, after a year's interruption, the *Partisan Review* resumed publication in 1937, with a new editorial committee that included Dwight Macdonald, Philip Rahv, William Phillip and Mary McCarthy, it announced a new political orientation, more definitely Marxist, but specifically anti-Communist. It now opened its pages not only to radical writers who had become disenchanted with Communism, but to all artists regardless of their political involvement. E. E. Cummings, John Dos Passos, Elizabeth Bishop and Wallace Stevens all felt equally at home in the new *Partisan Review*.

When Agee's work appeared in the *Partisan Review* that year, it was published there not because of his political opinions, but because of his experimentalism. It was also as an experimental writer that he was published in *New Masses* as well as in *Common Sense*—a capitalist, anti-Communist publication. It was unusual for pieces by the same author to appear simultaneously in magazines whose political stances were so different. But Agee, in spite of his sympathies with the left, was sufficiently neutral to be an acceptable contributor to both.

It was not only in his poetry that Agee strove for the reconciliation of radical and experimental literature expounded in "Art for What's Sake." He pursued the same goal in the writing of a work that inaugurated a new genre: the parable in the form of a cinematographic narrative. "The House" was published in 1937 in *New Letters in America,* a new periodical established the same year.[11] *Letters* appeared in book form and was intended to come out twice a year. "Most of the names listed in the table of contents of this volume are names of young writers, writers whose work has been deeply affected by a new conception of human consciousness which arose after the world war and began to be assimilated after 1930." In the preface Horace Gregory explained that though the majority of the forty authors represented in the first volume had been associated with the leftist and progressive causes (Horace Gregory, W. H. Auden, Muriel Rukeyser, Philip Rahv) the unifying principle of the collection was less political than aesthetic. Gregory spoke of a transformation of literary form in which poetry and prose would take on the nature of fable. It was certainly a fable that Agee had written.

From the outset the reader of "The House" is purposely disoriented and forced to follow the movements of an imaginary camera. A sequence of visual images charges the narrative with symbolic meaning: chimneys point upward like rifles; columns of smoke rise from them like shots that have been fired. The locale of the story is fairly specific: a provincial industrial city of one to two hundred thousand inhabitants, such as Knoxville or Chattanooga, Tennessee. (It is noteworthy that Agee chose his native region as the setting for his uncanny tale of violence and destruction, and doubtless he did so for several reasons: the reference to a precise geographical location gives the narrative a feeling of authenticity and shows that even the most remote and seemingly pastoral and sheltered places will not escape the decadence and utter decomposition that is facing the Western world. Furthermore, Agee was demythifying in his own eyes a place he was only too willing to associate with an illusory state of innocence and purity.) The camera is charged with the task of destroying the illusion that setting and decor could create for less practiced and less inquisitive eyes; it determines the rhythm of the narrative and the quality of the images, whether it closes in on objects or people, probing and revealing their strange and horrifying nature, or whether such objects and people meet and challenge the camera's eye in a cynical fashion. A desolate area of the city is singled out. Half-legible neon signs bear words in an international language, words for suspense and disaster. Images fade in and out, as in a dream. A legless man appears selling pencils. Two nuns approach, their faces hidden by their starched headdresses. As they draw near, the camera shows two fangs sprout from the lipless mouth of one of them. Sexual and animal excess is veiled in sacramental garments. A troop of Boy Scouts passes, carrying a crucifix on which is nailed a naked woman. The woman has neither hands nor feet, and her head is a classroom globe of the earth surmounted by the word MOTHER. These children turn out to be adult midgets, performing gestures of sacrilege and destruction and leading a long parade of other midgets: financiers, mothers and orators, all waving flags and throwing confetti. In their wake follows a gigantic hearse and a cortege of fifty limousines. Trying to cross the road is a short fat man with a derby, a brother of Joyce's Bloom. He struggles through the chaos of automobiles, which are now moving at an increased speed. A horn sounds just as a car drives over the body of the plump little man.

The second part of the narrative is centered around the house, a Victorian dwelling in the same city. From the front door of the house emerges a procession of characters whose dress and posture convey a strange mixture of dignity, ceremoniousness and obscenity. Their facial expressions are uniformly dignified, a calm and resigned despair that comes from the cold, clear knowledge of the fate in store for them. Agee makes free use of Freudian symbols and Surrealist and cinematic techniques to suggest the characters' deformities, eccentricities and most secret thoughts. As all these figures disappear in a limousine the camera moves cautiously toward the house, exploring it with a series of ascending and circular motions that reveal the extent of its past splendor and its present desolation. The house stands with a kind of intense rigidity made up of pride, a strength it has not yet relinquished, and a savage defiance of the menacing sky. Around an old woman (whose presence is foreshadowed throughout the tale) who alone has remained to be present at the destruction of her home, wreckage suddenly accumulates to the accompaniment of almost apocalyptic sounds. Finally a flood of rain, an enormous unleashing of waters, carries her and the house away. Then, gently, life begins again with sunshine, shouts and laughter. Some poor children collect the debris floating in the water that runs along the street: a goldfish, a derby hat, a white lace curtain. They solemnly proceed to bury the goldfish and to reenact a marriage ceremony. Their gestures offer a parody of human action but they are also a commemoration of the essential rituals of death and life.

Written at a time when the world was threatened by the rise of Naziism and by impending wars, "The House" may serve as a metaphor of the fall and destruction foreshadowed in those prewar years. It may also be given a broader historical significance. It pictures any time of upheaval, the end of an ancient order and the beginning of a new one. But the new era may turn out to be no more than a mock repetition of the preceding one. It is as though history brought no essential changes but only the cyclical return of similar events. The narrative may also be read as a parable of life and death. Symbols of decadence (represented primarily by physical deformities) and of the fall (represented by the collapse of the house and the disappearance of its occupants) are counterposed to symbols of redemption and salvation and to the hope that there exists a spiritual strength that can survive the most terrible cataclysms. The proud resistance of the old woman, the fate of the little man in the derby hat represent an individualism that is no less real for being ultimately defeated. Messages of hope are also transmitted by the children who appear at the end of the story, who are enjoying a genuine childhood, as opposed to the counterfeit childhood that was portrayed in the opening section. Between the image of the old woman, whose face is the only one to register changing emotions, and that of the playful children—between old age, which death will soon overtake, and childhood, which is courted by life—passes a stream of anonymous figures, cold and frozen as death itself.

"The House" represents Agee's effort to make the fable into a new literary structure. It was also a milestone in the evolution of Agee's art. Combining numerous literary techniques, from symbolism to Surrealism, in an "amphibious" style that was neither prose nor poetry, drawing on stories of fantasy or horror, it still remained a parable with a simple moral meaning. "The House" also made extensive use of story-telling modes newly discovered in motion pictures. Beginning that year, 1937, Agee's works would be characterized by a gradual shift from poetry to prose and by the reconciliation of traditional literary forms with experimental narrative techniques.

PART IV

DIFFICULT
AND
PRODUCTIVE
YEARS

CHAPTER ONE

HAVANA CRUISE

"Our marriages are imagination of choice; we meet and mate like apples swung together on a creek." (*C.S.P.*, 144)

THE MOST INTERESTING ASSIGNMENT AGEE RECEIVED DURING THE year after he returned from Alabama was to research the tourist industry in Havana and the steamship lines linking Cuba with the United States. Accompanied by Via and Walker Evans, who was again the assigned photographer, he took a cruise on the *Oriente,* sailing from New York. His immediate task was to investigate the opportunities open to the tourist and to find out which social classes tended to select the cruise in preference to other forms of travel, and for what reasons. Therefore, in addition to looking up the statistics, he needed to speak to as many cruise passengers as possible. In order to avoid arousing suspicion, the three decided to separate and to conceal their relationship from the other passengers, but they tried often to meet secretly in order to share impressions. When they met in public they occasionally spoke to each other with an intimacy that would have betrayed them had they not been able to quickly and cleverly restore the illusion. By the end of the voyage, however, their connivance had become apparent to many of the tourists.[1]

Agee worked enthusiastically during the six-day cruise. For most of his *Fortune* articles he merely had to write the piece based on facts gathered previously by a researcher. This time, as in Alabama, he was doing his own research, without an intermediary. His senses and his intellect were thus free to receive direct impressions. As in Alabama, he took notes as the journey progressed.

"Six Days at Sea" was submitted to *Fortune* in the early part of July, 1937.[2] In spite of some concessions to journalism—statistics and general reflections on the financial aspects of running a cruise ship—the article reads like a superb piece of fiction. The central character, the tourist in his many guises, is taken from the beginning to the end of his voyage in the space of a few pages. All the experiences and emotions of a pleasure cruise—excitement, curiosity, boredom, torpor, flirtations, drunkenness, newfound friends, disappointment—are captured in the course of the narrative. And Agee raises his piece to the level of profound social criticism when he describes the tourist as the helpless, anonymous, middle-class victim of the unscrupulous tourist industry, whose main motive, of course, is profit. It is the essential emptiness of middle-class life that makes the exploitation possible, Agee suggests, and it is this lesson that the tourist inevitably learns on board as he attends his "school of disenchantment."

During the weeks following his trip to Havana, Agee worked constantly, his own serious writing alternating with purely hack work, such as an article he wrote for a travel agency on crime in ten Southern cities. He was living as a lone wolf in New York now, spending most of his time at home, unshaven; at his side the *Daily Worker,* his cat Gilbert, and a few books. He only went out to see a movie, or the newsreels, which he followed with devotion. The truth was that Via had left him in August.

In "Six Days," in fact, there are several allusions to the inevitable lassitude that occurs after years of married life. At the end of the story there is a shattering account of a domestic squabble on the last evening of the cruise. It was no coincidence either that constantly in his writing, and in long passages in his letters to Father Flye and to his other friends, Agee expatiates on the grandeur and servitude of conjugal love. And hostile as a rule to institutions, he mistrusted the institution of marriage more than any other. True, marriage compensated for the heart's insecurity, but the ties so formed were too unconditional, Agee felt, to make much sense in the long run.

The break with Via had taken place brutally while they were staying in Clinton with the Saunders', but it was in fact the end result of a gradual process of change. It was one of a series of instances in which Agee gave in to his impulses toward rebellion and liberation and rejected constraints and past influences. Shortly before his death he described the circumstances of their separation in an unpublished story, "Bigger Than We Are," in which he insisted that destiny, not human will, decides the course of human lives.[3] Thus, twenty years later, he was still trying to understand what had motivated his decision, so profound had been his turmoil at the time.

In the story he did not even change the names of the characters. Although certain elements are transposed, it is likely that most of the events are true. As such, "Bigger Than We Are" is the best available account of what took place in Agee's life that critical summer. Against the background of Greenwich Village life in the late thirties—parties, drunken discussions, Sunday morning walks along Bleecker Street and Washington Square—Agee describes the fragility of love in the lives of couples: the unmarried, the newly married and the married with children. Agee also introduces his encounter with Alma Mailman, a friend of the Saunders' whom he had originally met in New Jersey. The Saunders' had practically adopted her as their daughter, and she was then all but engaged to their son. She too was a musician, and she played in the concerts they gave for their friends. When Agee met her again she had just arrived in New York, where she decided she wanted to live. In the

story Agee describes their meeting at a party and his being struck
by the qualities that set her apart from the other guests: the modesty
of her manner, the simplicity of her appearance and the shyness of
a newcomer to the city. Agee also perceives and is annoyed by the
tinge of protectiveness and condescension in Via's attitude toward
her. Quick to transpose his impressions into terms of social consciousness, he felt that Alma, who came from a lower social class
than the Saunders', was a victim of bourgeois snobbery, against
which he was becoming more and more openly rebellious.

He recalled that he, too, had in his time been seduced by the
bourgeois world and had lived for years under its influence. Only
recently had he become aware of his enslavement to it, and since
then, he had succeeded to a certain extent in detaching Via from
it, forcing her to share his bohemian life. He had often regretted
having to impose the consequences of his own rebellion on Via,
but if she wanted to stay with him, she too would have to free herself from the constraints of a society he felt was too rigidly structured.

During this summer Agee and Alma became increasingly involved with one another until, on impulse and ignoring Via completely, they took off together in a rented car for a trip to the South.
Traveling through the Shenandoah Valley they came to Knoxville,
where Agee met a few family friends and made a pilgrimage to his
grandparents' house. He also took the time to explore the changes
the TVA had brought to the region. In Birmingham the Negro staff
at the DeSoto Hotel still remembered him, and he played jazz on
the piano for all the hotel guests. With Alma, he revisited New
Orleans. They saw Nashville, with its somewhat disquieting atmosphere, and Louisville, the drinker's paradise. In Tuscaloosa, Alabama, they found themselves staying near the families about whom,
two years earlier, he had written in his article for *Fortune*. And
wherever he went he introduced Alma as his wife.

If departures are exhilarating, returns are proportionately agoniz-
ing. Being back in New York brought increasing confusion to Agee.
He felt deep guilt at having abandoned Via and offended the

Saunders'. And he not only reproached himself for his cruelty to Via, he resented the new dependence his love for Alma implied. In spite of his better judgment, he began to blame Alma for the predicament he found himself in, and his esteem for Via increased in turn. During the weeks of indecision he saw himself as a donkey caught between two bales of hay, as he wrote in "Bigger Than We Are." Nevertheless, in his urge to rationalize the situation, he came to see that Via remained a product of her class, molded by its tradition of bourgeois respectability, the very elements against which he was now in full rebellion. He no longer had any desire for an orderly existence, a prudently accepted conformity. He was committed to a life of material, intellectual and emotional bohemianism, for which Alma now seemed the ideal companion.

In October, 1937, Agee applied for a Guggenheim grant for the last time. Now published as "Plans for work: October, 1937," the account of his present and planned activities was more detailed than his earlier presentations had been. It included many projects: the book on Alabama, a collection of letters, a new kind of dictionary, essays on color photography and portraiture, a study on the pathology of laziness, a survey of sexual literature, love, the adaptation of Shakespeare to the screen and the stage, jazz, a history of motion pictures, an autobiographical novel, a study of the roles of imagination and realism in description, the introduction of musical techniques to literature, the development of cabarets and new forms of theater. And, once again, he did not hesitate to sabotage his chances by including the usual frank remarks in his application.

CHAPTER TWO

NEW JERSEY:
THE CHALLENGE OF
A NEW RETIREMENT

"All escapes are relative and bestow
their own peculiar forms of bondage." (*C.S.P.*, 201)

As the end of the year 1937 approached Agee resolved to
get a divorce. At the beginning of 1938 he and Alma left New York
and settled on a farm in Frenchtown, New Jersey, not far from his
friend Wilder Hobson. He planned to take no more regular jobs
and to work for money only when he was in urgent need of it. He
felt that the security he had had as a salaried writer was a hopeless,
illusionary trap.

By leaving New York he hoped to make the transition from "the
man he was to the man he had to become," to establish some order
in his personal life after the emotional turmoil of the preceding
months and to complete his book on the South, the manuscript of
which he had nearly destroyed earlier in a fit of depression.

At first this new life was hard to bear. After his many activities
in New York the solitude of Frenchtown caused him to seek dis-

tractions: tennis matches, walks, visits to his friends and books. He read Céline (*Mort à Crédit*), Thomas Mann and Kafka, who seemed to him spiritually akin to Shakespeare, Joyce, Proust, Dostoevski and Malraux.[1] He was able to relax, but he still had no appetite for work. He wished that an illness would confine him to his bed, insuring him against ever-present temptations and forcing him to work. He did develop boils in one ear, which he treated with his habitual indifference, and when—though he continued to play two hours of tennis every day—the resulting fever only lasted one day, he humorously complained that he had thus lost the opportunity to fall seriously ill. When Alma found a job in New York for several weeks Agee discovered he had even more free time, but the result was only increased solitude and increased idleness. He made frequent trips to New York; he enjoyed making surprise visits to his friends in their offices at *Life* and *Fortune* and pursuing his war against Luce and his crowd.

It was not until May that he finally settled down to work (he was then living on Second Street in Frenchtown), and resumed contact with the literary world. Recalling that he had sent one of his poems, "Dixie Doodle," to *Partisan Review,* he wrote Dwight Macdonald on May 3, 1938, proposing some changes in the poem and recommending that a line be deleted. He later learned that his suggestions had arrived three months too late; the poem had been published in February.

His trips to New York grew less frequent. He devoted himself more to his work and completed a lyrical piece called "Knoxville: Summer 1915," which first appeared in the August/September 1938 issue of *Partisan Review* and was later used as the prologue to *A Death in the Family*. Feeling that it would be futile to spend much time and effort looking for a title,[2] Agee had originally wished to call the work simply "Short Story," since nothing more original came to his mind. This would have had the additional advantage of startling those readers who truly expected his piece to be a short story, for it differed considerably from the conventional definition of that form. Agee felt that it was necessary to restore life and freshness to both the concept and the word *story,* which were in danger of extinction. Eventually he renounced this supposedly provocative gesture, which very likely would have gone unnoticed.

"Knoxville: Summer 1915" is a continuation of Agee's literary experiments. Summer nights in Knoxville are perceived through a child's eyes at the ritual hour when fathers are peacefully watering their lawns, when the last noises are silenced and the night becomes "one blue dew." The child's own language describes the colors (the pale luminosity and blue of night) and the sounds (the song of water in the hoses and the song of crickets and swallows) that compose these nights like elements of a symphony. This world of sensations is described as though it were perceived at that very instant, and, as a result, the reader is impressed with its immediacy. He hears the text as though it were music, and reading it, he joins with the child creating it. The text moves imperceptibly from prose —a lyric and flowing prose that unrolls like the long hoses that the water swells and then leaves inert—to a poetry that through the juxtaposition of single words and images evokes the mysterious quality of summer evenings. In the quiet of descending night the immobility of the bodies resting on the moist grass seems a fore-shadowing of the silence and repose of death.

At about the same time Agee returned to his book on the tenant farmers of Alabama. He was more mistrustful than ever of art and of everything literarily and self-consciously "written." Nonetheless, his book had evolved beyond a simple piece of reporting. He now envisioned it both as an autobiographical narrative presenting its author as an ignorant and unworthy journalist confronting an absurd and unjust system and as a meditative poem based on the sociological materials of the situation of the working poor in Alabama. On a level deeper than his anger at the oppression of a social class, his denunciation of abuses and defense of the oppressed, Agee wanted to demonstrate that the very issue of human existence was involved. It was necessary, in the end, to place the Southern tenant farmer in the wider context of humanity as a whole. To express this an infinity of possible forms suggested themselves to him: social tract, journal, realistic narrative, documentary, poem of cosmic scope. He ultimately decided he could not limit the work to any one particular form; instead, he attempted to integrate all the possibilities into a single narrative that would make use of each within a unified whole. He was determined to achieve a new art form by ignoring the outmoded rules that these forms of literature followed. At the same time he also intended to defy the conventions of *art* and *literature* in the commonly accepted sense of those words. It also happened that in June, 1937, Agee had reviewed two novels about the South for *New Masses*.[3] *Black Earth,* by Cochrane, was the story of a Negro child from the deep South and a study of society around Memphis. The analysis of the relationship of the tenant farmers to the class that controlled them and the emphasis on their desire for respectability and on their need to feel assimilated particularly intrigued Agee. This and the second novel, *River George,* by G. V. Lee, probably provided him with new ideas about his own work and put him on guard against committing certain faults common to literature about the South.

At first Agee saw his opus as a "nonbook," a book only by necessity. He told Wilder Hobson that he ought to have written simply an explanation of why such a book should not and could not be written (an entire section of the final book was written in this vein) and left it at that. In the final work whole chapters denounce art, others confess his alleged ignorance and his incompetence to deal with the topic without mutilating it. The book was thus conceived of as an inevitable failure, and with a mixture of irony, indignation and contempt in the actual writing Agee simultaneously reviles and accepts the failure he was predicting. He was trying to provoke the reader, and he shamelessly imposed on him the disorder of the thoughts and feelings, the shortcomings and rebelliousness of an angry young man. He felt it was essential that the reader be aware of the author's unworthiness, so that he could blame the writer, not the subject, for the book's supposed failure.

Meanwhile Agee had begun negotiations with a publisher. But

Fortune had gotten wind of Agee's and Evans' plans and at first refused to relinquish the rights to the material, insisting that a project they had commissioned could not be published without their consent. *Fortune* subsequently relented, and Agee eventually signed a contract with Harper's, the contact having been made through Edward Aswell, the husband of his friend Mary-Louise White. As it turned out, he was no longer satisfied with his original conception of the book, and by August, 1938, he asked for an extension. Publication was postponed to midwinter, 1939.

During the final months of 1938 he found a new style. "I made a try lately of writing the book in such language that anyone who can read and is seriously interested can understand it" (*F.F.*, 114). Having succeeded, he thought, in alienating the cultivated and righteous reader—which was how he ironically saw himself—he now wished to dedicate his book to new readers, to the kind of people who were its subject, for these families' lives belonged first to their peers and only incidentally to a more sophisticated audience. Like Whitman, his purpose was democratic; he wished to return to the farmers of Alabama the spiritual material he had taken from them. However, the new and the old styles soon became confused. Agee found that he could not do without the educated city reader whom he had wanted to provoke or exclude. If the book were directed solely to the tenant farmer, many passages would end up being dull or even offensive. And if he were writing in order to do injury—and that was one of the main intentions of the book —it would be better to address himself to intellectual readers as well as to the defenseless farmers.

From Frenchtown, Agee resumed a more regular and frequent correspondence with Father Flye. His letters reflect his confusion during this period of retreat, as he tried to get his bearings amidst his social, political, religious and artistic obligations. Some letters are continuations of the same thoughts that run through his formal writing, and also provide a definitive portrait of Agee at the age of twenty-nine. He depicted himself as a social anarchist, a declared enemy of rigid authority who lived only within the dictates of his own conscience. He criticized the contentment of a society that deceived itself as readily as it deceived others. Saddened to see how good intentions were pressed into the service of evil causes, he concluded that sincerity was the most destructive of virtues. Although innocence and simplicity appealed to him, he felt that nothing was more pernicious than unthinking and defenseless docility in the face of a manifestly tyrannical reality. It seemed to him that education encouraged prejudices and the easy and unconditional acceptance of false and dangerous ideas. He dreamed of an unregimented form of education that would take place in the streets, a type of individual instruction as practiced by Socrates and Jesus that would teach people to remain free and independent.

Looking around him, Agee saw only people "tragically deceived in part by self-deceived men" (*F.F.*, 12). Agee accused the revolutionaries and reformers of the time who surrounded moral words and concepts with deceptive ambiguity. Words like *loyalty, love, honesty, duty* no longer meant much, and their opposites were words that people invoked constantly but carefully refrained from defining. It was when attempting to find real causes that most errors were made whether by putting too much violence into the accusations or by being silent about matters deserving more attention. To Agee it seemed as inadequate to say that the oppressed suffer from ills such as poverty, sickness and misery, for which they are not responsible, as it was unjust to say that they deserve their fate. But he was as enraged by the Christian idea that poverty is a necessary evil as he was by society's indifference and cruelty. He denounced the Christian arguments that encouraged resignation. On the other hand, he felt that science and Communism were guilty of a facile optimism for the future. In the meantime most people continued to suffer from afflictions they never desired and which they would never understand. What attitude should one take, what comfort should one offer? As a writer and a poet, Agee had no illusions about the powers of literature, but he did hope, at least, to give his work a moral justification. It is in the light of these concerns that Agee's book on tenant farmers must be read.

In a way Agee saw himself also as one of society's victims. He feared that anyone who refused to capitulate would sooner or later be driven to madness or to death. A random news item offered him a symbol of the situation of all young rebels such as himself: a young man had leaped to his death after spending eleven hours meditating on a window ledge of a New York hotel, stationed between the city, which opened like an abyss below him, and the hellish room from which he had fled. Like this young man, Agee felt subject to too many pressures, trapped with no way out. It seemed that two forces were fighting within him, pulling him in two opposite directions; one would ensnare him into some kind of compromise, the other would precipitate his disintegration. It is known that he was tempted to try psychoanalysis, but he did not have enough faith to submit himself to it at this time, and his ambivalence ran too deep for him to pursue the matter.

In December, 1938, he married Alma. He needed to feel that there was something stable in his life, and he decided to assume the responsibilities from which he could no longer flee. In marrying Via Saunders, he had put himself under the protection of her milieu, her maturity and her wisdom. This time his responsibility was greater. Alma was younger than he and defenseless. It was she who had a right to his protection.

His marriage did bring a new serenity to his life. Suddenly everything became easier. In the subsequent weeks he finished his book on the South, but in spite of his relief at completing the project, he feared that it would be a long time before he would find another project that would inspire him so.

He spent his additional free time reading. He read Eckermann's *Conversations with Goethe* and concluded that Goethe suffered from a lack of integrity. There were, according to Agee, two kinds of artists, the artist-bishop and the artist-saint, and Goethe, he felt, belonged to the first kind and had betrayed his God. By contrast, though on a more modest scale, Agee felt that his friend Walker Evans was an example of the second kind, a true artist (*F.F.*, 113).

The experience in Frenchtown had thus been both gratifying and excruciating. Having removed himself from the world, he could better defy and condemn it. He perceived a certain contradiction between his declaration of independence, his vehement accusations and the acts he was committing. Betrayed by society, he knew that he was also betraying himself by accepting certain ties, functions and compromises. The whole experience in Alabama, the writing that describes it as well as the retirement in Frenchtown, appear as one sustained effort to abolish the distance between his proclamations or beliefs and his outward activity.

CHAPTER THREE

ANGER

A FURTHER CHALLENGE BROUGHT AGEE'S RESOLUTION TO A HEAD.
He would soon be obliged to borrow money. Thus, in early spring,
when *Fortune* asked him to write an article on Brooklyn, he accepted promptly. He returned to the city and moved into the house
of Wilder Hobson's in-laws in Brooklyn. It was a gabled house on
Saint James Place, and he lived in the garret, where he actually
kept a goat with him. That was doubtless the reason why one day
someone scribbled in chalk on his front door, "The man who lives
here is a loony." Oblivious to the reactions of the people around
him, Agee worked with a furious intensity. When he had finished
the article he found that he was not satisfied with it, and he rewrote
it completely. He then presented the two drafts to his editor, only
to have both versions rejected. *Fortune* wanted accurate reporting
based on facts and statistics, not an impressionistic text, and that
is what Agee had submitted to them twice over. The assignment
was therefore given to another writer who, surprised that *Fortune*
thought he could succeed where Agee had so honorably failed,
quoted a sentence from Agee's original manuscript at the head of

his own article. And though the rejection of his article partly caused Agee to leave *Fortune* for good, the use of his words as an epigraph in the magazine in fact gave him a kind of boost; it made him feel that he was bidding farewell to *Fortune* as an independently recognized author.

The pages Agee wrote on Brooklyn try to give a description of the "physique" and "tone and meter" of an American city that differs from other cities because of its proximity to "the mad magnetic energy" of Manhattan. Brooklyn suggests at the same time the qualities of a small town—the provincialism, the casualness—and the characteristics of a large city, where "the whole of living is drawn up straining into verticals tightened and badgered in nearly every face of man and child and building . . . and nevertheless relaxed upon horizontalities . . ." [1]

In May, 1939, Agee became involved in a new dispute, this time with *Partisan Review*. He was one of a group of writers who had been sent a questionnaire by the magazine on the situation of the American writer. The questions dealt with the artist's ties with his country's literary heritage, his opinion of literary nationalism, the audience for whom he wrote, his opinion of literary critics, his financial concerns and the problem of making literature an economically stable profession, his attitude toward religion and his reaction to politics and the war. Agee was annoyed by the tone and the futility of the questions. He wrote his answers out immediately, before his anger had cooled, interspersing the replies with a direct attack on the naiveté and pretentiousness of the survey, conducted by a magazine that prided itself on being in the vanguard of the nation. He then realized his reactions had been written out too hastily, but when he was no better satisfied by his revisions he decided to send in his first answers. *Partisan Review,* it turned out, now refused to publish them; protesting that criticism of the questionnaire and of the magazine itself was irrelevant to the matter at hand.

Agee's response, in fact, could be considered a pamphlet which, in spite of some confusion in his ideas, expressed many of his deeply felt convictions. Literary nationalism, he claimed, was a pointless chauvinism. He urged that a true international community should be established among artists and that literary tradition itself should take on an international character. To the names already mentioned in his poem "Dedication"—Whitman, Beethoven, Blake, Christ—Agee now added other artists to his pantheon, among them Céline. Many of the ideas he expressed here had in fact already figured in "Dedication," but the tone had become angrier and the formulations more categorical. Agee further declared that he had grown away from both Communism and Catholicism, which had at different times appealed to him. Dwight Macdonald returned the rejected manuscript to him, but Agee was later able to publish this piece as part of his book on the South. It makes up the chapter entitled "Intermission. Conversation in the Lobby" (*F.M.,* 349-357).

Regarding his book on the South, Agee was involved in continuing discussions with Harper's. It had been suggested that selections be published as a magazine article before the book appeared in its entirety. Harper's would pay him in advance for this article, which its editors would select from his manuscripts. At the same time he also intended to submit extracts to Dwight Macdonald for *Partisan Review.*

In early July, after three difficult months, Agee left New York once again. He and Alma had decided to spend the summer at Monks Farm in New Jersey, not far from Stockton. There Agee wrote the concluding pages of his book. In early August, 1939, he sent the completed manuscript to Harper's and settled down to await their reaction. By that time his friend Selden Rodman, who was head of the magazine *Common Sense,* had also offered to publish selections from the book. Although Agee would have preferred to wait until he knew what selections Harper's had decided to use, he let Rodman choose the passages that interested him most and discussed a possible title with him. He rejected the title "Preview" (it might lead the reader to place unfounded hopes on the book), and he suggested instead "Three Tenant Families—A Selection." [2] At that time he expected the book to be partially or completely published in the fall of 1939.

Meanwhile Agee enjoyed himself at Monks Farm. He and Alma received visits from Father Flye, Agee's sister Emma and friends from New York. He played tennis, his favorite sport, saw movies (among them *Good-Bye, Mr. Chips* and *Mädchen in Uniform*) and read Cocteau and Joyce. Joyce's *Portrait of the Artist as a Young Man* gave him the disturbing feeling that he could have been its author, and it is likely that it later inspired him to write *The Morning Watch,* his novel about adolescence. As for his work, as someone had suggested to him that he prepare a collection of various kinds of letters, he became momentarily involved in the process of gathering, editing and organizing the pertinent materials.

In October, 1939, *Common Sense* published the first selections from "Three Tenant Families." By this time Agee no longer wanted to use the title he had suggested. He wanted to save it for a longer work he was planning to write, of which the book he had written would be only the first volume. For this first part he found another title, *Let Us Now Praise Famous Men,* a line from a verse in the forty-fourth chapter of Ecclesiasticus he had often sung as a hymn with the Exeter Glee Club. Agee liked the title's solemnity and the irony of the word *famous.*

He also conceived of a different format for his book. Since it was inspired by the tenant farmers of the South and dedicated to them, he decided that it should be made available in an inexpensive edition, to be sold for no more than $1.50. The cover could be a facsimile of the old hymnals that are found in the South or made of the cheap cardboard that government publications used. Needless to say, Harper's found these demands somewhat singular; they refused to agree. Soon another aggravating incident occurred. Through a young editor's inadvertence, Agee learned that the editors were suggesting that certain passages be cut from the book. After one of his finest fits of anger Agee withdrew his manuscript from Harper's altogether, thus wasting the effort of many months' negotiations. Wilder Hobson recounts that two hours before Evans and he were to meet for the last time with their editors Agee spent the time discussing whether he should wear a dark suit, like Evans, or whether he should dress in his own usual careless way. In spite of his concern that Evans not suffer for Agee's own audacities, he opted for casual dress.

Disgusted and bitter, Agee now resolved to "take revenge on Harper's and on the world." But he was equally intent on not letting petty quarrels control his life. He was now thirty years old, and failure stared at him from all sides. He sensed that his rebelliousness had led him to an impasse that threatened to be irremediable.

Agee found temporary relief in a new job, to write a film adaptation of a scene from *La Condition Humaine* by Malraux. He had discovered Malraux's work, along with Céline's, several years earlier, and felt that he was one of the great prophets of his time. Moreover, Agee's interest in motion pictures and in the possible fusion of literature and film made the experiment attractive to him. Agee's brief scenario "Man's Fate" appeared in Volume I of *Films,* probably at the suggestion of Lincoln Kirstein, a friend of Agee's and a member of the magazine's editorial board.[3]

Agee found in *La Condition Humaine* themes by which he was constantly obsessed: revolution and struggle, courage and cowardice, innocence and cruelty, loneliness and death. The episode he chose to adapt is the scene in which the hundreds of prisoners of the Kuomintang, who are about to be burned alive, are awaiting their death. Agee imagines a camera moving among the two hundred or so prisoners, who are lined up in a schoolyard. Still living but already on the brink of death, pressed one against the other, they seem almost "printed on the earth." The dull sound of their lamentations is as constant as "the humming of bees." Suddenly one of them is thrust head-first into the boiler of a locomotive ("like a shell into a gun"). The scene is followed by several rapid shots in counterpoint: Chiang-Kai-Shek with a "Methodist" smile, a woman in a nightclub, another in a nursery. The camera then returns to the faces of three more condemned men, each one absorbed in his own fate, surrounded by the noise of the machine that will remove them forever from the world. Such is the bloody tale from which gilded legends are made. More lives are extinguished amidst whistles and screams, while a multitude of men's and women's voices rise in a dense murmur. Then Kyo, emotionlessly and with a kind of sensuality, kills himself—not through fear of torture but because he does not want to be robbed of his own death. Indifferent to the slaughter, the "little executioner" nevertheless for a moment stops giving commands. He is determined that the whistle of the sinister locomotive be repeated in a particular rhythm only.

In a footnote Agee specifies that the scene must not be romanticized or contrived but rather that its literal character must be intensified "to become formal out of its own substance." It is said that Malraux himself was astonished by how skillfully Agee had rendered his text in cinematic terms.

In fact, Agee had become more and more attracted by motion pictures and several months earlier had submitted to Dwight Macdonald a lengthy study of the movies, suggesting that he publish it as an article. Moreover, after "The House" and "Man's Fate" he felt ready to go even further with his experiments. The exchanges between cinema and literature offered a new stimulus for his talent, as well as a temporary solution to his financial problems. Perhaps Agee also hoped to emulate the example of Malraux, who, in 1937, had produced a kind of diptych, a film and a book, entitled *L'Espoir*. Agee was to return to this ambition several years later.

In the autumn of 1939 Agee set out in search of a new job. He had left *Fortune* for good, and his financial difficulties were becoming more pressing. He gloomily realized that sooner or later he would have to return to being a salaried writer. Torn between his desire to preserve his freedom and independence, and his need to earn a living, he understood that the only way he could continue his personal work was to use his talent in the performance of thankless but well-paid jobs. He contemplated this new betrayal of his art and the return to a semisuicidal vocation with a mixture of coldness, cynicism, helplessness and guilt. It was a capitulation, but he was in no position to choose. As it turned out, though, the choice he made was not without its rewards.

PART V

JOURNALISM AND THE FILM ADVENTURE

CHAPTER ONE

AGEE AT TIME

IRONICALLY ENOUGH, IT WAS JUST WHEN HIS REBELLIOUSNESS was at its peak that Agee forced himself to return to the milieu he had boldly renounced some months before. He renewed his ties with his old employer, Luce, Inc., by signing a contract with *Time* Magazine. In spite of his noisy and repeated altercations with his editors there, they still held him in high esteem. *Time*'s editors knew that Agee was a good catch, a truly original talent, and though his quarrels with *Fortune*'s staff were legendary, the editors of *Time* still hoped they could tame him. T. S. Matthews, in particular, who was in charge of the art section, was intrigued by Agee's strange reputation and offered him a contract as a staff book reviewer.

For Agee, *Time* was a somewhat lesser evil. Where he had formerly been a mere reporter, he was now a critic. The experience might turn out to be intellectually more satisfying. He suspected, however, that he would be required to conform to an even stricter discipline and to meet greater demands than at *Fortune*. Aware of his distaste for submitting his talent to standards he felt were arbitrary, he foresaw further battles with the editors and thought this job could be no more than temporary.

Nobody saw Agee during his first months at *Time*. He chose to work at night. The only two people who occasionally met him were Whittaker Chambers, who shared his office as well as his nocturnal habits, and T. S. Matthews, to whom he submitted his articles. In the evening he would arrive at the office unshaven, in a threadbare velvet suit and a black or checked shirt, tieless, resembling, as Matthews describes him, a daguerreotype of Abraham Lincoln as a young man.[1] He and Chambers became known as the "night owls." At first Chambers, mistrustful by temperament, was not pleased with the intrusion of the newcomer. He liked to surround himself with mystery and had very few friends; it is said that when he invited someone to dinner he required his guest to go through several skyscrapers, ascend and descend elevators or take the subway first downtown, then uptown, in order to throw off the trail anyone who might have wanted to follow him or spy on him. Agee, however, won his confidence almost immediately and soon became his friend. This friendship is referred to in several passages in Chambers' book *Witness*.[2]

Every week Matthews called a meeting of his staff and presented them with a list of the books to be reviewed in the next issue. Each writer was therefore more or less able to choose the books he would write about. Agee reviewed books by Aldous Huxley, Erskine Caldwell, William Faulkner, Thomas Mann, Gertrude Stein and Carson McCullers as well as by lesser known authors. He was a watchful, generous and indulgent reader; however mediocre the book, he looked carefully for some redeeming quality, but he could also become ferocious with works he judged to be dishonest or pretentious. He recorded a multitude of judgments and impressions about each book. Careful as he was to leave nothing out, his finished articles were invariably too long and often had to be cut by more than half. Amused and annoyed by so many cuts, Agee returned to the ruse he had used at *Fortune;* he deliberately stated every important idea in three different sentences, so that at least one of them had a good chance of appearing in the final text. For his part, the editor, who was almost always T. S. Matthews, was pleased with the work he did on Agee's pieces; the thought came out clarified and the overly verbose style gained density and conciseness.

Agee himself was too aware of his imperfections not to accept criticism. His relationship with his editor was extremely cordial. He appreciated Matthews' humanity, a quality he rarely found among *Time* editors, and he trusted his judgment. During their brief conferences he was able to sense immediately whether or not Matthews was satisfied with what he had turned in, and if he noticed the slightest reservation, he would offer to rewrite the article. The magazine went to press on Monday, but Agee's contributions were seldom finished before Saturday night. Often, after he had rewritten it entirely, an article would be little better than the original version, but Agee was unable to do any job by halves. Since he considered himself a writer, he could not allow himself to make casual judgments of other writers' work. As for *Time*'s notorious style, it had not taken him too long to learn it (what with his parody in his Harvard days) but in using it he was, in a way, also parodying himself. When he adopted the tone and the clichés of superficial journalism, he felt he took the risk of making the style so completely his own that he might later have difficulty abandoning it. In effect, the demands Agee made on himself were greater than those of his editors and readers. Having just accepted the constraints and pitfalls of journalism for the second time, he considered his situation with anguish. Throughout the rest of his life he would try a wide variety of jobs and accept various assignments, searching in vain for a solution to his problems. When he came to work for *Time* in September, 1939, he had no idea that this "temporary" solution was to last for nine years.

With the outbreak of war in Europe, Agee spent the first months of 1940 in a daze. The image of a drowned man recurs constantly in his letters to Father Flye. "Between jobs, occasional attempts to write of my own, personal worries and a smattering of ill-organized social life, I am so generally drowned, I am incapable of time and clarity of mind" (*F.F.,* 124). "I have a fuzzy, very middle class, and, in the bad sense of the word, Christian mind and a very clouded sensibility" (*F.F.*, 129), he further wrote. Perhaps out of weakness, he clung desperately to values that had been important to him in the past: his religious faith, his parents, his childhood. But he still felt his world was just about to disintegrate (*F.F.*, 123). He had lost all hope and confidence and had been disappointed in Communism, like many radical intellectuals; "If I weren't an anarchist I would probably be a left-wing conservative" (*F.F.*, 126). He could still be moved or excited by ideas and he was thus assured of some kind of intellectual survival, but when he considered his own life and his artistic career, his despondency was complete.

Alma was expecting a child. Agee awaited the birth with a mixture of hope and fear, joy and sorrow. Their son, Joel, was born in March, 1940.

CHAPTER TWO

LET US NOW PRAISE FAMOUS MEN

TROUBLED BY WORLD EVENTS, DISAPPOINTED IN HIMSELF AND more uncertain than ever, Agee nevertheless decided to try once more to get his book about the South published. In the spring of 1940 his friend Eunice Jessup showed the manuscript to Paul Brooks, an editor at Houghton Mifflin, Boston, who made Agee an offer. Brooks held no illusion about the book's potential commercial success; he was interested solely in what he judged to be the work's major literary significance.

Before he submitted the manuscript to Houghton Mifflin, Agee asked Walker Evans to go over it for possible cutting and revision. Evans declined, citing lack of qualifications. It was a measure of Agee's esteem for Evans and his art that he made the request in the first place. He felt that Evans' somber photographs were the better half by far of their joint work and that by comparison, his own text was still unfixed, unfinished and unworthy. "If I could do it, I'd do no writing at all here. It would be the photographs; the rest would be fragments of cloth, bits of cotton, lumps of earth, records of speech" (*F.M.*, 13).

The contract with Houghton Mifflin was signed in the spring of 1940, but Agee knew that this did not completely settle the matter.

His experience with Harper's made him wonder whether the Boston publisher would also insist on a great many cuts and react negatively toward his own suggestions. On several points he still intended to refuse to give in. He now wanted the text to appear in its entirety and insisted more strongly than ever that it be published in a low-priced edition. And by this time he was even more attached to the idea of using the format and binding of the reports published by the Government Printing Office. The friends to whom he broached this plan agreed with the editors that his plans were impractical; they accused Agee of reverse snobbery and found an element of extreme preciosity in his claims to simplicity.[1] They further felt that it would be wiser to give up the demands rather than to risk the project falling through again. Agee reiterated that these seemingly minor details meant more to him than the publication itself.

Before the book actually appeared in 1941, an excerpt entitled "Colon" was published in *New Directions,* the magazine edited by James Laughlin.[2] Meanwhile Agee was surprised to learn that the only concession asked of him by Houghton Mifflin was the deletion of certain words that were "illegal in Massachusetts." He accepted this censorship but made note of it in the preface, in which he recounts the adventures of the manuscript since the autumn of 1936, when the first article was delivered to *Fortune.*

The book finally came out in August, 1941, bound in the conventional fashion; on this matter at least Agee had been forced to yield. It contained thirty-two photographs by Walker Evans and 471 pages of text. Its various phases reveal the process of continual effort and gradual approximation, spontaneity and slow maturation, through which Agee developed his experience in Alabama into an artistic work.

Designed to disorient the reader, surprise him and little by little cast a spell on him, *Let Us Now Praise Famous Men* is composed like a symphony consisting of themes and variations. Major and minor themes are introduced and repeated with modifications, now tangled, now disjointed. The variations are numerous, in either tone, movement, form or intensity. In the preface Agee stresses that the book should be read aloud, without interruption, as one would listen to a simple piece of music or watch a film. The reader must bring to it, he emphasizes, not only his eyes, but his ears; not only his intellect, but his entire being. Agee tried to facilitate this communion by beckoning his reader from all sides, continually provoking his interest, holding his attention, appealing by turns to his mind, his sensitivity, his moral and artistic senses.

The book opens with a rather dense account of its own intentions: It is to be a personal inquiry into certain normal conditions of human "divinity," seen through the daily existence of men of flesh and blood who suffer, die, eat, drink and love in the back country of Alabama. As specific as his inquiry may be, Agee wants it to transcend the context in which it originates. He further intends to promote to a kind of fame these men whose existence had hitherto been ignored, thus encompassing the religious and ironic meaning of the title.

The book opens with three quotations: lines from *King Lear* (III, 4); a familiar Marxist slogan that Agee explains in a footnote must not be taken for a profession of faith in Communism but is simply an introduction to one of the themes of the book; two passages from a geography textbook used in Alabama schools that in their naive simplicity offer an ironic commentary on Agee's own approach. These references were meant to show the starkness of wretched lives, the obsession of unfulfillable vows.

After these preliminaries the dramatic nature of the book is announced through a list of people drawn up as a cast of characters: the three families, several witnesses including the two spies, Agee and Evans, and unpaid agitators. This is reminiscent of the listing of people in the poem "Dedication," where obscure names appear side by side with names of famous men. The reader is already somewhat bewildered by the time he reaches Book II, with which the arabic pagination begins.

A new table of contents sets forth the structure of Book II, announcing that there will be three "Parts" and an intermission, as in a play. In fact, Part I of Book II does not begin until page 46. It turns out that the parts are not general headings for the major subdivisions of the book at all, but isolated chapters, separated by other independent sections. But this seeming confusion hides an organic structure that only a closer scrutiny can reveal. Farther along, Agee supplies several clues to the book's composition, explaining that he borrowed techniques from musical polyphonic structures and from the art of the film.

The three chapters called "On the Porch," numbered as if to indicate variations on a single theme, were, he says, all written in 1937. Originally intended to serve. as an introduction to a much longer work, they were retained as prefaces or overtures; they also serve as a framework and foundation, a central point with respect to which the other components of the book are flashbacks, preludes and "foretastes," explanations or contradictions. The singularity of the work and its technique, which borrows from all genres, cannot be overemphasized. Agee first awakens the reader's curiosity by intriguing him, by annoying him, and then contradicts his anticipations. Yet he spurs him on in the hope that he will eventually come to perceive through the artificial complexity of an apparently puzzling structure the true complexity of the subject. The book was thus designed to checkmate the casual reader, the one who reads with preconceived ideas, determined to see nothing that he does not already know.

To the preface Agee adds a preamble (pp. 7-16), which begins with excessive apologies and self-criticisms but soon turns into another manifesto. It offers a definition of the work with respect to the three characters involved in the adventure: subject, author and reader. It rages against "honest journalism," which presents a particular kind of merchandise to an extended public that will approve of it. The information they receive in comfort is sufficient to appease their conscience. Agee intends to achieve just the reverse; his work is not meant to please, entertain or flatter. Agee deplores the calm welcome that works written in anger often meet, the "emasculation of acceptance" they achieve: "the deadliest blow the enemy of the human soul can strike is to do fury honor" (*F.M.*, 13).

Having thus prepared and warned his readers, he lets them penetrate more deeply into the work, whose intentions, he hopes, have been made sufficiently clear. The execution of those intentions is another matter. Appropriate forms and techniques will be derived from the work's contents, from the reality it perceived and treated. It will thus find its own unity and equilibrium in spontaneous development free from rigorous, narrow, conventional principles of composition, logic and symmetry.

The first movement of the book consists of two lyrical prose pieces, "The house had now descended" and "All over Alabama the lamps are out," which themselves frame three short anecdotal and descriptive scenes. The prose poem introduces one of the work's major themes, the night, and associated minor themes: silence, rest after weariness, solitude in sleep, the return to the primordial state of innocence. Sleep seems to strike and stun all creatures, men and beasts, who inhabit the earth. From its impenetrable depths the protagonists of the book will slowly emerge with the day.

The anecdotes that follow are based on encounters with people: an official meeting with three Negro singers, a meeting at a crossroads and the meeting on the road with a young Negro couple whose rhythmic gait seemed to Agee like a song. These tableaux show the author striving to establish contact with the people he met and to overcome the obstacles he encountered. They also picture the beauty and sacredness of the simplest things.

"All over Alabama," marking the end of the first movement, returns to the theme of night. Here, though, the earlier tone of anger and somber wrath is transformed by respectful and reverent humility into a mood of tranquil elegiac contemplation.

A long meditation follows, entitled "A Country Letter." It portrays Agee at work, having retired like a monk to his cell, full of meditative intensity, scribbling in pencil in a schoolchild's notebook by the light of an oil lamp. As his thoughts center on the lamp he minutely analyzes the quality and odor of its flame; the wick sleeping at its core is like an embryo bearing the pallor of death or like flowers in a museum, exposed to the fatal gaze of visitors, in the dishonors of an accepted fame (*F.M.*, 50). The globe that encloses the flame serves as a central metaphor for this passage and for the entire book, describing as it does the globe of the earth and those separate spheres, the villages of Alabama, isolated in the great desert that surrounds them. Agee later returns to this image and develops it further to include the all-engulfing sea. It was important, Agee felt, to describe his manner of composition. He was thus inviting the reader to approach the book and its subjects in the same meditative and respectful spirit.

He wrote as if possessed, his thoughts expanding to the point where they sometimes seemed truly prophetic. The night was his accomplice, and no part of what it communicated to him could be unimportant. He waited for the secret hour when the night attained its fullness, when sleep was finally conquered and the senses abandoned themselves to silence and darkness like "ships" sighting land for the last time before setting out to sea or like a city when the ending of a festival leaves a kind of enchantment (*F. M.*, 51-52). Such is the nocturnal realm of the imagination, which has become receptive, relaxed, passive and nostalgic. In the profound silence and solitude of the darkened world he assigned himself the task of trying to communicate with the solitary beings around him. Under the sheltering roof beneath the Alabama sky, in the intimacy of the tenant farmer's family, he tried to go beyond merely imagining their lives; he tried to experience them as his own.

The section that follows is again more purely dramatic. Agee introduces members of the families: Merry Lee Katy, Clair Bell. He then withdraws to permit them to communicate directly to the reader in a kind of imaginary chorus, where, as in Greek tragedy, each character comments on the fate of his companions.

In these few pages the lyricism becomes intensely dramatic. Themes expand and multiply. Sleep comprises the notion of death, the one possible salvation, yet an ironic end to lives of trial. From this point on, as the first episodes have suggested, the book develops on two levels—an evocation of the beauty of innocence and a recognition of the cruelties of life.

The third section returns to purely lyric expression. After the triumph of night comes its exhaustion, at the hour when the day is reborn and once again everyone takes up the burden of living. Agee suggests the full beauty and cruelty of the hour when the day takes possession of the earth, pitilessly delivering man to his destiny and revealing each object in its stark splendor. Meanwhile man accepts with simplicity the new day's servitude.

The cycle is complete in the fourth section. The return of the day is also the call to work. Night, sleep and rest are replaced by their opposites. Labor follows rest as inevitably as day follows night.

This motif of the cycle of unending return, which gives the book its poetic unity, did not entirely satisfy Agee. Thus "Colon," a meditation on the essence of the farmer's soul, another attempt at definition, marks a pause in *Famous Men*. Agee speaks here of the tenant farmer "as a furious angel nailed to the earth by his wings." This passage contains many religious references; the style, in fact, is a conscious attempt to imitate the eloquence of sermons: long periods, repetitious syntax, enumerations, rhetorical questions, direct address to an audience that is sometimes specifically the farmer or the reader, sometimes both, or the world in general.

In order to describe a life, a multiplicity of incidences and circumstances must be taken into account. It is into this more specific universe, the physical world of emotion and sensation, that Agee now descends as he proceeds to transcribe this world with precision or to make conjectures about it. The reader's task is to transform the information given him into a clear and unified image.

Part II of *Famous Men* opens with a statement of the tenants' economic status, their position with respect to the land owners, the resources at their disposal. Here Agee adopts a direct and simple journalistic style. "Money" merely states facts without comment. "Shelter" presents the tenants' physical surroundings—fields, houses, a spring, a garden—in their organic mutual dependence. Agee does not merely list the features of the countryside but describes each one in great detail: the texture of the wood, the quality of the light. This section is reminiscent of *Walden* in its pragmatic approach to the economic facts of existence. At the same time, as in *Walden,* there is a concern with communicating nature's singular beauty and the rapture it offers the senses. For Agee the beauty entitled to most reverence is simple and pure, untainted by any intentions of art or elegance. A combined work of nature and of man, born of chance, circumstance, tradition and necessity. Agee's descriptions reveal the influence on his writing of the camera eye. He tried, in fact, to equal in his prose the force of Walker Evans' photographs, whose savage realism burned in his imagination. Compared to Evans' shots, Agee's prose sometimes seems awkward and labored, not only because of the lengthy descriptions but because of the excessive use of adjectives such as *human, poor, humble.* Affected images and similes also mar the text, as do the repeated references to music and the too frequently made comparisons of a house to a sanctuary or a temple. His prose thus sometimes confirms the failure of words, which he had himself predicted.

Yet it is often by simple enumeration, by careful inventories, that Agee obtains the most felicitous effects. Naming an object, no matter how insignificant, and describing it in great detail, gives it particular importance. The enumerations become a sort of litany, intended to induce a mood of prayer and celebration. The intensity of Agee's feelings as he writes is such that each object appears to him as in an "epiphany" and is transfigured. Perception is no longer the isolated act of sensing but rather a mystical and religious experience in which the individual consciousness loses itself totally in the object. What these precise and sometimes fastidious descriptions give us, in the end, is an eminently poetic universe in which every object has been reevaluated and assumes a portentous significance.

The oratory function of description is particularly evident in the presentation of the house. By inviting the reader to become conscious of each of its parts, of the simultaneous existence of the various rooms as a sort of musical counterpoint, Agee guards himself against "the counting mind." It is essential, he says, to perceive with one's entire body, with all of one's being. One must identify completely with the object or, rather, reconstruct it in a kind of reverie, in which the walls of the house rise up and come together "like the petals of a flower," the roof rests itself on the walls "like the wings of a butterfly." Each part of the house is revealed as if through an invisible camera that approaches an object slowly, stops; inspects and illuminates it before continuing its investigation. It is as though Agee were officiating at a religious ceremony. Certain objects are even presented as an altar (the mantelpiece), or tabernacle (the drawers of a table), and this section actually ends with a hymn: "Recessional and Vortex."

In Agee's universe all things are alive and interdependent; the vegetable and animal kingdoms have close ties with man, and at all levels of existence there is both joy and suffering.[3] But Agee also sees much of man's misery as society-induced, the society that tolerates the exploitation and degrading poverty of the sharecropper system. Yet society is not entirely to blame. There is a self-destructive as well as a sadistic instinct in man quite apart from the social order he finds himself in. And his cruelty to his own mule is not entirely explained now as a means of seeking release from his oppression. There is sadism, a violence, Agee says, that is inherent in nature. The beaten mule is also a victim of the natural condition, enslaved and doomed to thankless labor. Life is thus an irresistible "vortex," in which the same frustrations and cruelties are repeated.

The next section, "On the Porch II," deals with the direct sensual pleasure of Agee's Alabama experience (in spite of all)—and discusses the ability of art to recapture the lived moment. The recreation of those instants is the test of true art, though art, in trying to describe them, often cannot help distorting, falsifying or even destroying them. Agee is led once more to reflect on the problem of the transcription of reality into language. Words, he concludes, are instruments of communication; art is inferior to life. Agee planned his work on four sometimes conflicting levels: night and meditation, direct inspiration, recollection at a distance and literary recreation. "On the Porch II" is unique in that it moves freely among these levels, becoming in turn a simple narrative, a nocturnal meditation, an evocation of memory and a reflection on writing itself.

The essays that follow this long interlude and that complete the second part of the book assert anew Agee's resolution to be as faithful as possible to perception and experience. Writing represents a communion with life, an effort to reproduce the totality of existence.

Considerations of accuracy take priority over aesthetic concerns. But many passages do nevertheless attain the artistic perfection Agee seems to disdain and are a source of delight for the reader, who can rejoice that the shoes of the Alabama tenant farmers inspired one of the book's most striking descriptions. In "Education," as in the later section "Conversation in the Lobby," Agee temporarily leaves the tenant farmers in order to inveigh against the abuses of the educational system. "Work," an epic tableau of the farmers' daily lives, brings the book back within its familiar limits. Labor, in which man finds both dignity and a threat of destruction, is seen as a sacrament as well as a form of bondage. And the powerful, infernal machine that crushes the cotton is symbolic of the menace to the individual, a menace implied by an inhumane and degrading job.

This section completes the cycle. When the day is over, the tenant returns to his house, to the evening rituals and to the night. As Agee portrays one day's work, he also includes the larger cycles of the seasons and of the years. Each summer day, as though driven by an unseen force, the farmer returns to the same field, to prepare a new load of cotton until, by a series of slow changes, winter closes in, and so on. In his poetry, notably "Ann Garner," Agee had already used similar seasonal imagery, to represent the desolation of winter, for example. Thus the lives of simple people are carried on from season to season and from generation to generation; obscure, anonymous, but real. The humblest existence takes on cosmic dimensions; the structures of an individual life are repeated infinitely—they are part of the infinity of the universe itself.

At this point Agee's answers to the *Partisan Review*'s questionnaire on the writer's position fit easily enough into the text. The interlude, entitled "Curtain Speech, Conversation in the Lobby," has the same function as an intermission in the theater. Here, the actor being interviewed is the writer, an actor-in-words, explaining his views about his art. Once again the tone is angry, as when Agee charges that much of literature betrays the reality it is intended to illuminate.

The manner of composition of Part II is borrowed directly from the liturgy. It returns to the motif of the meeting that had originally appeared at the beginning of the book. To tell the story of these "Inductions" and of the various incidents that mark them, Agee adopts the structure of a religious service. He prefaces the chapter "Inductions" with a passage from the Forty-third Psalm, "I will go unto the altar of God," and portrays the encounters, described therein as a succession of introits. The encounter is viewed from two points in time: the time of its occurrence, the summer of 1936 in Alabama, and the present moment of writing. It seems reasonable to assume that certain passages, undoubtedly those written in the present tense, were kept just as they were written in Alabama. Others, written in the past tense, are memories interspersed with older personal recollections. Agee recalls, for example, his fit of despair when, at the age of eleven in his grandfather's house, he was overwhelmed by the white crushing heat of a gloomy Sunday, an emotion he relived during his Alabama stay. This section of the book more than any other reminds the reader that Agee is a Southerner. In Alabama he had renewed his participation in the rhythm of the land: "I was stationary in the middle of a world of which all members were stationary and in this stasis a sour odor of the earth and of night strengthened into me steadfastly until at length I felt an exact traction with this country in each twig and clod of it . . . in the plain rhythm of a human being in his basic relation to his country" (*F.M.*, 409).

The stormy night that brought him back to the tenant's house was a kind of rebaptism in the land of his forefathers, but counterpointed with his rediscovered sense of identity was a sense of betrayal and alienation. Agee was still a foreigner in the South, in spite of the loving intoxication he felt at returning to it; it was his homeland only with respect to his past, and the circumstances of his present life had forever cut him off from it. He concludes he no longer has the right to call himself a Southerner. On a personal level Agee's adventure in the South resulted in a partial failure.

The last movement of the book, paralleling the preceding one, takes parting as its theme: the farewell to the dead in "Shady Grove" cemetery and Agee's farewell to the farmers of Alabama. Like the dead who are interred with their mementos, Agee takes his leave of the living with two images: a peaceful tableau of a baby at its mother's breast, and a luminous picture of a second newborn infant. The survival, if not the divinity, of man is symbolized by both. A long prayer inspired by the Bible verse that gives the book its title closes the movement.

The notes and appendices that follow are for the most part ironic. They contain references to other books, to maps and postcards of the South, as well as reference to a newspaper clipping in which it is claimed that it is impossible to disturb the peace by playing Beethoven. Agee also quotes an article on the photographer Margaret Bourke-White, but the absence of comment clearly indicates his reservations about the surrounding publicity and the content of her book on the South, *You Have Seen Their Faces*, published four years earlier. Agee was particularly indignant about the contrast between the compassion evidenced in her portraits and her alleged indifference to their actual subjects. There follows an attack on the manner in which the word *tenant* and many other words as well have been misused by the intellectual left, which, in its strings of loosely connected words, its fascinating juxtapositions of ideas, ends up being a meditation, a kind of chant on the magic of language.

Next in sequence a list of aphorisms from Blake's "Marriage of Heaven and Hell" reaffirms the sacred character of all life. The book concludes with a final lyric passage, "On the Porch III." The cries of mysterious animals calling out to each other in the night affords Agee one last moment of exaltation, a mixed emotion of joy, at hearing the world talk to itself, and grief, "the grief of incommunicability."

Let Us Now Praise Famous Men was published in the wake of a number of other books on the South: Margaret Bourke-White's picture book; *The River*, by Pare Lorentz; *Tobacco Road*, by Erskine Caldwell; *Land of the Free*, by Archibald MacLeish; and *American Exodus*, by Paul Taylor and Dorothea Lange.

Agee's book, resembling, of course, none of these—nor any other, for that matter—was bound to disconcert any reader with a preconceived notion of what a book about the South ought to be like. It was neither an ethnic study of a "primitive" society nor a sociological novel; a pleading for a cause nor a slice-of-life description of the tenant farmers. *Famous Men* offered, in addition to its multifaceted descriptions of the South, the description of a book being written about Southern existence—whole sections examine the relationship between life, or experience, and art. Various clues are given about the composition of the work, its similarities to a religious service, a piece of music, a photographic or film transcription of reality—but it seems that none of these intentions is followed consistently. The reader of the early forties might resent the repeated digressions, the long inventories. He could also find some discrepancy between Agee's extreme humility toward his subject and the scope of his ambition.

A number of critics praised the work when it first appeared and even hailed its publication as a major event in contemporary literature.[4] Harvey Breit wrote approvingly of Agee's honesty in exploring his own recesses of consciousness where one's feelings are not always to one's credit. He also admired Agee's rare understanding of the black man's psychology. On the other hand, Lionel Trilling felt that the book was not a success, that it was a failure for the very reasons Agee himself had given. But it was not, he amended, a literary failure; the book contained, Trilling wrote, unforgettable passages. The failure was on the level of the work's claim to moral realism. Agee had falsified reality by seeing his tenant farmers as the embodiment of perfect virtue—if only because of their impoverished existence. The falsification, he supposed, was owing to Agee's uncontrollable sense of guilt, which Agee himself analyzes at great length in the book.

While several critics, such as Trilling, dealt with the ethics of the work, most evaluations dealt with its artistic merits—this despite Agee's firm denials that he was creating a work of art. And when *Let Us Now Praise Famous Men* was reissued in 1961, it was hailed by most critics as a classic on the grounds that Agee, on its first publication, had so passionately disavowed.

In 1941, however, the book was neither a commercial nor a critical success. It sold fewer than six hundred copies the first year, and before it was eventually remaindered, the total sales had not even amounted to four thousand copies.[5] But what disappointed Agee more was that the book did not reach the people he was writing for, nor did it gain the attention of those whose indignation he had hoped to arouse. A polemic written with fury and passion, *Famous Men* was met only with indifference. The failure was partly because of the vicissitudes of time. Russia and the United States had just entered the Second World War, and the country that had been so long preoccupied by its own economic problems now turned its attention toward Europe.

The book market was thus understandably dominated by war novels—but even then, not of a notably sophisticated literary level.[6] Thus Dwight Macdonald, deploring the apathetic response to *Famous Men,* lamented that truly great works of art were rarely appreciated in their own time.

In any event, *Famous Men* was irrevocably out of date by the time it was initially published. Had it appeared several years earlier, it is still not certain that it would have been successful. But at least its true genius as a work belonging to the international protest literature of the fears preceding the Second World War, of which Malraux and Ignazio Silone were the best European examples, would have been more easily recognized.

Agee's book is situated between two poles. On the one hand, anger and indignation link it to the embattled literature of documentation and polemic prevalent during the thirties; on the other, prayer and meditation, and celebration of life, anticipate the spirit of the forties, with its insistence on the individual, the secret, the particular.

But although it is important to see *Famous Men* in the context of the years during which it was written and the literature that was contemporary with it, the work, in the end, defies all classification. *Famous Men* is a mobile creation, an ongoing inquiry that offers no definitive solution to the social problems it describes or to the literary problems it poses. The work is an intense spiritual adventure, a search for innocence, and along the way all literature, all culture, is brought into question. It is an experimental, polyphonic work in which all the arts—literature, music, film—fuse. And though Agee repeatedly disavows its artistic purposes, it is as a work of art that *Famous Men* is ultimately valued.

CHAPTER THREE

CRISIS AND DISORDER

ALTHOUGH HE WAS RELIEVED TO BE FINALLY DONE WITH A BOOK
that had taken him so long to write and whose publication had
involved so many complications, Agee now felt a postpartum emptiness. He would have liked to begin to work immediately on another
project and so to avoid confronting the ongoing turmoil of his life.
For it happened that soon after the birth of their son Joel, Alma
left him. Though Agee did not know at this point whether the
separation would be a temporary or permanent arrangement—
Alma had gone to Mexico with Helen Levitt to work on a photographic project—he certainly must have admitted to himself that
his second marriage had been a mistake, and the realization, coming so soon after his break with Via, left him still more bitter.

Disturbed by the ebb and flow of his affections, Agee again put
most of the blame on himself. He saw a self-destructive impulse in
himself and deplored the harm it did to other people. Freedom in
his life seemed as difficult to achieve as freedom in his art; he had
dreamed of writing an untrammeled, new and courageous work and
of modeling his own life on this ideal. And like his life, his art, too,
had failed. Altogether, his spiritual anguish and uncertainty
granted him few moments of real happiness. Agee once more

wondered whether psychoanalysis could help him, but in the end he decided against it. He feared it would only bring him a new source of humiliation and failure; he also remarked he could see no wisdom in further turning attention on himself. Reflection and analysis made him more cruelly aware of his inconsistencies and left unresolved the conflicts that set him against himself and against others.

During these months of crisis Father Flye served both as his confidant and confessor. The letters Agee wrote him reflect his deep confusion and trouble. There emerges in the correspondence the image of a person tragically self-deluding and subject to a seemingly incurable melancholy.

Yet Agee always retained a lively sense of humor and was at times capable of a frank gaiety that allowed him to poke fun at himself. At the same time that he drew this rather dismal self-portrait to Father Flye, he was painting—for a less compassionate viewer—a vivid and amusing caricature of himself as an artist-intellectual grappling with an indifferent world: "Born scarcely 100 years after the birth of Lincoln . . . pronouncedly schizoid and a manic depressive as well, with an occasional twinkle of paranoia . . . tall, faintly rustic in appearance, with slightly walled eyes, gentle when not aroused, and always kind to animals, thanks to an inexcusable bit of carelessness he has lost several teeth but still retains a legal sufficiency to bite the God of War, should their paths cross . . . does not like to be called Aggie, Uhgee, Egg'gee, Ag-you, Aukyow or Rufus. Due to some domestic or Christian trauma sustained in early youth, he is kindly, in proportion to his hatred." [1]

A new element had entered his character—rage, brought on almost certainly by his sense of continued frustration. Rage was almost constantly with him, ready to explode at the slightest provocation. Regrettably, its effect only aggravated the cause: It decreased his ability to communicate and sped him further along his destructive path.

CHAPTER FOUR

WAITING

1942 MARKED A PAUSE AFTER THE TURMOIL OF THE PRECEDING years. Ideologically, in his relation to Communism and Christianity, Agee felt himself less involved, and his emotional involvements were likewise less intense. He sought out the friendships of Walker Evans and Helen Levitt and formed calm and more stable relationships. His work had also gone into a dormant phase. He now felt only a vague need to write another book and had not yet decided what its subject would be or what form it would take. It was a period of waiting, during which he reorganized his life and his activity.

At *Time,* his work became more diversified. His book reviews now alternated with short pieces on films. He had turned away temporarily from the world of literature, where he no longer felt welcome, and deflected some of his energy toward the movies, seeing sometimes four or five films a day. Occasionally, when a first viewing left him with an uncertain reaction, he would return to see the same film again and again until he knew the work as thoroughly as if he had made it himself. He submitted his reviews in the form of lengthy essays that, when edited, became the brief, anonymous yet opinionated pieces in the *Time* manner. It was the combination of opinion and anonymity that left Agee dissatisfied with the work. Thus, when several months later, in December, 1942, Margaret Marshall suggested that he write a similar column for *The Nation,* Agee agreed. Starting in 1943 and continuing for five years, his signed articles appeared regularly in the pages of that magazine. At *The Nation* Agee was able to write more freely than at *Time;* he had more space at his disposal, and his articles appeared pretty much as he wrote them. Sometimes he would expand on thoughts already outlined in *Time* and sometimes he would discuss in an extended fashion ideas that first appeared in his letters to Father Flye. Critically astute though they were, his pieces were very personal, and for the first time in his life he found a regular, loyal audience to whom he could confide his philosophy and his opinions. It is somewhat ironic that Agee first gained a certain degree of renown not as a poet or author but as a journalist, the profession he thought so little of. While his notes in *Time* were read by film enthusiasts who wanted quick information about what to see, the readers of *The Nation* had different interests. In Agee's columns they found fine prose and opinions that revealed an attractive and original personality. They enjoyed his witty turns of phrase, his enthusiasm and unquestioning faith in an art that was still frequently regarded with suspicion. Letters to the editor congratulated Margaret Marshall, then in charge of the magazine, for having introduced Agee to the pages of *The Nation.*

As much a polemical essayist as a critic, Agee did not hesitate to broach controversial issues in his pieces. Thus in May, 1943, he was vehement in his denunciation of *Mission to Moscow,* a film he judged to be a pernicious mixture of Stalinism, New-Dealism, and Hollywoodism: [1] "It indulges the all but universal custom of using only so much of the truth as may be convenient and of regarding aesthetic integrity, human verisimilitude and psychological credibility as scullions." He found this sort of irresponsibility "insulting and inimical to its producers, appraisers and consumers alike."

An angry response from Dwight Macdonald published on June

19 under the title "Double Talk" accused his friend of having contradicted himself over and over again in the piece. Macdonald also bitterly criticized what he felt to be Agee's prejudgments on matters about which he claimed to have a neutral opinion. Agee replied to Macdonald's biting sarcasm in the same tone; he should, of course, have left such questions to those men who were so obviously versed in political matters that they were forever hitting each other over the head with circumstantial evidence to prove their respective positions; his opinion, he claimed, had been that of an unpretentious, not to say detached, individual. He admitted that he was incomparably less well informed than Macdonald, but he did not care at all to have an outlook that adhered to any political system. Nor did he now back away from the views that had so enraged his friend. He would not try to defend them any further, for he neither knew enough to do so, nor believed in that kind of knowledge. If Agee's opinions on politics in the forties—a time when current events were arousing everyone's passions—often contradicted themselves, it was because he remained distrustful of adopting any formal stand. Doubt and skepticism seemed to him the healthiest political attitude. His formulations were not part of any political creed but the effort of one anguished individual attempting to understand the horrifying and bewildering events of the day.

At that time the possibility of his own mobilization (the draft board changed his status from 3A, temporarily exempt, to 1A, immediate call) caused him to reflect further on the role the United States proposed to play in the war. He wrote to Father Flye that he expected "the worst" from his country and from England and not much better from Russia and China. He criticized the paternalistic attitude of the great powers toward the small and would have liked to encourage the underdog to forgo submissiveness and gratitude in favor of clearsightedness and rebellion. His constant motto was "Don't bite the hand that feeds you, reach for the throat." He also condemned the condescension shown to refugees.

The readers of *The Nation* were receptive to Agee's opinions when he went beyond the bounds of film criticism and dealt with broader political issues. In October, 1943, for example, in an article entitled "So Proudly We Fail," he analyzed America's unique situation—comparing it with the position of nations geographically more involved in the war—as an evil situation and one that could have dire consequences for the future of the country. It seemed to him that schizophrenia menaced both the men who were fighting the war in foreign lands and their countrymen who were outside the event and remained intact, virginal or "prenatal" at a time when all the other peoples, in a certain sense, had come of age.[2] America, he thought, was fundamentally incapable of deep involvement in the war. For the fraction of the nation that participated in it the experience would remain sterile, bitter and isolated, while the abyss that separated them from the rest of the people would deepen as the great majority emerged from it as though the war had never taken place.

In another controversial piece Agee wrote that film makers were often guilty of falsifying the American people's idea of the war. The media offered potentially an undreamed of means of information and participation, but the current films, he felt, were pandering to the audience's cheapest emotions. Agee was not hostile to the majority of Hollywood productions. He did not hesitate to praise those films that seemed to give an honest, unsentimental portrayal of the war.

After an article for *Time* on Eliot's *Four Quartets,* written in collaboration with Harvey Breit, Agee abandoned book reviewing altogether and devoted himself almost exclusively to film criticism. He soon specialized in writing "cover stories" several pages long. Often a cover story would trace the entire career of an actor or director or discuss a film at much greater length than was possible in the regular film column. Normally the writer had to turn in his article earlier than usual to allow the editors several days to organize the layout of the magazine. Agee soon became an editor's nightmare; he rarely turned in his manuscript on time. T. S. Matthews, who was still his editor at *Time,* recalled how Agee showed up in his office one Saturday morning with the manuscript of an article on Olivier's *Hamlet*.[3] He had worked on it for several nights and had come to deliver it, even though he was still dissatisfied with it. Watching Matthews' expression as he read the manuscript, Agee understood that his editor was not overly impressed with the piece, and he left without saying a word. He returned with a completely rewritten manuscript on the very day of the week that *Time* appeared on the newsstands, but of course it was too late. The first article had already gone to press. When Matthews read the second article he found that although it was different from the first, it was not all that better. The anecdote does, however, illustrate how conscientiously Agee worked for the magazine. He would spend entire nights writing, rewriting, tirelessly correcting an anonymous article, with the same passionate concern as though it were one of his poems or signed pieces. It was no more possible for him to do a job carelessly than it was for him to discipline himself to do it on time.

Although Agee's friends and even his editors tried to persuade him to quit journalism so that he could direct his energy toward more serious work, Agee persisted, perhaps out of necessity, perhaps out of genuine interest and commitment, perhaps also because he had lost the hope of ever becoming a full-time writer. He certainly did not hide the fact that he needed money. Journalism, which offered him good pay and fairly regular work, made it possible for him to earn a living. Nevertheless, he needed to feel that he was earning his money honestly. Perhaps, though, it was to redeem the job in his own eyes that he brought to it so much professional conscience. In addition Agee respected certain of the men he worked for, especially T. S. Matthews, and he did not want to disappoint those who had shown faith in his talent. It is true, too, that through journalism he finally reached the broad audience for which he had always secretly longed.

Agee may also have been throwing himself so completely into journalism to fill the void left by the completion of his first book. It is likely that the reserved welcome accorded *Let Us Now Praise*

Famous Men had led him once more to doubt his talent. Once the ambitious young poet of the thirties, Agee had practically given up poetry; though he continued to write poems, it was as if by habit. The sad truth is that at this point in Agee's life poetry had temporarily, it turned out, lost its power.

CHAPTER FIVE

AGAINST THE AMERICAN GRAIN

"O My Poor Country I Have So Much Hated" (*C.P.,* 157)

As he lost interest in poetry Agee became more and more involved with journalism and criticism. In response to an article written by Louise Bogan in 1944, he published a long piece on popular art in *Partisan Review*.[1] In it he deplored what happens to art forms when they are cut off from their source. Authentic jazz, for instance, was no longer played except by little-known musicians. Artists, he felt, were just as much to blame for this as their public. And the corruption that had overtaken popular art affected the lower classes as well as the bourgeoisie, blacks as well as whites. In spite of the talent and creativity of certain artists, popular art had lost its innocence. It had been spoiled by publicity, distorted by too much refinement. Agee's article aroused many reactions, including a response in *The New Yorker*'s "Talk of the Town" column, accusing him of the conceit of passing judgment on movies he had not even seen. In fact, in a postscript, Agee had mentioned that on the recommendation of his friends he had purposely not attended the productions he had criticized most harshly: *Oklahoma,* Robeson's *Othello,* and *Carmen Jones.* James Grossman took Agee's side in *Partisan Review,* arguing that one should not dispute Agee's right to avoid bad films. Had Agee spoken favorably about them, no one would have cared whether he had actually seen them.[2]

Agee, obviously, expressed his opinions bluntly and impertinently. His article was an indictment of prejudices, fashion, the commercialization of art and the vulnerability of most artists. His method, as he said, was to work "against the grain," against the tradition of commonly accepted ideas. He pursued this campaign on two fronts: that of current affairs and public life, and that of cultural realizations. Culture he held to be a sacred domain. Although he was an anarchist in his fashion, he was neither a reformer nor a revolutionary. He was open to experience but attached to traditional artistic values. He was also a resolute individualist, lamenting the disappearance of authentic liberalism. He wished someday to write a weekly column dealing with the subjects important to him: education, advertising, attitudes toward war criminals, the decline and perversion of individualism and "of virtually all nominal rationalism," the "mock revival" of religion. The wish, however, seemed to him unlikely ever to be realized.

It was at this time, however, that he accepted a new job at *Time* that enabled him in part to realize his project. For two years, 1945-1946, he was no longer attached to one specific department of the magazine. He abandoned his regular film reporting in order to write lengthy articles on a variety of subjects dealing with domestic and foreign affairs as well as with the press and religion. The job was a welcome relief from what had become the tedium of going from one movie theater to another, and he enjoyed the job's greater freedom. But he also confessed to Father Flye that he was not altogether easy in his mind about it, since he feared that he was displacing other more specialized writers who usually wrote on these topics (*F. F.,* 149).

His first assignment was on postwar Europe, "Europe, Autumn Story," [3] in which he blended the themes of hope and disillusionment and introduced a diffuse symbolism of the seasons man's life passes through. He also returned to an idea already expressed in *Famous Men,* that the goodwill and generosity of Americans might be more damaging than helpful, bringing little comfort to a long-suffering people. In another piece he held out little hope for the success of the laws recently passed against racial discrimination. He could not see how the situation portrayed in Richard Wright's *Black Boy* (a book that made a great impression on him) could ever be remedied. Laws might offer protection to blacks, but they could not abolish prejudice. Agee felt he had a better understanding of the Negro problem than the theoreticians of equality. He certainly can be criticized for having chosen for the most part to be silent in the face of the most prolonged injustice the country had lived through. Agee was a moralist but not a reformer. As an artist he was increasingly convinced that art should not become involved with polemics, but he also believed that the writer could participate in the production of meaning, that he could organize the signs reality offered him so that some degree of intelligibility would emerge.

He once again tried to find through writing an answer to the problems with which contemporary events confronted him. In "Dedication Day," published by *Politics* in 1946,[4] Agee returned to a form he had experimented with in 1937, in "The House," allegorical satire. Just as "The House" reflected the political atmosphere of the thirties in the United States, "Dedication Day" is a fable of American society and of the world scene in the midforties. Intended as an outline for a film, it is in fact less clearly designed for motion pictures than "The House" and is closer in structure to straight fiction.

The narrative unfolds as a satirical fantasy. The satire is built on the initial premise that the bomb represents a great accomplishment in which man can rightly take pride. To see it as a criminal enterprise and to try to atone for it is considered a sign of madness. Agee spares not one of the participants in the ceremony, the entire cultural establishment. The polemic enlarges into an attack on the American way of life, its slogans, its advertising, its utilitarianism,

its conformism and its blindness—all the complacencies and fatui-
ties of a self-satisfied society. The bomb is represented by an
enormous fuse, not unlike a cotton spindle, whose manufacture has
been cunningly planned to solve various tricky economic and social
problems. The cotton comes from the formerly doomed region of
the Nile Delta, which has been rendered fertile by a Sharecropper
Rehabilitation Project. The fuse is manufactured in an air-condi-
tioned workshop and its production provides an honorable and
profitable occupation for numerous unemployed men and handicapped veterans and Hiroshima or Nagasaki survivors. They are
treated with civility and provided with a healthful, standard American diet: steaks, toothpaste, and liquid editions of *Time,* the
Reader's Digest and the New Testament administered orally, rec-
tally and intravenously. Everything is set up to prevent possible
deficiencies. There is one lone shadow to mar this careful planning.
An American scientist has obstinately demanded to be made part
of the Japanese team making the fuse, requesting that an exception
be made to the rule of segregation. His appearance causes a dangerous disturbance. He eventually dies, a victim of his own madness,
at the very hour when the project to which he has devoted his lifetime is tested.

The script, whose adaptation to the screen would be difficult to
envision, has the full moral significance of a fable. A passionate
outcry against the fragmentation of the world, it is derived both
from the utopian and the futuristic novel, borrowing from them the
use of an imaginary situation and fictional characters in order to
criticize existing institutions and develop hypotheses about the immediate future. Agee's purpose was to forewarn the reader, remind-
ing him that the past was not completely dead and predicting a
future that seemed only too plausible because it so cruelly resembled the present.

Agee's satire, which masqueraded as the advocate of the things
it condemned, spared no one and nothing, particularly America's
role in the tragedy of Hiroshima and the noisy celebration of a dis-
putable victory. As the story progresses allusions multiply, giving

a broader field to the parody. Nothing is spared—government, army, university, Church, modern art, science, psychiatry. High praise is given to a nation that can bring rapid and efficient solutions to the most serious problems (unemployment, the handicapped, the mentally ill), to a civilization oriented toward a promising future based on science, power and progress. The large audience that has come to participate in the inaugural ceremony seems to give unanimous approval to the policies of its country. Yet the significance of these outward gestures is questioned through the presence of a troubled individual, who, ironically, is one of the scientists the nation takes such pride in. He reintroduces values hitherto overlooked. The old scientist is no threat, yet his fate is a tacit condemnation of the civilization around him. Agee intentionally chose as his spokesman a somewhat ludicrous character who acts out a pantomime of piety. It is also fitting that he be insane, since only from madness is true reason born. Perhaps, to a certain extent, Agee projected himself into the scientist of "Dedication Day," for he lent him, in addition to his idealism, his sense of failure, guilt and deception. The message of the tale is no less clearly apparent through all the irony, and is, if anything, more cogent because it is skillfully concealed. Agee attacks intolerance, racism, blind optimism and condemns a society that not only rules its members' daily life (their leisure, their diet) but measures its strength by the extent to which every personality is integrated and submissive. The tone of the script is by turns light and amused or somber and bitter.

The themes of "Dedication Day" also appear in a letter Agee then wrote to Father Flye, expressing his anger at a deceptive democracy (a dog would, he said, "disdain the kind of freedom it offered" [*F. F.,* 165]). It is also tempting to connect the title with his early poem "Dedication," in which all these subjects are tested for the first time. But the word *dedication* is now used with much more bitter connotation, the intervening years having had a marked effect on Agee's optimism. Agee's tone had changed since the first work; his art had also matured. The old lyricism is now supplanted by a pungent irony. The later work is also endowed with a much vaster symbolic meaning, reverberations of innocence and guilt, atonement and death, echoing throughout.

Agee had always attached a superstitious importance to his thirty-sixth year, since this was the age at which his father died, and when in 1945 he turned thirty-six he believed that it would mark the end of his own life. Nor would he have thought it inopportune to die then. His own life, he felt, had been wasted, and he contemplated his own demise with complacency. He even joked about it with his friends. He imagined all possible ways for death to come to him: a sudden death like his father's (a strange foreshadowing of the death that awaited him nine years later), death by torture (inflicted by some enemy, possibly the Stalinists, as he wrote sardonically to Father Flye) and any of a dozen forms of accidental death. Around that time Agee was unexpectedly called to the bedside of his stepfather the Reverend Erskine Wright, who was gravely ill. In the airplane that was taking them to their mother he confided to his sister Emma that, having reached the age at which their father had died, he could not help thinking that his own death was drawing near. But he insisted that if he managed at all to survive this difficult turn in his life, he was certain his situation would improve. It turned out that his stepfather survived the immediate crisis, as did Agee, the crisis of that fated year.

In this period of his life Agee's companion in his distress was Mia Fritsch, a woman he had met at *Fortune* and had known since 1941. He was now legally separated from Alma, who was living in Mexico with their son Joel, and he again considered the promise of happiness in marriage, with a new partner. Thus, in 1946, the foe of matrimony again renounced his bachelorhood. In an article he wrote in January, 1946, for *The Nation,* Agee had expressed his concern about the false glamour the movies were attributing to bachelorhood. Agee also seemed much more open to paternal emotions than he had been when his son Joel was born. (He had seen Joel only briefly, when, in March, 1945, Alma had brought him to New York from Mexico.) Fascinated as he was by his relationship with his own father, he regretted that he had not yet formed the same ties with children of his own. Having lost faith in the quality of his work, he began to feel a passionate conviction that children were his only hope of immortality.

Significantly, this conviction provided a new direction to his writing. He now entered upon a quest that lasted until his death and that eventually led him to explore and recreate the lost world of his own childhood, a world infinitely richer than the one he presently lived in. At about this time Agee agreed to write the narration for a film that his friend Helen Levitt was planning to make with Janice Loeb. *The Quiet One* is the story of a Negro boy who lives at Wiltwyck, a charitable institution for maladjusted children in northern New York State. Agee's recent interest in films dealing with childhood (*Zéro de conduite, Mädchen in Uniform,* and *La Cage aux Rossignols*) inspired him to apply himself completely to the project. The hero, Donald, imprisoned by his confused memories, lives behind a wall of solitude that no one can penetrate. A seashell he finds himself unable to model in class opens the gulf of the past for him. He slowly begins to control his life. Transformed by recollection, the hell that was his childhood is turned into a lost paradise. But when he can find no satisfactory replacement for the material affection denied him—he is too desperately jealous to share his advisor Clarence's attentions with the other children—he decides to die. He flees toward the railroad tracks, but during the brief and tumultuous moment when the train rushes past the boy jumps back. He returns to the institution resigned and peaceful. The film's title acquires a second meaning.

At first glance *The Quiet One* is seen as a sociological study, and it is true that the film presents a warning that young people must be given help. But Agee's ultimate concerns are much more private. In the film *The Quiet One,* Donald's victory, his adjustment, his acceptance of the world and of himself are brought about at the price of a painful renunciation. This is the voice of Agee the introspective artist talking. Nor can one fail to perceive throughout the film the element of disguised autobiography. Agee, whose childhood name was Rufus, identifies strongly with the Negro child. And the child's problems strongly echo his own, his relationship with his mother, the separation from her that he found humiliating, the sometimes painful loneliness of life in a boarding school. The story of Clarence mirrors Agee's emotional experiences, first at Saint Andrew's and later at Exeter. And the course he chose for Donald is the one he himself eventually followed, freeing himself from his memories by learning to accept them.

In 1947 Charlie Chaplin's film *Monsieur Verdoux* opened to cold and hostile reviews and, six weeks after its release, disappeared from the moviehouses. A virulent slander campaign began against the film and against Chaplin himself, who rapidly fell from public favor because of his apparent Communist sympathies. The film was labeled immoral; it was seen, not unjustifiably, as a sharp attack on capitalism, war and religion. The campaign against the film awakened Agee's combative instincts. He expressed his consternation at the critics' lack of discernment. He went on to surmise that the audience was disappointed because Chaplin had unexpectedly changed his comical tone; they were blind, Agee insisted, to the cold and savage gaiety of the film. He became its self-appointed champion and defended *Monsieur Verdoux* as vehemently as if he himself had made it.[5]

Chaplin's character, Verdoux, took a very significant place in Agee's system of values. To Agee his fate showed where the veneration of innocence could lead if carried to its extreme. Verdoux's criminal activities involve a kind of sublimation. Since reality contradicts his dreams, in his mind he converts the most perverted reality into the subtlest and maddest of dreams. The story of Verdoux, as Agee interpreted it, can be likened in some ways to that of the scientist in "Dedication Day." The two characters, doomed to isolation, symbolize two possible expressions of an insane devotion to innocence. One pursues ferocious involvement, the other seeks complete self-effacement. Agee's scientist, in fact, bears a possible resemblance to Chaplin's "Charlie," whom Agee saw as a figure out of Christian mythology. In their anarchism and detachment both try to preserve a purity that more involvement in the world would destroy.

In 1947 selections from *Let Us Now Praise Famous Men* were reprinted in *Spearhead,* an anthology compiled by the editors of *New Directions.* The work had aged well, despite the experience of the intervening war. Postwar America still deserved the criticism Agee had made in 1939-1941, and his somber predictions of a dire future still seemed believable.

Meanwhile, tired of the incessant controversies in which his profession as a journalist and critic involved him, Agee once more thought, like the scientist in "Dedication Day," of resigning. The reappearance of the *Famous Men* excerpts in *Spearhead* probably contributed to his desire to return to serious writing, and soon he was at work on two separate projects: a poetic novel in the form of a family chronicle, set around 1910, covering the first six years of his own life until the day of his father's death; and a novella on the religious fervor of adolescence, drawn from his experience at Saint Andrew's. The National Institute of Arts and Letters, whose director was now Stephen Vincent Benét, offered him a two-year grant so that he could devote his full time to their realization.

The situation seemed promising, but for Agee the year 1948 began inauspiciously in other respects. He passed the first months of the year in a long depression he was unable to shake off. In April he was operated on for appendicitis, an experience he found no more dangerous than a walk in New York during rush hour but one which caused him again to reflect somberly on life and on death. And he regretted, he wrote Father Flye, that under anesthesia he had not been able to consciously feel the nearness of death.

Still, he decided to write less for the magazines, and in July he finally bade farewell to *The Nation* in an article paying homage to D. W. Griffith. In November he stopped writing for *Time* as well. But his activities in the world of the cinema were not at an end, for as he was making resolutions to set aside more time for his work, he was signing new contracts involving films, one with Huntington Hartford for an adaptation of a story by Stephen Crane, and another with *Life* for an article on silent movies. Writing screen plays, as Agee now started to do, was, in general, quite lucrative work, and would insure a certain degree of financial stability. In addition, film work, far from betraying his artistic vocation, was an extension of—if not something already embraced by—his serious literary interests. Indeed, composing screenplays would once more involve him in his exploration of new structures of artistic expression and might perhaps one day lead to his being able to direct his own film. In the light of these ambitions, it seems strange that the screenplays he finally wrote were all adaptations. He was, in fact, relegated to a very secondary role in the productions he worked on. Furthermore, the films were rarely faithful to his original scenarios. His friends were thus on the whole dubious about his new career and feared that following twelve years of journalism films would prove a further waste of his energies. But what was their skepticism compared to Agee's fascination by the movies? Nothing could check the dynamism that carried Agee toward new experiments.

CHAPTER SIX

A WAY OF SEEING

"And all of consciousness is shifted from the imagined, the revisive, to the effort to perceive simply the cruel radiance of what is." (*F.M.*, 11)

IN HIS FIRST REVIEW FOR THE NATION, IN DECEMBER, 1942, Agee had presented himself to his new readers as an amateur critic, starting on the same ground and under the same handicaps "as the average movie-goer. If I were a professional, my realization of the complexity of making any film would be so much clarified that I would be much warier than most critics can be in assigning either credit or blame . . . as an amateur I must simultaneously recognize my own ignorance and feel no apology for what my eyes tell me as I watch any given screen."

Informal as they are, the reviews written over the next six years, taken as a whole, constitute a fundamental reflection on the nature and significance of motion pictures. Agee had grown up with the movies, and they were his first love. To that spontaneous love he added in his pieces the keen analysis of a sensitive and critical mind. Agee's criticism was by turns indulgent and ferocious, benevolent and aggressive—all in terms of his very personal conception.

Having long been familiar with photography through the work of his friends Walker Evans and Helen Levitt, Agee was convinced that it succeeded in capturing both the surface and the mystery of reality better than words could.[1] Derived as it was from photography, the motion picture was a potent new way to explore reality. Carefully manipulated, it could capture what was in large part lost to all other arts; it could record reality without altering it.

The purpose of a film is to reproduce life without distortion. Agee focused much of his analysis on the director, as the person in charge of the shooting, editing and selection process resulting in the finished film. This fascination with the director's original conception of a film sometimes led him to give more consideration to that than to the final product. In his imagination Agee would often reconstruct a film as it could have been if its creator had carried out his plan and then tried to explain why its potential had not been realized. At times, he would even forget to discuss the film itself, imposing, sometimes arbitrarily, his own point of view. He was rebelling against two equally false assumptions, which both director and audience seemed to be responsible for, that viewed the movies as an escape and took for granted the passivity of the audience. If a film presents the reality of life itself, that confrontation demands active participation. Agee condemned "art" films that used material for the glory of the artist; it was the responsibility of the film to pay homage exclusively to reality.

But no matter how faithful the motion picture might be to reality, it was no mere imitation of it. It was not an objective truth but a creation: reality experienced and sensed intensely through the mind of one witness, the creator himself. Again, Agee saw the director as critical to the process. At the heart of Agee's criticism is the passionate faith in the infinite possibilities of film, explaining both the scrupulous attention he gave to certain motion pictures as he searched for qualities he greatly hoped to find in them and the disproportionate praise he gave to others. It is no wonder that his criticism is also an indictment of the deficiencies of the cinema of his time, of the mediocrity of most productions and of the debased artistic, political and social values they professed. Agee raged against commercialization of the motion picture and the conditions in which actors and directors had to, or agreed to, work as well as against the power of that anonymous collectivity that René Clair has called the "Hollywood Trust." [2] He likewise attacked the common conceptions of the set and the actors. He insisted that films be shot on location and not in a studio. The image must not be commercialized, mass-produced in a warehouse; nor should the cast necessarily consist exclusively of professional actors. Agee preferred nonprofessionals, chosen because their voice, appearance or sensitivity made them right for the role.[3]

Infinitely curious to see what the future had in store for the seventh art, Agee studied the problems of all genres of film. He had no preconceived ideas about the value of any particular genre; he was ready to recognize excellence in any type. Yet he maintained, counter to the opinion of the progressive critics, that novel and admirable sentiments did not necessarily make good films and that during the forties, in fact, it was the thrillers which had maintained a high level of movie production. However, three genres seemed especially important to him in the postwar years: the historical film, the best of which shed light on the present; the documentary, a source of significant information; and the war movie, the record of society's most tragic ordeal.[4] He was particularly interested in the poetic documentary, which was for him the ultimate cinematic art form, in which photography often succeeded where words were inadequate. It was, he called it, a "humble" cinema, close to the earth, an illumination of life. And speaking of *Farrebique,* Agee showed how Rouquier's film magnificently brought to the screen the poetic message he himself had endeavored to express in *Let Us Now Praise Famous Men.*

As for political films (and political propaganda films) Agee often feigned his usual political agnosticism. But still he railed against the facile cant of most of the Hollywood efforts in this vein —the anti-German war film, which he found mean-spirited and vengeful, as well as pro-Stalinist films like *Mission to Moscow,* whose naive conceptions appalled him. And in one of his pieces he did own up to the fact that inevitably the movie critic was "involved as much in the analysis of an industry, a form of government and the temper of a civilization as in the analysis of a film." [5]

But it was the silent film that Agee admired most. In an article for *Life* he described the great era of the comic films, declaring that it was at the beginning of its career that the motion picture had been most truly creative.[6] The absence of sound, far from being a limitation, had given free rein to the moving image. The infancy of the silent movies—the great era of Mack Sennett, Charlie Chaplin, Harold Lloyd, Harry Langdon and Buster Keaton —truly won his heart. From 1912 to 1930, he wrote, the silent film had achieved an exultant vitality, an eloquence that had never been equaled, in which the comedic movement was the bearer of emotion and beauty. The actor was an acrobat, a clown and a mime. The image existed in its pure state and spoke to the eye alone.

In evoking the heroic age of film, Agee's prose became nostalgic and lyrical. He sought not only to revive interest in the early movies but to resuscitate the entire bygone era in which he and his parents had lived, when the movie audience was enthusiastic, receptive and without pretentions and opened itself gladly to the magic of the show. He turned to the silent films to find an image of his own childhood projected on his memory as on a screen. He recalled the wonder he had felt at Chaplin's earliest films, the atmosphere of the movie theaters in Knoxville and Sewanee, the mingling odors of perfume, tobacco and perspiration, the unrepressed laughter that arose from the spectators, "as violent and steady and deafening as standing under a waterfall." Throughout the piece one is aware of Agee's deep regret that the communion and solidarity that had once joined the audience and the films (an empathy he had always demanded of himself, even for mediocre productions) had been lost. The essay also attempts to prove that the motion picture, as a popular form of entertainment, could perform the same function and attain the grandeur and universality for our time that the Elizabethan theater achieved for its era.

Because of the questions raised and the polemics involved, Agee's film criticism often touched on the ongoing debate between mass culture and elite culture.[7] On the one hand, Agee defended the movies as a popular art form; on the other, he feared that they might become a mediocre form of entertainment and dreamed of an unsurpassed excellence for them. But oblivious to cliques and feuds between critics, Agee did not ally himself either with the majority or with a progressive minority. His interest was not in discussing whether film was an inferior medium or not, whether it should satisfy the tastes of the elite or of the masses. His concern was rather to communicate his understanding of the intimate nature of movie expression, his keen sense of perception and his fierce love for motion pictures. As a way of seeing, film making bore witness to the unique and sacred character of reality. Agee's insistence was ultimately on the function of the "naked eye," and he eagerly looked forward to "films that would be works of pure fiction, played against and into and in collaboration with unreleased and uninvented reality," films for which the ideal moviegoers would be "those who have eyes capable of seeing . . . and minds and hearts capable of caring for what they see."[8]

CHAPTER SEVEN

THE SALVE OF RECOLLECTION

"Now as awareness of how much life
is lost and how little is left . . ."
(C.S.P., 143)

HAVING FREED HIMSELF FROM THE WORLD OF JOURNALISM, AGEE
fell into the habit of going to an old farm in Hillsdale, in upstate
New York. He went there with Mia whenever she could arrange
a short vacation and with their infant daughter, Julia Teresa, who
had been born in November, 1946. He would frequently revisit
this spot in the years to come. Far from the city, he could gain
a sense of perspective, recover from his recurring depressions and
find the courage to write.

But in spite of Mia's support, the apathy, self-pity and fits of
rage persisted. It is said that one day, while attending the type
of reception at which he was never completely at ease, he became
so exasperated by the banality of a particular remark that he
smashed at the face of the woman who had made it and broke
two of her teeth. He did not regret the incident, nor did he apol-
ogize. Agee vented the same anger on himself. Once he pounded
so hard on a table with his hand that he could not write for several
days. On another occasion he punched his fist through a window

pane. When such explosions occurred he felt no remorse; he preferred the show of lightning anger to the painful brooding that was his usual state.

The celebration of his fortieth birthday in 1949 brought more bitter reflection on his wasted life. And he indulged in further presentiments of approaching death. Having passed the age at which his father died, Agee looked at the extra years as a reprieve —granted him, he felt sure, for a purpose. Writing thus became for him a matter of life and death, a race against time. He again picked the two autobiographical projects he had dropped during the long months spent on the article for *Life* and turned his full attention to his childhood. Animated by the "simplest and most primitive of the desires" [1] that can move a writer, he explored the lost paradise of his infant world. Reaching back to the first memories and the most remote experiences, he wanted to represent them in their stark reality, "far beyond the transmutations" that he had made in poetry or fiction. In those moments of most intense recollection, experiencing emotions he had not felt in forty years, passionately reliving the key moments that had formed his being, Agee was led to a reconciliation with himself.

A Death in the Family and *The Morning Watch* were written simultaneously and have similar sources of inspiration. In the one, Agee returns to his first great emotional crisis, his father's death. In the other, he describes his first great religious crisis, the time when his young mind first rebelled against the religion in which he had been raised.

These narratives deal with two successive periods of his life and with two experiences that explain and complement each other. Each is organized around a central tragedy: the death of the father and the death of Christ. If the Crucifixion story touched him so deeply and had such a hold on his imagination, it was only because he understood it in the light of the other, more personal tragedy. Conversely, Agee did not truly experience his father's death until he profoundly understood the meaning of the death of Christ.

The death of his stepfather, of cancer, in 1949 gave rise to further meditations on the subject of death. Reverend Wright had died with the differences separating stepfather and stepson still unresolved. His passing seemed as ironic and absurd to Agee as that of his own father thirty-three years earlier. Why speak of Providence, he bitterly wrote to Father Flye, when there is only chance? (*F.F.*, 176).

At about this time Agee was asked to participate in a symposium conducted by *Partisan Review* on the ongoing religious revival among intellectuals in the United States.[2] In his response he declared himself to be personally a dilettante, or more precisely "amphibious" in the matter of religion. Even though he had received an intensive religious education, he found it difficult to speak clearly and coherently of an experience that had affected him on such a deep personal level. In a general way it seemed to him that intellectuals were the victims of the same illusions as anyone else. He asserted that people commit equally grave errors in the name of religion as in the name of science and reason. But at least a true religion, he felt, could restore a sense of personal responsibility in which each man answers for his own thoughts and acts. Taking religion to mean religious consciousness and not the established Church, faith could inspire respect, compassion and a sense of mystery—all life-enriching qualities. Agee concluded by citing the difficulty of judging the validity of a conversion that seemed to him more a social act than a personal one.

In September, 1950, Agee wrote to Father Flye that the religious feelings about which he could speak from experience seemed to him quite amorphous and hard to define. He thought that the feelings could also be experienced by nonbelievers and people who had never had a religious education. In such people the emotion would take the form of a certain sense of existence, an attitude of veneration and respect for life. As for himself, though his faith had weakened with time, he confessed that he was more preoccupied by religion than he had been in years and that he was curious to rediscover the faith that had seduced and shaped him as a child.

PART VI

1949-1955
THE FINAL
PILGRIMAGE

CHAPTER ONE

SCREENWRITER

In July, 1945, Agee signed a contract with Huntington Hartford to write two screenplays for projected feature films. The first of these was an adaptation of the story "The Blue Hotel" by Stephen Crane.[1] His first scripts, "The House" and "Dedication Day," had not, of course, been seriously intended for actual production; Agee was thus writing for the first time for the real screen. (It turned out that "The Blue Hotel" was never produced either, but that was for other reasons.) In the screenplay Agee successfully accomplishes the best of translating into visual terms Crane's tale of the implication of several men in the murder of a Swede. The screenplay itself is structured around a simple sentence pronounced by the Easterner, the story's "conscience":

Cowboy: "That feller was lookin' for trouble."

Easterner: ". . . like all troubled men. And we helped him find it and we trapped him into it." [2]

The sense of a predetermined fate hanging over the lives of the six men and the Swede (an alternately sympathetic and repellent figure) haunts Agee's script. His one major deviation from Crane's text has the effect of further dramatizing and unifying the story.

In the original, the Easterner does not reveal that Johnnie, the innkeeper's son, was cheating at cards until several months after the Swede's death. In Agee's screenplay Johnnie is accused immediately after the game, after the Swede has left the inn but before he is killed. We know beforehand, then, that if something happens to him, Johnnie and the witnesses are responsible. By this device the death of the Swede takes on a tragic character. No longer a mysterious accident, it is the foreseeable conclusion of a series of events. The scenario ends with a closeup of the Easterner's face, expressing sadness, pity, tenderness and a need, however useless, for atonement. Agee thus transforms him into a mystical figure; he can be likened to Frankie in Nelson Algren's *Man with the Golden Arm,* published in 1949, a character who has a sense of having betrayed himself and others, is unsure of his innocence and seeks a form of redemption.

Crane had already given the story a moralistic ending; Agee goes even further. He pays much more attention to the motifs of responsibility and guilt, often in a heavy-handed manner. Crane has the Swede fall into a trap created by his own bad temper, suspiciousness and irritability. In Agee's version the trap is set by the others as well. Agee also dwells longer on the Swede's behavior, expanding one paragraph of the story into a five-page description of a meal in a passage reminiscent of "They That Sow in Sorrow Shall Reap," one of his own short stories written at Harvard. In fact, the screenplay seems a return to the same source of inspiration as the short stories Agee wrote at Harvard after his summer in the West in 1930.

Agee's screenplay is shot through with powerful visual imagery. At the moment of the Swede's death, Agee directs the camera skyward; the cold stars suddenly become brighter, and then, very slowly, like an enormous wheel, the entire sky begins to turn. Agee also uses the symbol of the color blue ("The Blue Hotel," its signboard) and at some time or another in the script each of the characters is identified with that allegedly arrogant bird, the blue-legged heron: the Swede, for instance, who is portrayed as strong in words but not in action. A final image is that of the blue hotel itself standing alone in the desolate countryside swept by wind and snow (Agee indicates that special sound effects should make the storm seem supernatural), and echoing the splendor and isolation of the central character.

At the beginning of the winter of 1950 *Life* commissioned Agee to write an article on the film director John Huston. When he met Huston for a first interview the two men formed an immediate friendship. Huston later spoke of Agee's extreme gentleness, his understanding and sympathy and his profound respect for other people's feelings. Agee saw Huston as one of the titans of Hollywood, an artist of the American cinema, the living proof that great films could come out of commercial studios. He admired Huston's inventive and intransigent talent, the vitality and joy he showed in his work and the enthusiasm with which he lived. Drawn toward action and the present moment, Huston was, Agee thought, a born film director, who could trust his instinct, unencumbered as he was by superfluous thought or theory, and who never doubted his own effectiveness. These qualities assured him of a spontaneity that Agee could not help but envy, for his own talent was much more thought out and self-critical.

Agee, who liked to recall that he had "hillbilly" blood, was attracted by this "cowboy," the son of an actor, who had led an adventurous and bohemian life. He envied the way he had spent his youth, unfettered by the rigors of a formal education. But Agee and Huston also shared a great deal: a predilection for drinking, smoking, tennis and intense late-night conversations. Both were also incapable of self-discipline and subject to fits of temper. In their own way they were anarchists, antiauthoritarian and obstinately individualistic.

In his article "Undirectable Director" [3] Agee analyzed Huston's particular talent, stressing its vitality and spontaneity. He praised Huston for having freed the motion picture from rhetoric and the "shot-for-shot's sake," for being equally skillful with the active camera, which seizes a moment of the story and tells it, and the passive camera, "whose business is transparency," to receive a moment of pure action and transcribe it. Instead of trying to seduce or enslave his audience, Huston respected them enough to work at opening their eyes and awakening their curiosity and intelligence. Although he was still dissatisfied with it, Agee turned in his article on Huston at the beginning of May. It had now become imperative for him to finish "Maundy Thursday," his original title for *The Morning Watch,* and he managed to complete a first draft in one week, shortly before his second daughter, Andrea, was born. Family duties took up most of the following weeks, but he did manage to put the finishing touches to the story before leaving for Hillsdale for the summer, where he planned to complete his other book. A letter he wrote to Father Flye at this time asks about the hours of sunrise and sunset at Saint Andrew's and in Knoxville in April and May (*F.F.,* 181).

As it turned out, Agee did little work on his book during the summer. He began a new project, collaborating with Huston and Peter Viertel, for the shooting of Huston's next film, *The African Queen.* Agee wrote the screenplay, adapted from a story by C. S. Forester. The script follows the riverboat trip of two characters, Rose, a dry and puritanical old maid, and Allnutt, a simple boorish pragmatist who gradually causes Rose to abandon her posture of unruffled British dignity as their shared danger brings them together. Their union, which is affirmed just when it seems they are going to die in a mishap, conforms to the true Hollywood tradition. Yet the attention to meaningful detail, to the humblest and most familiar gestures, the excellence of the comic scenes, make the screenplay infinitely richer than the original.

Despite these qualities, which two years later earned it an Academy Award nomination, there is no denying that this script is a fairly commercial and conventional one, a disconcerting fact considering that for eight years as a critic Agee had been the passionate advocate of nonconformist experimental cinema.

By the time he had completed *The African Queen* and finished typing the manuscript—which, he confided to Father Flye, was a still more terrible task—Agee had no desire to return to his book. He was at the stage of correcting the drafts before preparing a typescript, but he deferred. As autumn, his favorite season, approached he tried to arrange to stay permanently in Hillsdale, making only occasional visits to New York. But when Huston wrote inviting him to join him in California, he accepted. Fatigued by the summer's work, obviously unable for the while to return to his book, he decided to satisfy an old longing to see California. He planned to go alone, by way of Texas, so that he could visit his friend Irving Upham there.

When he left, his mind was almost easy. His novella, which he had titled *The Morning Watch,* was finished, and his book was in its final stages. Yet Agee unknowingly was at another major turning point in his life. A significant creative period was at an end. He would never again return to that intense and agonized inquiry into his childhood roots that, amid screenplays, articles and symposia, he had been involved in for the past three years and that had produced his greatest fiction.

CHAPTER TWO

THE MORNING WATCH

THE MORNING WATCH APPEARED FIRST IN 1950 IN BOTTEGHE
Oscure [1] and was published the following year by Houghton Mifflin.
It constitutes the first part of a diptych that was not completed
until the posthumous publication in 1957 of *A Death in the
Family*. It is in part a deliberate pause, a "watch," in the midst
of the tumult of Agee's life, a meditation not only on himself and
his childhood, but on life, art and the writer's vocation.

The story is an account of three hours in the life of a twelve-
year-old boy in an Episcopalian school in Tennessee, on the morning of Good Friday. These intensely lived hours turn out to be a
synthesis of Agee's years at Saint Andrew's. The opening pages
present a portrait of young Richard (a name Agee had already
used in his early short stories), written with tender irony; they
depict the child's efforts to live the last hours of Christ's agony
with the proper devotion in order to be worthy of the watch with
which he is entrusted. Richard will spend several hours in a suf-
focating chapel filled with the smells of incense, burnt wax and
faded flowers before he is permitted to escape into the freshness of
a new day.

The atmosphere of community life among adolescent boys is

evoked as they are brutally awakened in the middle of the night. Like the Apostles, Richard has succumbed to sleep and abandoned Christ during his night of torment, a reference that lends the word *watch* in the title its full meaning. The betrayal motif is introduced in that the watch Richard undertakes in the little chapel with two of his schoolmates should have been preceded by another night-long watch that he had secretly demanded of himself. The theme of failure, accompanied by shame, is added to that of betrayal. Richard is obsessed by sin (here, sin by omission), by the idea that transgressions must immediately be punished by the conscience, in which each action or thought is judged as it occurs. As in Agee, in Richard impulse is stopped and spontaneity strangled. The boy watches himself attentively for even the smallest faults, but he feels trapped: for if he happens to find himself innocent or contrite, he will be pleased with himself, a feeling tantamount to the supreme sin of pride and pharisaism. This creates the necessity for renewed contrition, and the cycle is complete.

The original title of the piece, "Maundy Thursday," is the liturgical term for the night that precedes Good Friday, marking the passage to the most solemn day of mourning in the Christian year.[2] Agee exchanged this title for one with a broader meaning, relating this watch to other watches—from the simple sailor's watch to the funeral watch. Ever present in Agee's mind, no doubt, was the watch his mother kept the night of his father's accident. With its connotations of responsibility, waiting, solemnity, excitement, the title provides the story larger dimensions, a richer symbolic meaning. And Richard himself compares his present watch to other important occasions in his life—his birthday, Christmas, Easter, the morning following his father's death (*M.W.*, 342).

The second major theme of the story is that of celebration. In the following sequence, the child abandons himself to joy and jubilation. This exaltation gives the narrative its particular tone, a certain chantlike rhythm reminiscent of the liturgy. But *The Morning Watch* is a celebration not only of a religious event, but of any event that can cause such ecstasy in the soul. The story throughout unfolds on two levels: the mystical—Richard's genuine religious awakening and awe, described though they are in childlike and conventional terms—and the ordinary—his response to sounds and colors and smells of the Easter pageantry or of the outside world.

Once in the chapel, many sensations alter the course of Richard's thoughts and turn his mind to prayer: The sweet smell of pine and incense, burnt wax and flowers and the thousand spears of light thrown by the flowers and flames have a hypnotic effect and remind him of the funeral chamber in which his father's body had rested after he died. Dizzy with the atmosphere of the chapel, Richard takes refuge in the prayer "Blood of Christ, inebriate me," but the literal meaning of the words brings a flood of skeptical and irreverent thoughts—the memory of good old whiskey that had hung like a heavy shadow over his childhood (an allusion later explained through several anecdotes in *A Death in the Family*), and of the way the children of Knoxville drank soda pop, thrusting the neck of the botle to the back of their throat and raising the bottle vertically, rubbing their belly with satisfaction. He makes a desperate effort to return from these pagan reflections to more solemn thoughts. The ticking of the clock reminds him of tiny thorns that cannot be removed from the flesh. The flames seen through his almost closed eyelids resemble tongues of fire poised above the heads of the Apostles.

But his imagination plays tricks on Richard (the ticking of the clock also reminds him of a cat's licking eagerly at a saucer). Instead of helping him in his religious exaltations, it brings him back to everyday reality, the realm of blasphemy.

Between these two conditions, pagan and religious, the world in which the hero moves remains suspended. Richard is no more able to keep himself from interpreting the world in religious symbols than he is able to achieve a properly religious frame of mind during his watch. The cock that the children see as they are leaving the chapel reminds them that the cock crowed three times when Peter betrayed Christ; the fluttering and shaking of its feathers also ludicrously evokes the image of a priest preparing to say Mass.

The split shell of a locust seen through the bark of a tree recalls the Crucifixion of Christ, and the mottled branches of the tree seem as if they are about to bleed.

In the second part the children walk out into the country instead of taking the path back to the dormitory. It is the antithesis of the first. The shift from the chapel to the outside world signals the arrival of spring after winter, of day after night. After the closed atmosphere comes the open air; after torpor, energy; after death, life. In the pure air of the morning that has just been born Richard prolongs the religious experience of the chapel. His dive into the icy waters of a pool has the ambiguity of all the experiences evoked in the book: a gesture of defiance asserting his courage and masculinity before his two schoolfellows, it is also a religious act performed in atonement of his imperfect watch—a baptism out of which he comes regenerated and purified. In the course of his dive he experiences the sensations of death (associated with the metallic coldness of the water) and thus fulfills his pledge of assuming the death of Christ. As he reaches the deepest part of the pool he is filled with a burning and serene energy. After the cold of death, the fire of life. And the return to the surface (rise after the fall, which takes him much longer than the dive) appears as a reenactment of birth.

After their swim the children spy a large snake, which inspires feelings of attraction and revulsion, admiration and terror. After vainly trying to keep his schoolmates from hurting it Richard finally kills it in a scene reminiscent of the story "Boys Will Be Brutes." But the animal holds for Richard a much greater fascination than had the frail birds of the earlier story. Its scales shimmering on its new skin, it captivates the child with its princely elegance, its calm and menacing power, the piercing coldness of its glance and the soft lines of its sinuous body. Its beauty thus carries a challenge, a provocation of the murderous act. Richard must test himself against its power. Justice triumphs, though, when he finally administers death like a sovereign deity, for the snake is symbolic of Satan, evil and sin. And by refusing to wash the venom from his sticky hand (because the stain has to come off by itself, like the ashes on the foreheads of the penitents on Ash Wednesday), Richard once more defies death. By throwing the stone with which he killed the snake into the very pool into which he has just dived, he links up the experiences of death and rebirth. Watching the snake's slow death, an agony that doubtless will last all day, Richard compares its suffering to that of Christ on the day of his Crucifixion. The memory of his own father's death also comes to his mind. The killing of the snake finally emerges as an act avenging his father's death as well as an occasion to relive it.

The story is composed of two movements: one bringing the children to the chapel, and one taking them away from it. Each movement offers variations on antithetical themes, treason and loyalty, failure and success, fall and redemption, death and resurrection, suffering and joy, cold and heat, night and day. And they are all connected to the major motif of the book, life and death. The haunting synthesis of themes is achieved through a language containing a profusion of images and metaphors, a great variety of rhythms and tones, a style suited to the ebb and flow of Richard's thoughts and actions. Lyricism dominates; the story is written like a hymn, a liturgical chant, the verses of the New Testament.

Yet Agee sometimes sacrificed substance to artificiality both in form, which seems exaggerated and out of proportion, and language, which seems too polished and ornate. He was too zealous in his writing, just as his young hero proved too zealous in his piety. He accepted the promptings of his imagination unquestioningly and let himself be carried away (the complexity and sinuosity of the sentences along with often obvious images is irritating); his style does not seem in this story to have matured or found its equilibrium. The form he chose—a short, quick, dense narrative, halfway between prose and poetry—imposed a certain amount of discipline on him, but it also tempted him to do too much arranging and polishing, to create a language that was too diffuse to encompass the reality of his subject. The Morning Watch does not have the vigor of the stories by Chekhov that Agee had hoped to emulate, nor of Joyce's *Portrait of the Artist as a Young Man.* The latter book probably served him, consciously or not, as a model, in that it too is the story of an initiation—a religious and aesthetic experience—and of a quest, a discovery of oneself and of the world. But even though the subjects are similar, Agee's presentation differs from Joyce's in being less controlled, less direct, less objective.

CHAPTER THREE

CALIFORNIA

AGEE'S FIRST IMPRESSIONS OF HOLLYWOOD WERE LESS HORRID than he had imagined. Soon after his arrival he saw Billy Wilder's *Sunset Boulevard,* and in an article he wrote for *Sight and Sound,* November, 1950, acclaiming the film one of the best ever, he showed a gentle indulgence to the milieu he had in the past been so critical of.[1] If the huge factory could create a film about Hollywood that was so free of complacency (Agee felt that it was in some ways even too pitiless), the industry must be less rotten than he had believed.

During his visit he also attended the filming of *The African Queen.* He found it fascinating to work in close collaboration with the film makers and to watch the film taking shape before his eyes. "The work is a great deal of fun," he wrote to Father Flye, "treating it fundamentally as high comedy with deeply ribald undertones and trying to blend extraordinary things—poetry, mysticism, realism, romance, tragedy with the comedy" (*F.F.,* 185).

He was leading a kind of life that was new to him; he was constantly busy meeting a great number of new people. He had little or no time to read or write or listen to music and did not miss any of it. After the intellectual and literary scene of New York, the West seemed relaxing, less irritating to him. People were open, friendly, seemed happy. Though he did not go out of his way to do so, he met Charlie Chaplin and became a regular guest at his home. Agee openly admired Chaplin. He discerned and respected in him the sensibility, tenderness and coldness that he thought were major factors constituting his genius.

Agee spent much of his time during these first weeks in Los Angeles with Huston, adopting Huston's routines and way of life: tennis early in the morning, then a filming session, followed by meetings, drinking, socializing and ending with a riotous evening of drink, long drives and impassioned discussions. He lived in a constant state of near intoxication, drinking and smoking to unhealthy excess. He was under Huston's spell and was happy to share for a time his vitality, his inexhaustible vigor. Furthermore, Huston's presence helped Agee to forget his problems, his melancholy, his mania for introspection. He accepted the lack of moderation and discipline he had always deplored in himself but never remedied. He had discovered a new way of living—to glorify the present, to live instinctively, intensely and unstintingly—and he found it good. But he was reckoning without the reaction of his body, which was unused to such dissipation. In January, 1951, Agee was struck by three heart attacks in three days. Hospitalized in Santa Barbara, where he was taken after the third attack, he was ordered to submit to five weeks of complete bed rest. With a docility that surprised his friends, he agreed to undergo the necessary medical treatment and to obey the strict rules imposed on him: no drinking, no smoking, no excitement. He was promised that after a slow convalescence he would be able to return to an almost normal life.

The weeks spent in the hospital were not unpleasant, and Agee was amazed to see them pass so quickly. But when the time came for him to leave, he did not know where to go. He arranged for his mail to be sent to his agent, Paul Kohner, in Los Angeles and, for the time being, he stayed from day to day with various friends who generously offered him their hospitality.[2] The future was a blank. He did not know whether he would return to the East Coast once he had recovered or take a job out West that would enable him to pay the bills accrued during his illness. When several job offers came up, Agee opted, at least temporarily, for the West. He remained in California.

He signed a second contract with Huntington Hartford and wrote another screenplay based on a short story by Stephen Crane, "The Bride Comes to Yellow Sky." [3] It is essentially a tale of East meets West. The running battle between the incorrigible Wilson and the sheriff of Yellow Sky, Potter, becomes meaningless on the day that Potter, who at the time is bringing home his new bride, confronts Wilson unarmed. The conflict can no longer be a fair fight. Allegorically, Potter has married the code of the East, and Wilson sees in its wake the collapse of his own.

This time Agee took considerable liberties with the original story. The film begins first with the introduction of the town of Yellow Sky, then of some of its leading personalities. Agee even introduced a comical character of his own invention, the jailbird. As the only occupant of the jail, the jailbird receives a special diet, gets drunk regularly and complains about the monotony of the reading matter he is given. When Potter crosses the threshold of his home with his new wife he throws torn-up illustrations from early murder stories of the West into the wind. When the film was shot the following year (it was paired for distribution with another short film under the collective title *Face to Face*), Agee played the role of the jailbird. It was a character with whom he doubtless identified to a certain extent; he even named him Frank Gudger, after one of the tenants in *Let Us Now Praise Famous Men*.

Working closely with the director, his assistants and the technicians, Agee learned a great deal about film. He wanted to experience as many aspects of movie making as he could, and in *The Bride* he worked as scriptwriter, technical consultant and actor. It was a prodigious feat.

At the end of November, 1951, he experienced a second round of heart trouble. Although less serious than the first, it was no less ominous. After two near-fatal attacks in the same year Agee began seriously to worry about his chances for survival. He was given the same advice—not to drink or smoke, to get regular sleep and to lead a quiet life. But discipline was not his forte; he felt it would be impossible to give up the simple joys he had never been able to deny himself. Moderation, he asserted, was contrary to his nature; and in any case, he detested all categorical imperatives. In the end, he told his friends, he could promise nothing.

In the hospital Agee read Boswell's *London Journal,* regretting that he himself had never been able to keep a journal for more than six weeks, and *Heavenly Discourse,* by Charles Erskine Scott, whom he found an interesting personality. Most important, during these few days in the hospital Agee again took stock of himself. Heavily in debt, he feared that the necessity of earning money quickly would send him back to journalism. He did not want to blame circumstances for what appeared to him a personal failure, but it seemed that he was still mired in self-pity. At the same time he felt there was no reason to bewail the fact that he had written little, since he took more pleasure in conversation than he did in writing. Writing, he thought, was a monologue, whereas conversation was the immediate exchange of ideas. Agee remembered with emotion the weeks' worth of late evenings spent talking with Chaplin, and while he regretted not having made note of what they discussed, he swore to himself that he would never use these conversations as journalistic material.

In spite of these reservations, he was once again filled with the desire to write. In the hospital, within a few days, he composed "A Mother's Tale," an allegorical fable dealing with human destiny and written with a sad humor.[4]

A young calf has seen a vast herd of cattle making its way across the plains and asks his mother where they are going. In reply, the mother tells the story of The One Who Came Back and The Man with the Hammer. It is a humorous tale about the departure of the herd, the long and painful voyage in a train, their arrival in a new and unfamiliar land, their life in proximity to men, whose smell is disagreeable to them, and the sudden, inescapable confrontation with The Man with the Hammer. The One Who Came Back miraculously escapes the intended death and returns to tell the herd left behind all he has seen and suffered. But he dies while delivering his message, leaving it uncertain whether it has been a true story or a dream.

In spite of the warning, long herds still move blindly toward the mysterious train that will take them to the same unknown destiny, until one day, perhaps, one of these young steers will recognize The Man with the Hammer in time, and a new chosen one will save his race.

This short allegory retraces man's history—his joys and his trials, his awareness and his ignorance, his solitude and his solidarity with other living creatures, all experiences that precede his inevitable death. The story may also be read as a Christian fable about the trials that must be gone through to attain salvation. There will be the elect and the damned; but it is uncertain whether the elect will be those who choose to stay behind or those who, having gone, one day manage to return. The story remains intentionally ambiguous. The One Who Came Back seems like a Messiah; his words are Revelation. Enigmatic as they are, the words transmit in almost biblical phrases a message that is both warning and prophecy. But in the end the Christian doctrine of endurance of suffering is rejected. Although The One Who Came Back is somewhat of a Christ figure, his message is more somber than the Christian message: each individual is born a victim and must attain salvation on his own through rebellion, disobedience or disbelief. "Obey nobody. Depend on none" emerges as the philosophy, not unlike that developed in *Let Us Now Praise Famous Men*. Those who remain will not be saved, for they "betray themselves . . . forever" by raising their children to be new victims. The story indirectly raises the question of faith, which alone can achieve the impossible. Between the world of experience of those who know, and the world of innocence of those who do not yet know, there are many who refuse to believe and run blindly to their fate as if The One Who Came Back had never existed. The young calf, impatient to leave the warmth and security of the maternal universe and listening attentively to his mother's story, represents youth eager for experience, stagnating in a narrow environment and anxious to discover the world, a reminiscence of Agee's own eagerness as a child.

In "A Mother's Tale" Agee returns, in a new Kafkaesque form of allegory, to some of his favorite themes: the denial of freedom, the individual struggling with a cruel and brutal world. Suffering is man's lot, whether it is collective, as in the first part of the journey, or individual, like the solitary return of the calf, maimed and hunted. Certain details inevitably suggest implicit reference to not too distant world events: the forced evil or expatriation, slow-moving trains taking men to an unknown destination, violence and torture in camps. One may also be tempted to read in "A Mother's Tale" an appropriate metaphor of this particular moment in Agee's life, speculation on his impending fate. The hopelessness of the story's message is somewhat mitigated by the portrayal of the relationship between the mother and her young calves. Life, Agee insists, can be beautiful. Nothing can destroy the mother's love for her children, her unsurpassable tenderness. Nor can anything impair the young calf's joy in life, his eagerness to explore the world. Words like *train* and *wagon* evoke the magic of an unknown world. Humanity is thus glorified in the face of the pitiless nature of existence. And alongside the central story the whole gamut of human emotions is explored.

At the end of November, Mia came out West to join him with their two children and a friend, Mary Newman. They all settled in Malibu, where the presence of his family brought Agee some temporary distraction. To fill his days he read, rewrote and typed his story. But the compulsory inactivity seemed to him all the more unbearable because it did nothing to alleviate the financial straits he was still in. Only alcohol, perhaps more enticing because it was forbidden, could bring him solace.

In December his prospects became less gloomy. He sold his story to *Harper's Bazaar,* where his friend Harvey Breit's first wife was working, and would now have enough money to make it through Christmas. For Emmanuel Conde he wrote a screenplay on the youth of Genghis Khan; the actual film was to be shot in the Philippines. That work, though, kept him from writing the screen version of *Moby Dick* for Huston. He considered writing another story in the form of a long, anguished love letter analyzing the course of a hopelessly unhappy affair. God would be the author of the letter addressed, but not delivered, to the human race. The story would attempt to show that liberty and free will are necessary if there is to be love. But Agee was dissatisfied with the way he had illustrated this idea and soon abandoned this project for another. He now dreamed of a movie whose hero would be a storm: he would explore the storm's effect on people, animals, crops and the land. The project, though, again quickly fell through. Agee began to tire of the West where, to him, only the film milieu had any life to it. For the present he was in a state of limbo, waiting until he had sufficient money to take his family and himself back East.

CHAPTER FOUR

LAST PROJECTS

WHEN, AT THE BEGINNING OF 1952, THE OPPORTUNITY CAME TO write the script for a television film on Abraham Lincoln for a Ford Foundation workshop, Agee responded enthusiastically.[1] Lincoln, the self-educated poor man's son, had always been one of his heroes, and he more or less consciously associated his own father with him. He also saw Lincoln as a towering and mythical figure, an embodiment of certain specifically American values: courage, tenacity, integrity and pioneer individualism.

He set to work immediately. He had decided to focus on Lincoln's boyhood, the age that interested him most. In the screenplay a train ride carrying Lincoln's body back to his native Kentucky acts as a symbolic link with the past. Lincoln's last voyage, the final tribute to the murdered President as the train and its retinue progress slowly through the American countryside, is described in a lyrical mode as a chant that seems to come from nature as well as from men. The narration then shifts back to the place and time of Lincoln's birth. Several tableaux, interspersed with dialogue in dialect, recreate the atmosphere of 1816, the pioneer life of Lincoln's father among Kentucky farmers, who lived under conditions that still prevailed when Agee had stayed in

Alabama. The screenplay also pays homage to the country folk, their courage and simplicity, and brings to the fore the hardships of their existence. At the same time Agee pursues his exploration of boyhood. A episode in which young Lincoln berates a friend for having willfully hurled a live turtle against a tree is reminiscent of the children's slaughter of birds in Agee's early story and of the episode of the snake in *The Morning Watch*. Another tableau set in New Salem, Illinois, in 1831, a new America in miniature, shows a mixed assemblage of Yankees, Southerners and Europeans, their hopes high for a new sort of democracy, gathered about the young Abraham Lincoln. Other episodes (some entirely out of Agee's imagination) deal with his courtship of Ann Rutledge and his fight with two bumbling characters, the Grimsby brothers.

Agee intended his completely personal interpretation of Lincoln's character to be simple enough to appeal to children—then he would know, he claimed, that he had done justice to Lincoln. In fact, he spent an entire year working on the script—fascinated by the technical differences involved in television and film.

During the same year Agee took part in making several other films with Helen Levitt and Janice Loeb. One was a documentary about Harlem called *In Our Street*, which shows the sort of images Agee had always been striving to convey in words. The constant and enveloping movements of the camera, back and forth, advancing and withdrawing, indicate the camera being handled much as he handled sentences—to achieve, one supposes, a multilayered picture of reality.

That October, the shooting of the Lincoln script began, and Agee was invited to accompany the crew on the trip to Kentucky and Illinois for location shooting. He hesitated at first because of his health, but he felt so committed to the work that he finally went along. The mood of depression he had been in during the previous weeks was dispelled by a period of intense activity in which he worked six days a week. In addition to assisting Richard de Rochemont and the director Norman Lloyd in the shooting, he played the minor role of a drunken citizen who shows up at the ballot box to vote—another caricature of himself, quite similar to his former part in *The Bride Comes to Yellow Sky*. It may be significant that Agee always chose the role of a drunk, either to parody himself or to justify his reputation for being a heavy drinker. Furthermore, those parts gratified his sense of humor and comedy. He had hoped on his way back to make a short visit to Tennessee, but lack of time and money compelled him to return directly to New York.

Further trouble with his heart led to his hospitalization for several days in New York's Memorial Hospital, but he was soon back at work again. It was at this time he wrote for Helen Levitt the scenario that was a barely disguised version of the story of his breakup with Via in 1937. He originally intended to call it "Love Story" but its title was eventually changed to "Bigger Than We Are." In spite of the sometimes quite cruel irony with which he treats the character based on himself, Agee was not in control of his subject. In reviving the confusing events of that critical year, he sought to exorcise his familiar demons; he was trying to rescue himself from his past by doing it justice, to eradicate all the painful misunderstandings and put an end to the meanderings and reversals that had marked his whole life. This script meant much to him. He continued to work on it without, however, making any notable improvements.

In January, 1953, Father Flye suggested that the two of them go on a retreat to a Trappist monastery in Kentucky. Agee would have liked to go, if only to contemplate his early death—a possibility that, now that he was seriously ill, haunted him more and more. But he was already too involved in various jobs to disentangle himself, and he had to be content with the occasional retreat to Hillsdale. He was going there with increasing frequency, living in a primitive way, reading voraciously and writing as much as he could.

One of the projects he had already agreed to was to write the screenplay for a biography of Gauguin. He set to work in March, reading as many biographies of the painter as he could find as well as Gauguin's own journal, on which he drew very freely, sometimes quoting directly from it. Gauguin became for him, as Lincoln had the previous year, an exemplary figure. The splendor and solitude of his obstinate quest for beauty and innocence made a success of a life that often seemed close to failure. *Noa Noa*[2] offers a portrait of the artist. A dive into the water on the day Gauguin goes fishing with the aborigines serves as a metaphorical representation of the goal he constantly pursued. Commercial success, illustrated by Gauguin's immersion in the asphyxiating atmosphere of the Paris salons, is shown as a threat to talent since the artist's inspiration is likely to die in bourgeois and domestic comfort. Writing about Gauguin gave Agee the opportunity to examine again the problems of the artist's function and identity. The artist, he averred, was the purveyor of beauty and truth. In order to pursue his solemn vocation with integrity, he must live on the outskirts of society. It is futile to try to improve the world or even to think about doing so. Marriage, too, is a mistake for the artist, as financial, material and family responsibilities overwhelm him. Likewise, Van Gogh's dream of a community of artists living in harmonious poverty is neither possible nor desirable, for the artist must carry out his task alone, at peace not with the world but with himself.

Agee, though, was not entirely uncritical of Gauguin. He deplored his egotism, his rages and the lack of consideration that led to the death of his daughter Aline. For Agee she was a blood sacrifice to a pagan artistic ideal.

In contrast to that ideal, *Noa Noa* presents an almost Christian image of the artist in the portrait of Van Gogh, whose self-denial contrasts with Gauguin's categorical and egotistical individualism. Whereas Gauguin is desperately seeking primordial innocence, Van Gogh is still living in an "innocent" world. In Agee's mythology Gauguin is the hero, Van Gogh the saint. He was, of course, in these two men parodying the two sides of himself: one rebellious, cynical, sarcastic and violent; the other sentimental, mystical and reverent. And like most of Agee's work, the screenplay reflects the three moods, anger, sorrow and love, which dominated his entire life.

In spite of its thematic importance, *Noa Noa* is marred on artistic grounds by its obvious and facile symbolism and a certain stylistic complacency in the telling of various anecdotes. It is, however, the longest and most ambitious of Agee's scripts for the screen, and it is unfortunate that the film was never produced. In late 1952 he spent several weeks in California editing the screenplay with the director, but the work never got off the ground. His death two years later ended the project permanently.

The script for *Noa Noa* occupied Agee for a period of several months, but it did not keep him from writing other screenplays: a scenario based on Davis Grubb's *The Night of the Hunter,* an English version of the French story *"Crin Blanc"* (*White Mane*) and a scenario for an Italian film, *Green Magic.* Following his return from California, Agee and Howard Taubman began work on *A Tanglewood Story,* a film on the well-known music school in Massachusetts.[3] Playing on the title, Agee imagined a story so complex that he despaired of ever untangling it. Taubman recalls how enthusiastic Agee was about this story; but even after long weeks of arduous work on the project, he did not come close to finishing it.

Unable to refuse the people who sought him out for commercial writing, Agee was also incapable of treating the job for what it was, a means of earning money. It is useless to deplore the lack of discrimination that led him to treat hack work as though it were a major undertaking. It is nonetheless true that, though he was unable to concentrate on a single activity, he at least found a measure of satisfaction in diversity. Doubtless, too, he was gratified that he was always in demand as a writer. In 1954 he undertook the greatest number of projects ever: a television serial on crime, a film on Heine, another on George Washington, a screen adaptation of Kafka's *Trial* and a film on John Wilkes Booth. Most of them, though, remained in an embryonic state.

When he learned of the sudden death of Mrs. Flye in February,

1954, Agee left New York, accompanied by his friend David McDowell, to spend several days with Father Flye. He rediscovered places he had not seen in thirty years and was moved to plan other excursions at the end of autumn—to Boston, and possibly to Exeter—to visit some of his former teachers. He also decided to go on the retreat that Father Flye had mentioned to him before. But he was counting without his commitments. Work on the Italian film, *Green Magic*, which had been interrupted the previous year by the producer's death, was now resumed, and Agee found himself pressed for time.

In December he agreed to write several scenes for Leonard Bernstein's and Lillian Hellman's musical comedy, *Candide*.[4] The project is described at length in a letter to Father Flye (*F.F.*, 216-220): It would be written entirely in verse; the characters would sing their lines and there would be almost continuous dancing. The conception of a terrestrial paradise gave him the opportunity not only to dramatize certain of Voltaire's ideas that interested him most, but to picture, in a lyrical but parodic mode, an Eldorado very much after his own heart. His proposals on the use of wealth, his indictment of culture, his treatment of the various petitions presented to the king are wholly original.

Only a few songs have actually survived of this initial project. The most interesting is doubtless the derisive "Culture Song," in which Martin, the governor of Buenos Aires, and Candide discuss art. In its mocking way the song, as does the preface to *Let Us Now Praise Famous Men*, puts all "culture" on trial.

Other songs were also developed at length. "Pure Child Song" expresses the people's faith in the child-king who will deliver them from doubt and sorrow; the Marquise's song extols love as it is taught by nature; the love duet between Cunegonde and Candide; and the chorus "finale," contrasting the platonic and metaphysical ideas of love. Agee also indicated numerous stage directions specifying the orchestra's role, the set, the movements of the crowd, of the chorus and of the characters. His plan, as he submitted it, seemed completely unworkable to the people who had requested it, and in the end Lillian Hellman finally decided not to use the poems at all. *Candide,* a comic operetta, nevertheless takes its place among Agee's experiments with new media and shows his sustained interest in the musical quality of language and his humorous treatment of reality.

Toward the end of 1954, after almost a full year's respite, Agee's attacks began again. This time they were more severe and more frequent. He was subject to as many as eight a day, and few days were free of them. He was ordered to follow a very strict regimen, involving complete relaxation and nine to ten hours of sleep each night. For a few weeks he lived cautiously and took care of himself as though he were in a hospital, but as soon as he felt better he took on more work. He agreed to write the script for a half-hour film on Williamsburg, Virginia, at the time of the Revolutionary War. The quick trip he took to Virginia (where he was disappointed in the restorations) caused a relapse in his health, but he was determined to begin working. He chose to describe a fairly ordinary day of the period, using a discussion in a tavern and a quarrel around a table to show how divergent attitudes were beginning to take shape many years before the clash of powers occurred. His characters are political types: the Tory and the Loyalist, subtly complementing each other; the intellectual and the frontiersman; the demagogue and the cautious merchant. Agee saw the frontiersman as a member of a new race—hard working, independent, mystical, close to nature—as the spiritual father of Abraham Lincoln and the unsung hero of this, his "Virgilian" poem about the nation before its birth.

Another series of still more serious heart attacks struck Agee in March, 1955. He was confined to bed for several weeks. He regained enough energy to complete a draft of the Tanglewood story, which he had finally succeeded in unraveling after months of groping and hesitation. In spite of his poor health he was considering several other projects: a trip to Ireland with Huston to work on an adaptation of Kipling's "The Man Who Would Be King," a history of the Quakers during the Civil War, an adaptation of

A. B. Guthrie's *The Way West,* a novel about the migrations to Oregon and California and a translation of Jean Cocteau's *La Machine Infernale.* Encouraged by Samuel Barber, who had written the music for "Knoxville, 1915," he also thought he might write some opera librettos. Finally, he continued to be interested in acting and, according to Marie Mencken, he actually played in a stage version of W. H. Auden's *Age of Anxiety* with Judith Malina.

The one project he came close to finishing was "Williamsburg," devoting to it all the time his health allowed him. But of the three parts he had envisioned, only one was completed.[5] The notes that accompany the text contain instructions about how the film should be made. The director, he indicated, should draw his inspiration more from the techniques of painting and theater than from the motion picture; he should try to reduce the heroic dimensions and vast perspectives of the story to an ordinary, intimate and recognizable scale. The spectator must be given the illusion of the present tense, of participation, which could be done more easily if an important historical event were not central to the story and if the characters were presented as ordinary people instead of historical figures. Agee also noted that it was important that the film be shot in the spring, the prenatal season.

The action takes place in one symbolic day, starting before dawn and ending long after sunset. The characters are shown leaving their various homes in the countryside or in scattered parts of the town and meeting around noontime in a tavern. There a discussion begins, becomes bitter and then degenerates into a quarrel, the central moment of the story. Other episodic characters are introduced: a Negro slave abused by his master, an Indian on the river, a visiting Frenchman. The narrative, like *Let Us Now Praise Famous Men,* contains a cyclical representation of life in an extremely structured and stylized form. To conclude the story, Agee envisioned a scene in which the frontiersman, his hero, walks through the virgin forest toward a rise from which he sees a fertile and uninhabited valley, the America to come.

With Agee's death "Williamsburg" too remained unfinished. In a letter to Father Flye, which he never had a chance to mail, Agee complained of a slackening of pace that was affecting his work. He felt himself dying a slow death. He expressed though, once again, the resolution he had so often made and so often broken: to refuse all commercial work and to devote the summer to finishing his book, his only full-length novel, which he now called with pride and irony "my" book. In the same letter he shared with Father Flye a last conception, a fable about elephants (*F.F.,* 229-231).

God, having abandoned man, entrusts a herd of elephants with the mission of saving the world. On learning their task, the oldest elephant chooses to die, foreshadowing the many deaths to come. Shortly after, the rest are captured and put into men's circuses. One elephant is immediately slain because superstitious people believe he is a reincarnation of Behemoth. Another is crushed to death by a locomotive; yet another is hanged for having killed three men, and thirty-six more succumb when, after having been forced to perform a humiliating dance directed by a great choreographer, one of them sets a fire in which they all perish. Their souls, as weightless as clouds, alight like doves in the great secret African cemetery, and God once more speaks tenderly to them: "The Peace of God which passeth all understanding . . ."

A number of friends to whom Agee told his idea were enthusiastic about it. Although the taste of certain details is questionable, the outline of his unusual story bears witness to his predilection for parables. Unlike the hero of "A Mother's Tale," the elephants choose death instead of rebellion, or rather, death is their means of rebellion. If they are to remain faithful to themselves, as God has asked, they must disappear and reject the ridiculous image man wants to impose on them. In this refusal to assume a destiny not of their own choosing, their death becomes exemplary. Through it, they save themselves, and also invite men to emulate them. The rebellion conceived by God eventually turns against Him, and it is this mocking representation of God, ultimately powerless in the face of events, which dominates this strange tale. A parable of the situation of the individual and the artist in society, it is also an illustration of the submission of one race to another.

It is terrifying to think that this grim tale of elephant death, however affirmative its ultimate message, was the last accomplishment of Agee's artistic imagination. Shortly afterward, in a taxi on his way to an appointment with a doctor, Agee suddenly collapsed and died without regaining consciousness. And he who was so fascinated by coincidence and had hoped to die on an exceptional day would no doubt have been intrigued to note that the date was May 16, 1955, the anniversary of his father's death.

CHAPTER FIVE

ALL THE WAY HOME

"It's mine to touch with deathlessness their clay,
And I shall fail, and join those I betray."

(*C.P.*, 38)

AT THE TIME OF AGEE'S DEATH MIA WAS IN WYOONA, MINNESOTA, with her dying father, circumstances strangely reminiscent of those described in the unfinished novel, *A Death in the Family*.

James Agee was buried in Hillsdale, a few miles from his farm. There is no inscription on the headstone. The only image he might have found acceptable was that of a bird he had often admired in a book by Otto Rank. The bird symbolized absolute death.

His premature passing did arouse considerable attention in literary circles, and within a short space of time a number of works came to the public's attention. *The Morning Watch* was republished in *Thirteen Great Stories,* the film *Green Magic* began playing in New York the very week of his death and in 1956 W. H. Auden cited a poem from *Permit Me Voyage* in his *Criterion Book Of American Verse*.[1] The same year, the *Cambridge Review* dedicated an issue to Agee and published selections from his unfinished novel. Excerpts from it also appeared in *The New*

Yorker.[2] In 1958 "The Waiting" was published in *Best American Short Stories.*[3] But in 1957, after offers had been made by Farrar, Straus and Harcourt Brace, McDowell & Obolensky brought out *A Death in the Family* in a tentative organization of Agee's unfinished manuscript. Only three days before he died Agee had mentioned in the course of a long conversation with David McDowell that he hoped to spend the summer working on the novel. In view of this information the editor's task was not easy. As he left it, Agee's manuscript was difficult to decipher.

In a fragment descriptive of his work Agee had stated "this book is chiefly a remembrance of my childhood and memorial to my father." [4] The manuscript contains two projects that were distinct from the beginning. One consists of a family saga, with highlights from a period of five or more years, showing the differences that separate the generations and the love that unites them. The second, chronologically organized, is a story describing the few days preceding the father's death. These two narratives were to be integrated into a single work, ending on the day of the funeral. Love and life, which are celebrated in the first narrative, are confronted with death in the second, only to emerge altered but victorious. Some sections, whose final placement in the manuscript is uncertain, are told primarily from the point of view of the young child, Rufus. One deals with the father's death, while six others describe the life of the family at a prior time. The importance of these six vignettes and their function in the book would depend on where they were placed in the rest of the text. The task of alternating them artfully with the strictly narrative parts presented a serious challenge to the skills of the self-appointed editors. Finally, the prose poem "Knoxville 1915," which had appeared in 1938 and was very similar to the manuscript in style and theme, was added as a prologue. The narrative was thus divided into three dramatic sequences: the family before the death of Jay Follet; the story of the accident; and Rufus' reaction to his father's death. Three of the other six episodes were placed at the end of the first part and three at the end of the second. Printed in italics to set them apart from the other chapters, they offer a counterpoint to the direct narrative passages.

The story has a simple outline. After an eventful day spent walking, talking and movie-going with his son Rufus, Jay Follet is summoned to the bedside of his father. He discovers when he arrives that his father is not as seriously ill as he had been led to believe. In Knoxville, Mary tells her disappointed children that their father will not be home. The next day Aunt Hannah takes Rufus to buy the cap he has long dreamed of owning.

This first chapter describing the day father and son spend together serves as a transition between the lyrical mode of the prologue and the narrative sequences. The long walk after the movies is one of a series of walks that will all follow the same ritual. But it is only in the light of the father's subsequent death that this particular walk takes on a dramatic character, for it turns out to be the last. It already has the poignancy of memory.

While this first chapter is presented as Rufus sees it, the second takes place in the adult world. A telephone call from Jay's brother, Ralph, gives the news of Mr. Follet's illness. The chapter ends with an onomatopoeic description of the sound of Jay's car setting out into the night.

The scene then shifts from Knoxville to the back country. On the narrative level Jay leaves the outskirts of Knoxville and drives through the night toward the place where his parents live. On a symbolic level the chapter describes the passage from the urban to the rural environment, a major theme of the book. The ride is also a voyage in time, for Jay Follet is returning not only to his home but to his origins, to his childhood. Night is a messenger from another world, and the expression "all the way home," reappearing as leit motif, takes on several meanings.[5]

The following chapters shift between Knoxville and La Follette. The two places are symbolically connected by the road on which Jay Follet meets his death. Jay's brother, Ralph, is introduced— an ineffectual, cowardly drunkard. The character is Agee's invention entirely, and is not unlike the "personae" he presented in his

early Exeter stories. At the end of this first section the three inter-
polated episodes evoke an earlier time. The first is interesting in
that it illustrates the three major themes of the work: remembrance of things past, the continuity of life and the solitude of all
beings. One summer night Rufus has a nightmare. His father com-
forts him and sings him country songs, relieving the son's fear of
darkness. As they did during the course of the walk, father and
son experience one of those special moments of happiness that,
when over, leave them more bereft than ever. In the narrative Agee
moves gradually, almost imperceptibly, from the child's mind to
the father's. Once Rufus is asleep Jay finds himself alone with the
memory of his own mother stroking his forehead to calm his fear,
the ritual gesture repeated from generation to generation. And
years later Rufus, in turn, will experience these same feelings.

Part II, "The Waiting," is more traditionally dramatic. The news
of Jay Follet's accident elicits pained reactions in the members of
his wife's family, an increasing but unspoken certainty that Jay is
dead, an intense but weakening desire to hold on to a last shred
of hope. An interesting scene skillfully shows how the news, after
having exhausted the spirits, affects the imagination: The presence
of the dead man is felt for an instant as if he were alive, and everyone, including the reader, is to varying degrees subject to the illusion.[6] Jay, taken too unexpectedly by death, cannot resign himself
to leaving and still lingers among the living, and those who remain
grant a moment of survival to the dead. Agee's skill consists not
only in having made the phantom believable but in having used
this episode to deepen the sense of Jay's confusion and loneliness.
After this strange experience the beauty and the indifference of the
spring night, the silence of the dark and sleeping city, create a
mood of calm and comfort. The characters make peace with themselves and with the world and regain a certain amount of serenity.

The three episodes that end Part II are flashbacks that return to
the world of childhood. Rufus is teased by the bigger children on
their way to school. Such encounters on the street corner with an
unknown, enticing but hostile world foreshadow the experience of

his father's death, which will cause him the same perplexity, the same sense of frustration and exclusion. The image of his father leaving for work in the morning and disappearing down the street is closely associated with that of the children who invade the street a few minutes later. Rufus feels the same envy and admiration mixed with respect for the man and for the children, since they all belong to a fascinating but inaccessible universe.

The second episode, the visit to Jay's great-grandmother, a character who is definitely known to be fictional, illustrates what was initially one of Agee's main intentions: to portray, through several generations, the life of a family and the ties that through space and time link its various members. The conviction expressed here that each being has roots in a communion with others of the same blood and with specific places is almost antithetical to the message of the preceding episode. Rufus' aged ancestor represents the triumph of life and the foreshadowing of imminent death. Still quite alive, with a "vague light [which] sparkled in the crackled blue of the eye," she nevertheless seems to be no longer a part of the world (*D.F.*, 238). The old woman represents a past whose dimensions are epic, outside of time. When Rufus approaches her a pitiful smile creasing her wrinkled face is the only response. But contact has been established as she vaguely recognizes in the boy some of Jay, her favorite great-grandchild. While Rufus experiences the visit with an intense immediacy, Jay is reminded of other, similar visits. Now his own son has replaced the boy he once was. The long voyage that will bring him, too, to the point of death has already begun.

The last episode, the ride back from the great-grandmother's, returns to the book's central metaphor, the return home. It reasserts the ties that link man to certain geographic locations, in particular to his birthplace. The mountains and smoke-colored hills of the back country are Jay Follet's true homeland. Gray, calm, suffused with a shadowy light, they are, to Rufus, like the sight of his aged ancestor, a revelation. Standing in the same composed immobility as the old woman he has just left, they seem to open out a deep space adding to Rufus' life unforeseen dimensions and a sense of infinity.

Part III is written almost entirely from the children's viewpoint, as Rufus and his sister come to realize the meaning of their father's death. The word *death* itself denotes a massive and magical solitude to Rufus, but otherwise it is devoid of sense, despite his almost comical efforts to understand it. At first, the children feel their father's absence as a personal offense. Their routine is suddenly changed. Rufus is angry at his father for not being there to see the cap his aunt bought him. Forgotten by the adults and with a period of unexpected idleness on his hands, he suddenly realizes that his father's death might help him gain some prestige with his schoolmates. But at the very moment when he seems to have resigned himself to his father's death he becomes most painfully aware of it. Later, standing before the empty armchair, he begins to understand what his father's absence will soon mean. As always in Agee's writing, emotion is revealed as sensation. ". . . He smelled of the chair, its deeply hollowed seat, the arms, the back. There was only a cold smell of tobacco. . . ." Running his finger along the inside of the ashtray, he licks it and "his tongue tasted of darkness" (*D.F.,* 281).

There are few beings in Agee's fictional universe who can truly be called wicked or evil. Father Jackson, the priest who visits the house after Jay's death, is an exception. Agee is so pitiless toward this self-centered, unctuous and dangerous prig that it is tempting to speculate whether this might be a dramatization of his resentment of Father Wright, his mother's second husband. Be that as it may, the children's frustration is increased by the religious element introduced by the priest into Jay Follet's house. Their mother removes herself further from them and devotes herself to a world from which they feel excluded. Mary's piety is, for Agee, the object of caustic comment. Religion, he suggests, is no solace for the despair of death.

The children's slow approach to their father's coffin parallels Rufus' earlier approach to his great-great-grandmother. The same curiosity pervades both scenes. On the old woman's face the child has read the ravages of time; on his father's he sees the ineluctable presence of death itself.

The novel ends with another walk, this time with his uncle. Again a certain tacit understanding and harmony are achieved, but Andrew's words, though reassuring, bewilder the child. All he has finally been able to grasp of his father's death is that he has been left powerless, bereft and alone.

There is no certainty that Agee would have chosen this ending to the story, yet it is consistent with the book's cyclic theme: after death, rebirth and the continuity of life.

The many connotations of the word *home* provide another unifying theme to the book. It is the hearth to which Rufus and his father return after the movies, the home to which Jay is rushing as he drives to meet his death; it is also the land of one's ancestors in a time long past, a homeland alternately lost and rediscovered, and which survives in the great-great-grandmother and in the memories of each member of the family. It is the identity that each man acquires in going back to the sources of his life.[7] Finally and paradoxically, "home" is death—the ultimate "homeland" where all return at the end of the voyage—and it is also life, which, by the end of the book, the characters have rediscovered through their personal experience of Jay's death.

On a purely autobiographical level the temporal metaphor predominates. Like Jay Follet, who, more than the child Rufus, is the hero of the story, Agee makes a pilgrimage to the sources of his life (a continuation of the voyage already outlined in *The Morning Watch*), in order to rediscover a long-lost happiness. It is destined to be a melancholy voyage, as Agee reminds us, since despite such "homecomings," the past cannot really be recaptured.

Like other young American novelists of the forties, Agee gives an important place to poetry, metaphor and symbol in his novel. Lyricism takes priority over narrative, notwithstanding the dramatic structure of the book. The action takes place in feelings and emotions. With a precision that is both poetic and scientific, Agee captures the everyday events of existence with an increasing accuracy. The book is conceived as a series of revelatory moods and moments, and its structure is completely poetic. Indeed, by abandoning the formal writing of poetry, Agee created a type of poetic story, which best suited his talent and sensibility. *A Death in the Family* achieves greater lyric perfection than *The Morning Watch*. Image and form are fused, meaning and language coincide without being smothered under a mass of images, symbols and metaphors. There is also, here, unity of tone rarely found in the earlier works.

Since "Dedication" and *Let Us Now Praise Famous Men* Agee's artistic intentions had changed little; his purpose was still to reveal "the cruel radiance of what is" and to celebrate life. But the rebelliousness and indignation of his early works had given way to more serene vision. Agee seems finally to have found some degree of faith in his life and in his art.

THE CRUEL RADIANCE
OF WHAT IS

Among the crucial experiences of James Agee's artistic development, his stay in Alabama, which resulted in the composition of *Let Us Now Praise Famous Men,* appears to have been decisive. A confrontation with reality that abolished the separation between life and literature, setting in a new perspective the author's speculations on the artist's function and endeavor, it marks the beginning of a new orientation. In placing life above art, Agee became involved in bold and contradictory paths, where literature was experienced both as a necessity and as an impossibility.

Although Agee never expressed his views in a systematic fashion, they are affirmed throughout his work. Literature is seen as an homage to life, a celebration. The artist must catalog the real with precision and fidelity, observe it with an attention that will illuminate its most obscure aspects. Language should follow the shape of reality; since words are inadequate, the writer has recourse to the use of sound, multiple meanings and symbols. Agee's writing attempts to deal with all the various aspects of life, although it cannot succeed in following all its intricacies.

Agee was subject to all the pitfalls of such an ambition: excess detail, lack of discrimination, tiresome inventories, a style that is ambiguous, sometimes ornate, distorted and rhetorical. Although he wanted to come to grips with life, he never completely freed himself from a certain preciousness acquired from his reading of the Elizabethans and his affinity for their writings. His language tended to become distant from its living sources.

It was because reality is born and reborn through language that Agee hesitated over the choice of a word and could not eliminate any of the alternatives. Agee wrote with the conviction that all literature is destined to fail to a greater or a lesser extent.

Music, photography and the motion picture were models Agee would always strive to equal. He tried by means of images to give his prose a sonority, a visual dimension and movement, to force the reader to respond to words with the spontaneity with which the ear perceives music, the eye a photograph or a film.

At times, by his own criteria, Agee succeeded in his literary task. His sentences unfold in an enchantment. The perfection he so ardently sought appears less often in the poetry of *Permit Me Voyage,* which contains too much technique and conscious refinement, than in the poetic prose of *Let Us Now Praise Famous Men* and of *A Death in the Family.*

Because poetry and existence were inseparable for Agee, his literary strivings reveal an extreme respect for life and the conviction that every being is also unique. His predilection for the ordinary was both a moral choice and an emotional involvement. Agee approached everyday, concrete reality with instinctive tenderness. He was so open to the emotions aroused in him by his perception of reality that he discovered a degree of passion that enabled him to perceive things "from within." He claimed the complicity of nature, of animals, and especially of the night, when the mystery of the world was intuitively revealed to him. In all, he brought to life a sacramental attention. Such a poetry, elaborated into a way of life, finds its basic laws in childhood. The qualities Agee claimed for the artist exist naturally in the child, whose capacity for wonder is still unrestrained. In his faith in innocence—that faith which is one of the Great American literary myths, from Mark Twain to J. D. Salinger—Agee retained his nostalgia for childhood; it offered him the means of revaluing a dehumanized world and of maintaining a state of grace. This is the source of his insistence on rediscovering who he had been. This also explains why writing seemed to him like a dreaded maturity. He undertook each new project to compensate for the absence of the work he despaired of writing, and if his literary production appears fragmentary and incomplete, it is partly a deliberate dispersion, explained by the very nature of his creative endeavor.

It is easy to see why Agee never belonged to any movement or literary school; yet his love of the land, his nostalgia for the past, his attachment to traditions, his sense of guilt and his obsession with sin and redemption undeniably link him with other Southerners. On these grounds it would perhaps be appropriate to place him among those writers whom Maxwell Geismar calls "the last of the Provincials."

Historically, Agee unquestionably belonged to the literary generation that was scarred by the Depression, tempted by political involvement and courted by journalism and movie making. He examined the problems of his time, sometimes preaching nonsubmission with Swiftian irony, urging a rebellion that would express itself not through acts of violence but through an obstinate adherence to a personal ideal. His work sprang from the old humanist tradition whose position was growing increasingly precarious. But although he was loyal to the past, he was also an innovator. His hatred of injustice, his religious sense of humanity as a mystical body, his contempt for bourgeois morality, made him sometimes appear as a liberator, even a revolutionary. In a satirical and impassioned explosion, he examined problems that are still those of America and of the world today: the exploitation of man by man, the individual reabsorbed or banished by society, crimes committed against or in the name of democracy and freedom.

Agee also reaffirmed that commitment to actuality was both essential and dangerous to the artist. His own work, halfway between provocation and celebration, his search for a difficult equilibrium between life in society and solitary creation, could in that respect appear exemplary.

It is difficult to predict what place Agee will occupy in the literary history of the United States. Some signs are available, though. When *Let Us Now Praise Famous Men* was republished by Houghton Mifflin, it appeared to the readers of the sixties as one of the most important books of the thirties. *A Death in the Family* won the Pulitzer Prize and was adapted for the theater by Fred Coe and Arthur Cantor in 1960, for television in 1961 and for the screen in 1962 under the title *All the Way Home*. Although these adaptations could not be totally faithful to the original, they did indicate the continuing vitality of Agee's work. In 1962 the appearance of *Letters to Father Flye,* offering as they did a new "portrait of the artist" on the American scene, produced an effect comparable to that produced by F. Scott Fitzgerald's *The Crack-Up* and the letters of Thomas Wolfe. The two volumes *Agee on Film,* which had appeared in 1958 and 1960, made him further known as the film critic and screenwriter he had been.

Both Agee's career—its gropings, failures and achievements —and his life, in its unrelenting quest and its sense of urgency, exemplify the fate of the American artist whose predicament it was to come to terms with himself as well as with a society that offered him constant pitfalls, compromises and denials of his talent.

Agee made the difficult journey through anger and rage to simplicity and love. He knew all the grace and terror of living and celebrated it in its magnificence and in its cruelty, leavening his observations with irony and humor. He saw the deep mysterious connection between ethics and aesthetics and emphatically asserted it in a work in which the most casual remark has the quality of true poetic utterance.

A NOTE ON THE AGEE LEGEND

To a certain extent the Agee legend was formed around an exceptional personality who intrigued and attracted people. At Exeter and Harvard, where his eccentricities were legendary, the myth had already been created. At *Time,* although he existed on the periphery of office life, his admirers were numerous. Young writers and journalists used to accost him in the corridors to ask for advice. Consciously or not, several imitated his style, his methods, as well as his mannerisms—his way of walking, of dressing. It is uncertain to what extent Agee was aware of this cult. He never sought it. He certainly did not try to be ingratiating and even found a wicked delight in displeasing people he did not like. But he never refused a few words, a conversation, or a whole evening to someone he found congenial. He was grateful for his friends' trust in him and would never betray them. He spared them neither time nor effort. He enjoyed both listening and talking and knew how to give all of his attention and understanding to people who confided their personal worries to him. Most often he identified with them completely. There were no problems that he had not experienced at some time or another. Since he had never solved them for himself, he had no hope of solving them for others, but he could still discuss them and, in a way, shed light on them. Agee could become deeply involved in a conversation, not only for the sake of argument, but because of the fact that he was unable to speak dispassionately. He never abandoned a subject before he had exhausted all its possibilities, and every subject was worthy of attention. The topic was almost always specific, rarely general, and the discussion was intense and carried out like a ritual.

For those who did not know him intimately but saw him in the Village or in Hollywood, Agee had become one of the prototypes of the American intellectual artist, exemplified by his indulgence in tobacco, alcohol, women, the movies, and by his habit of staying up late at night. If the generation of the thirties had found its reflection in Fitzgerald, Agee's generation recognized itself in that anti-intellectual poet, musician, journalist, screenwriter. He shared its uncertainties and its enthusiasm, its hatred and its aspirations. For many, Agee embodied a magnificent dream, intensely pursued but never realized: the dream of a world from which all sterility would be banished.

After Agee's death people seized on the myth that he himself had helped to create. His untimely death, which left his work uncompleted, lent him a new prestige; it seemed a paradoxical fate for a man who had sought to live with an intensity that had been his own destruction. Of his life, nobody knew what to think. It had been incoherent, full of projects that had not always been brought to completion. People were equally puzzled by a vocation that had at an early stage affirmed itself as very ambitious but had resulted in only a few works that were scarcely noticed. Agee's life was seen as an exemplary failure, from which all writers should draw a lesson; he had been a captive genius, the victim of a society that paid him well but robbed him of the circumstances favorable to truly creative activity and the will to pursue it. It was a good illustration of the view that, of the many talented men alive during the thirties and forties, only a few succeeded in developing their gifts; most dispersed their energy. Agee, like many of his contemporaries, had first been ensnared by journalism's offer of security and later caught by the lure of a new art form, movie making, in which he passionately believed. He was also hampered by his overly glorious image of the past and his admiration for the great masters whom he sought to equal. On the one hand, he seemed like a man of his generation, the two decades through which he had lived so intensely, and whose aspirations and failures he symbolized; on the other, he was on the periphery of the major currents of his time, taking refuge in the past, his own past and the bygone days of the South, which he contrasted to contemporary America. He thus trod a solitary path. He was unable to reconcile himself with his era despite the impassioned dialogue he tried to established. For those who judged him still more severely, he had been a promising young writer who had failed because of his own deficiencies alone. The legend did not contest Agee's right to be thought of as a writer, but showed him more as a potential talent than as a fully proven one.

During his life Agee had little interest in seeing what he wrote appear in print. His articles and criticism were of course destined for immediate publication in newspapers and magazines, but he published the short stories, narratives and poems primarily on the suggestion of his friends. Whereas his collection of poems had appeared at the time of his greatest literary ambition, the many other poems he subsequently wrote were never gathered into a second volume during his lifetime. It took him four years to arrive at a definitive form for his book on the farmers of Alabama before entrusting it to an editor; it was to the same publishing house that ten years later he presented the manuscript of *The Morning Watch*. Considering that he wrote tirelessly throughout his life, it is quite ironic that at his death his published work consisted only of several scattered short stories, a number of articles and these three major pieces, which had little success and soon went out of print.

One may venture several explanations for this apparent lack of interest in publishing. It is improbable that Agee was so embittered by his experience with *Let Us Now Praise Famous Men* that he mistrusted all editors. Perhaps there was in his reluctance a component of disdain for commercial success, a refusal to treat literature as an institution. But it is more likely that the real reason lay in his artistic scruples, the constant and almost unhealthy humility he showed in regard to everything he wrote. For Agee, a work only deserved publication if it were finished, perfect, in its definitive form, and nothing he wrote seemed to him to have that quality. Every sentence, every partially finished manuscript, was an immediate source of doubts. His original goal of dedicating himself totally to the truth was too ambitious.

The Agee legend interpreted the writer's scruples differently, developing a theory of failure. During his life Agee, who was prone to self-pity as well as to merciless self-criticism, would not have contradicted those who listed his failings. To a certain extent he was responsible for the legend, in that he respected the artist's mission too highly not to mistrust the kind of achievement that would have made him successful.

BIBLIOGRAPHY

For complete bibliographical material consult the *Bulletin of Bibliography*, XXIV (May-August, 1965), 145-149; 163-166.

FICTION

The Collected Short Prose, ed. with a Memoir by R. Fitzgerald, Boston, Houghton Mifflin, 1969.

POETRY

The Collected Poems of James Agee, ed. with an introduction by R. Fitzgerald, New Haven, Yale University Press, 1968.

DRAMA AND FILM

"Catched, a Play in Three Scenes," *Phillips Exeter Monthly,* XXX (Feb., 1926), 87-97.
"In Vindication," *Phillips Exeter Monthly,* XXX (March, 1926), 122-126. (Play)

"Any Seventh Son," *Phillips Exeter Monthly,* XXXI (June, 1927), 107-109. (Play)

"The House," Sketch for a Scenario, in *New Letters in America,* edit. by Horace Gregory, New York, Norton, 1937, 37-55.

"Man's Fate," Sketch for a Scenario, *Films,* I, 1939, 51-60.

"Dedication Day," Rough Sketch for a Moving Picture, *Politics,* III (April, 1946), 121-125.

"Noa Noa—A Fragment," in *Film Book I,* edit. R. Hughes, New York, Grove Press, 1959, 109-121. Incorporated in *Agee on Film* (II), 1960.

Five Film Scripts by James Agee, in *Agee on Film* (Vol. II), New York, McDowell & Obolensky, 1960, 488 pp.

———— *The Blue Hotel,* written in 1948–1949, under contract to Huntington Hartford, 393-488.

———— *The African Queen,* written in 1950, assisted by John Huston and P. Viertel; released by United Artists in 1952, 151-259.

———— *The Bride Comes to Yellow Sky,* written in 1951–1952 for Huntington Hartford; released by RKO under the title *Face to Face* in 1952, 357-390.

———— *Noa Noa,* written in 1953, 3-147.

———— *The Night of the Hunter,* written in 1954; produced by Paul Gregory; released by United Artists in 1955, 263-354.

James Agee also wrote a number of film scripts which have not been published:

The Quiet One, commentary for a documentary film, released in 1948 (Museum of Modern Art Film Library, New York).

White Mane, an adaptation from the French *Crin Blanc,* distributed by Rembrandt Films and Contemporary Films in 1953.

Green Magic, handled by Italian Film Exports, New York, in 1955.

Tanglewood, on Berkshire Festival—in collaboration with Howard Taubman—bought by 20th Century-Fox.

Genghis Khan, a Filipino movie—Director Emmanuel Conde—released by Italian Film Exports in 1952.

Williamsburg (uncompleted), written in 1955. (Colonial Williamsburg, Audiovisual Dept.)

Abraham Lincoln, written for Omnibus Television Series in 1953.

In the Street, shot by James Agee with Helen Levitt and Janice Loeb, 1952.

NONFICTION

I. BOOKS

Let Us Now Praise Famous Men, Boston, Houghton Mifflin, 1941, 471 pp.
Let Us Now Praise Famous Men, Boston, Houghton Mifflin (second printing 1960).

II. ARTICLES

"Extract from the Diary of a Disagreeable Young Man," *Phillips Exeter Monthly,* XXX (Dec., 1925), 62.
"Largest Class in History of School Grades," *Phillips Exeter Monthly,* XXXI (Nov., 1926), 48-52.
"To What Extent Do the Ramifications of International Trade and Commerce Affect the Political Relations Between the United States and the British Empire?" (Brooks-Bryce Prize Essay), *Phillips Exeter Monthly,* XXXI (Mar., 1927), 135-140.
"Class History," *Phillips Exeter Monthly,* XXXII (June, 1922), 207-211.
"Housing," *Fortune,* VI (Sept., 1932), 74.
"Sheep and Shuttleworth," *Fortune,* VII (Jan., 1933), 43-81.
"Strawberries," *Fortune,* VII (Apr., 1933), 64-69.
"$100,000 Worth," *Fortune,* VII (May, 1933), 58-66.
"Cincinnati Terminal," *Fortune,* VII (June, 1933), 72-76, 125.
"Baldness," *Fortune,* VIII (July, 1933), 52-55, 79-82.
"T.V.A.," *Fortune,* VIII (Oct., 1933), 81-97.
"Steel Rails," *Fortune,* VIII (Dec., 1933), 42-47, 153.
"Quinine to You," *Fortune,* IX (Feb., 1934), 76-86.
"Butler's Ball," *Fortune,* IX (Mar., 1934), 68-69.
"Cockfighting," *Fortune,* IX (Mar., 1934), 90-95, 146.
"U.S. Ambassadors," *Fortune,* IX (Apr., 1934), 108-122.
"Arbitrage," *Fortune,* IX (June, 1934), 93-97, 150-160.
"Roman Society," *Fortune,* X (July, 1934), 68-71, 144-150.
"Cabinet Changes" (on Mussolini), *Fortune,* X (July, 1934), 126-127.
"The American Roadside," *Fortune,* X (Sept., 1934), 53-63, 172-177.
"Drought," *Fortune,* X (Oct., 1934), 76-83.
"Illuminated Manuscripts," *Fortune,* X (Dec., 1934), 90-98.
"Glass," *Fortune,* XI (Jan., 1935), 48.
"T.V.A.," *Fortune,* XI (May, 1935), 93-98, 140-153.

"The Normandie," *Fortune,* XI (June, 1935), 84-88.

"Williamsburg Restored," *Fortune,* XII (July, 1935), 69-73.

"Saratoga," *Fortune,* XII (Aug., 1935), 63-69, 96-100.

"Hercules Powder," *Fortune,* XII (Sept., 1935), 57-62, 110-125.

"The Modern Interior," *Fortune,* XII (Nov., 1935), 97-103, 164.

"U.S. Art: 1935," *Fortune,* XII (Dec., 1935), 68-75.

"U.S. Commercial Orchids," *Fortune,* XII (Dec., 1935), 108-114, 126-129.

"Jewel Spread," *Fortune,* XIV (Aug., 1936), 70.

"Art for What's Sake," *New Masses,* XXI:12 (Dec. 15, 1936), 48.

"Posters by Cassandra," *Fortune,* XV (May, 1937), 120.

"Smoke," *Fortune,* XV (June, 1937), 100-102, 130.

"Havana Cruise," *Fortune,* XVI (Sept., 1937), 117-120, 210-220.

"Three Tenant Families: a Selection," *Common Sense,* VIII (Oct., 1939), 9-12, partly incorporated in *Let Us Now Praise Famous Men,* 1941.

"Colon," *New Directions,* ed. James Laughlin, Norfolk, Conn. (1940), 181-192, incorporated in *Let Us Now Praise Famous Men,* 1941.

"Pseudo-Folk," *Partisan Review,* XI:2 (Spring, 1944), 219-223.

"U.S. at War" (on F. Roosevelt's death), *Time,* XLV (Apr. 23, 1945), 1.

"Victory: The Peace," *Time,* XLVI (Aug. 20, 1945), 19-21.

"New York, a Little Rain" (National Affairs), *Time,* XLVI (Oct. 1, 1945), 22-23.

"Europe: Autumn Story" (Foreign News), *Time,* XLVI (Oct. 15, 1945), 24-25.

"Godless Götterdämmerung" (Religion), *Time,* XLVI (Oct. 15, 1945), 62-64.

"The Nation" (National Affairs), *Time,* XLVI (Nov. 5, 1945), 22-24.

"Average Man" (The Press), *Time,* XLVI (Nov. 26, 1945), 58-60, 64.

"Voice of Reason" (Foreign News), *Time,* XLVIII (Aug. 26, 1946), 28.

"Syria: Triumph of Civilization," *Time,* XLVIII (Sept. 9, 1946), 34.

"Russia: Last Mile" (Foreign News), *Time,* XLVIII (Sept. 9, 1946), 34.

"Food—Harvest Home" (International), *Time,* XLVIII (Sept. 23, 1946), 30.

"Great Britain" (Foreign News), *Time,* XLVIII (Sept. 23, 1946), 32-33.

"Great Britain: Beyond Silence" (Foreign News), *Time,* XLVIII (Oct. 7, 1946), 31.

"A Star in the Darkness" (Education), *Time,* XLIX (Apr. 7, 1947), 55-56.

"David Wark Griffith," *Nation,* CLXVII (Sept. 4, 1948), 264-266.

"Comedy's Greatest Era," *Life,* XXVII (Sept. 3, 1949), 70-88.

"Religion and the Intellectuals," *Partisan Review,* XVII (Feb., 1950), 106-113.

"Undirectable Director" (on John Huston), *Life,* XXIX (Sept. 8, 1950), 128-145.

"Notes on Portfolio of Photographs 'Rapid Transit,' by Walker Evans," *The Cambridge Review,* No. 5 (1956), 25.

"Self-Portrait," *Esquire,* LX (Dec., 1963), 149.

"A Way of Seeing," an essay on photography in *A Way of Seeing,* presenting the photographs of Helen Levitt. New York, Viking Press, 1965.

III. REVIEWS

For complete listing of theater, book and movie reviews, consult *Bulletin of Bibliography, op. cit.*

"The Moving Picture," *Phillips Exeter Monthly,* XXX (Mar., 1936), 115-117.

MOVIE REVIEWS: MISCELLANEOUS

"The Marx Brothers," *Films in Review,* I (July-August, 1950), 25-29.

"Sunset Boulevard," *Sight and Sound,* XIX (Nov., 1950), 283-285.

Part of the movie reviews written for *Time,* and a major part of the movie reviews written in *The Nation,* have been published in *Agee on Film* (Vol. I), New York, McDowell & Obolensky, 1958, 432 pp.

IV. LETTERS

James Agee and Dwight Macdonald: Exchange of Letters. Agee's reply, *Nation,* CLVI (1943), 873-874. (About Agee's review of the film *Mission to Moscow*)

Letters of James Agee to Father Flye, New York, G. Braziller, 1962, 253 pp.

Letters of James Agee to Father Flye, with a new preface and previously unpublished letters, second ed., Houghton Mifflin, 1971, 267 pp.

ANTHOLOGIES

(NOTE: This list of Agee's works that have been anthologized is in chronological order.)

New Anthology of Modern Poetry, ed. S. Rodman, New York, Random House, 1938 and 1946, 272-275 (poems).

Modern American Poetry—Modern British Poetry, ed. L. Untermeyer, Harcourt Brace, N.Y., 1942, 278-282 (poems).

Partisan Reader, 1946, Scranton, Pa., 28-31, "Knoxville, Summer of 1915."

Spearhead (New Directions), Norfolk, 1947, 509-520 (excerpts from *Famous Men*).

One Hundred American Poets, ed. S. Rodman, 177 (poem drawn from Prologue of *Famous Men*).

Transition Workshop, ed. Eugene Jolas, N.Y., Vanguard Press, 1949, 200, "Lyric."

One Hundred Modern Poems, ed. S. Rodman, N.Y., New American Library, Mentor Books, 156-159, "Six Selections from *Famous Men*"; 120, "Lullaby" (poem).

Harvard Advocate Anthology, 1950, 228 (3 poems).

Best American Short Stories, ed. Martha Foley and Joyce F. Hartmann, Houghton Mifflin, 1953, 1-18, "A Mother's Tale."

Thirteen Great Stories, ed. Talbot, N.Y., Dell, 1955, 195-256.

Criterion Book of Modern American Verse, ed. W. H. Auden, N.Y., Criterion Books, 1956, 256-257, "Description of an Elysium" (poem).

Best American Short Stories, ed. Foley and Burnett, Boston, Houghton Mifflin, 1958, 1-20, "The Waiting."

The Art of the Essay, ed. L. Fiedler, N.Y., Thomas Y. Crowell, 1958, 372-384, "Comedy's Greatest Era."

Film Books, ed. R. Hughes, N.Y., Grove Press, Evergreen, 109-121, excerpts from *Noa Noa*.

CRITICAL BIBLIOGRAPHY

WORKS ABOUT AGEE

Barson, A. T., *A Way of Seeing,* U. of Massachusetts Press, 1972.

Coles, R., *Irony in the Mind's Life,* University Press of Virginia, 1976.

Ohlin, Peter, *Agee,* Obolensky, N.Y., 1966.

Seib, Kenneth, *James Agee: Promise and Fulfillment,* U. of Pittsburgh Press, 1968.

WORKS CONTAINING SECTIONS ON AGEE

Beach, J. W., *Obsessive Images,* ed. William Van O'Connor, U. of Minnesota Press, 1960 (see the Introduction).

Breit, Harvey, *The Writer Observed,* N.Y., World Book Company, 1956; 18.

Chambers, Whittaker, *Witness,* N.Y., Random House, 1952; 87, 478-479, 493-494, 504, 615 (biographical).

Chaplin, Charles, *Histoire de ma vie,* French ed., Poche, Laffont, 1964; 630, 638, 646-647 (biographical).

Deutsch, Babette, *Poetry in Our Time,* Anchor Books, Doubleday, 1963, second edition; 366.

Drew, Elizabeth, *Poetry: A Modern Guide,* Dell Publishing, 1959; 211-213.

Frohock, W. M., *The Novel of Violence in America,* second edition, Southern Methodist U. Press, Dallas, 1964, "James Agee, the Question of Wasted Talent"; 212-230.

Hoffman, F. J., *The Act of Southern Fiction,* Southern Illinois U. Press, 1964, "James Agee and Flannery O'Connor: The Religious Consciousness"; 74-85.

Kazin, Alfred, *Contemporaries,* Atlantic Monthly Press Book, Boston, Toronto, Little, Brown, 1957, "Good-Bye to James Agee"; 185-187.

Macdonald, D., *Against the American Grain,* N.Y., Random House, 1952, 142-166.

Macdonald, D., *Memoirs of a Revolutionist,* Meridian Books, 1959, "A Way of Death"; 262-266.

Tasker, Witham, *The Adolescent in the American Novel,* N.Y., F. Ungar, 1964; 17, 118-119, 179, 265-266.

BIOGRAPHY

Articles

(Listed alphabetically by name of periodical.)

Atlantic Monthly, CCXV (July, 1960), 74-75, "J. Agee in 1936."

Harvard Advocate, CV, IV (Feb., 1972), "A Snapshot Album, 1928–1932," R. Saudek, 18-22; "An Article of Faith," Father Flye, 15 ff.; "Agee at *Time,*" T. S. Matthews, 25.

Holy Cross Magazine, LVI (Oct. 10, 1945), 297, "Reminiscences and Reflection," Father Flye.

Hudson Review, XVII, No. I (Spring, 1964), 44, "Tudoresque," poem by Lincoln Kirstein.

Life, L (Jan. 27, 1961), 96, "Rare Legacy of a Poet."

The New York Times, May 18, 1955, "James Agee, 45, Poet and Critic"; Jan. 26, 1958, "On Local Movie Fronts," A. H. Weiler.

Partisan Review, XII (Winter, 1945), 111-119, "Mr. Agee and *The New Yorker,*" James Grossman.
Publishers' Weekly, Jan. 5, 1959, 66, "Rights and Permissions," Paul Nathan; Jan. 12, 1959, 54 (On Tanglewood).
Reporter, VIII (Apr. 14, 1953), 31-33, "A. Lincoln, Television Series," Meyer Levin.
Time, LXV (May 30, 1955), 70, obituary.
Wilson Library Bulletin, XXX (Sept., 1955), 70, obituary.

Books

Remembering James Agee, Madden, D., ed., Louisiana State U. Press, 1974.

GENERAL ARTICLES OR STUDIES

(Listed alphabetically by author's name.)
Behar, Jack, "James Agee: The World of His Work," D.A. XXIV 4690 (Ohio State U.), unpublished doctoral dissertation, 1963.
Bingham, R., "Short of Distant Goal," *Reporter,* XXVII (Oct. 25, 1962), 54.
Breit, Harvey, "In and out of Books: Tribute," *The New York Times* (Apr. 22, 1956), 8.
Burger, Nash K., "A Story To Tell: Agee, Wolfe, Faulkner," *South Atlantic Quarterly,* LXII (Autumn, 1964), 32-43.
Chase, Richard, "Sense and Sensibility," *Kenyon Review* (Autumn, 1951), 688-691.
Coles, Robert, "Agee's Famous Men Seen Again," *Harvard Advocate,* CV, IV (Feb., 1972), 42-46.
Da Fonte, Durant, "James Agee, the Quest for Identity," *Tennessee Studies in Literature,* VII, 25-37.
Davis, Louise, "The Agee Story," *Nashville Tennessean Magazine* (Feb. 8, 1959), 10-11, 20; (Feb. 15, 1959), 14-15.
Dempsey, D., "Praise of Him Was Posthumous," *Saturday Review,* XLV (Aug. 11, 1962), 24-25.
Dunlea, W., "Agee and the Writer's Vocation," *Commonweal,* LXXVI (Sept. 7, 1962), 499-500.
Dupee, Frederick, "The Prodigious James Agee," *New Leader,* XL (Dec. 9, 1957), 20-21.
Fitzgerald, Robert, "A Memoir," *Kenyon Review* (Nov., 1968), reprinted in *The Collected Short Prose,* Boston, Houghton Mifflin, 1969.

Fletcher, Angus, "Dedication to James Agee," *Cambridge Review,* No. 5 (Mar. 20, 1956), 8-11.

Flint, R. W., "Reply to John Updike, Article on James Agee," *New Republic,* CXLVII (Aug. 20, 1962), 30-31.

Frohock, W. M., "The Question of Unkept Promise," *Southwest Review,* XLII (Summer, 1957), 221-229.

Kaufmann, Wallace, "Our Unacknowledged Poetry: An Essay on James Agee," *Agenda,* IV, No. 3-4 (Summer, 1966).

Kramer, Victor A., "James Agee Papers at the University of Texas," LCUT, VII, No. 2, 33-36.

Lakin, R. D., "The Displaced Writer in America," *Midwest Quarterly* (Pittsburg, Kansas), IV, 295-305.

Levin, Meyer, "Abraham Lincoln Through the Picture Tube," *Reporter,* VIII (Apr. 14, 1953), 31-33.

Macdonald, Dwight, "Death of a Poet," *The New Yorker,* XXXII (Nov. 16, 1957), 224-241.

——— "James Agee: Some Memories and Letters," *Encounter,* XIX, No. 6 (Dec., 1962), 73-84.

——— "On Chaplin, Verdoux and Agee," *Esquire,* LXIII (Apr., 1965), 18.

Oulahan, R., "James Agee," *Life,* LV (Nov. 1, 1963), 57-67.

Phelps, R., "James Agee," in *Letters to Father Flye,* N.Y., Braziller, 1962, 1-9.

Presler, T., "The Poetry of James Agee," *Harvard Advocate,* CV, IV (Feb., 1972), 35-37.

Robertson, Priscilla, "Agee's Special View," *Progressive,* XXV (Jan., 1961), 44-45.

Ruhe, Edward, "James Agee," *Epoch,* VII, 3 (Fall, 1957), 247.

Simon, John, "Let Us Now Praise James Agee," *Midcentury,* XV, No. 6 (Nov., 1959), 17-22.

———, "The Preacher Turned Practitioner," *Midcentury,* XVIII, No. 27 (Summer, 1961), 18-21.

Thomson, Lionel, "Reply to D. Macdonald," *The New Yorker,* XXXII (Feb. 15, 1958), 120.

Updike, John, "No Use Talking," *New Republic,* CXLVII (Aug. 13, 1962), 23-24.

LIST OF
ABBREVIATIONS

*The following abbreviations have been used in the notes or in
the text. Page references are to the editions indicated below.*
HC =Hard cover   P = Paperback edition

P.V.	*Permit Me Voyage*	Yale University Press, 1934	P
F.F.	*Letters to Father Flye*	G. Braziller, 1962	HC
F.M.	*Let Us Now Praise Famous Men*	Houghton Mifflin, 1961	HC
M.W.	*The Morning Watch*	*Botteghe Oscure,* VI, 1950	
D.F.	*A Death in the Family*	McDowell & Obolensky, 1957	P
Film I	*Agee on Film* (Vol. I)	McDowell & Obolensky, 1958	HC
Film II	*Agee on Film* (Vol. II)	McDowell & Obolensky, 1960	HC
C.S.P.	*Collected Short Prose*	Ballantine Books, N.Y., 1969	P
C.P.	*Collected Poems*	Yale University Press, 1968	P

E.M.	*Phillips Exeter Monthly Magazine*
H.A.	*Harvard Advocate*

For complete references consult the bibliography.

NOTES

PART I

PROLOGUE

The information contained in this chapter was told to me in 1964 by Mrs. Wright, Agee's mother, and by Father Flye.
(1) This text was lent to me by David McDowell. It has since been published in *C.S.P.*, 143.
(2) *Ibid.*
(3) *Ibid.*

CHAPTER ONE

(1) "Tennessee Valley Authority," *Fortune,* VII (Oct., 1933), 81.
(2) *Ibid.*
(3) *Ibid.*
(4) The railroad, which was perhaps the most familiar and prominent feature of the countryside, became a correspondingly recurrent motif in Agee's writing, carrying several levels of symbolic meanings. It is near the railroad tracks that certain characters become aware of themselves, of their life, of their cowardice (in "Near the

Tracks," *Harvard Advocate,* CXVI, June, 1930, 9-20), of the uselessness of their despair (in the scenario "The Quiet One"). It is also on the train that the principal scene of *The Bride Comes to Yellow Sky* takes place, and it is a slow train that returns Lincoln's body to his native region in "Lincoln—A Television Script" and that carries the cattle in "A Mother's Tale" toward an unknown destination.

(5) Agee later signed his uncle's name to certain of his poems.

(6) This became one of the major themes of his work, which is expressed, sometimes with a certain amount of preciosity, in his love poems, notably "No Doubt Left, Enough Deceiving," in "Lyrics," *P.V. (C.P.,* 4).

(7) This anecdote was related by Mrs. Wright.

CHAPTER THREE

(1) Although this second death did not affect Agee as deeply as the death of his own father, it did cut him off even more thoroughly from his father's family, thus completing a break with a certain part of his past.

(2) The information on Saint Andrew's comes primarily from Agee's mother, Mrs. Wright, Father Flye and certain of Agee's friends. But I am especially indebted to John Stroop, who preceded Agee at Saint Andrew's and was kind enough to grant me a long interview. In addition, various teachers at the school, notably Harold Kennedy, who in 1952 wrote an important essay on the school's history, provided me with documents.

(3) A fable written late in Agee's life and published in *Harper's Bazaar* in 1952 (see *C.S.P.,* 249-275).

(4) *The Morning Watch,* Boston, Houghton Mifflin, 1951, 120 pp. References to this work will be to its first appearance in print, in *Botteghe Oscure,* VI (1950), 339-409.

CHAPTER FOUR

(1) *E.M.,* XXXI (April, 1927), 161-166.

(2) "The Scar," *E.M.,* XXX (Jan., 1926), 78.

(3) "The Bell Tower of Amiens," *E.M.,* XXX (Dec., 1925), 48-51.

(4) "Beauvais," *E.M.,* XXX (May, 1926), 177.

PART II

CHAPTER ONE

(1) Certain information dealing with Agee's years at Exeter is from documents in the "Agee Collection," which was established in the library of Phillips Exeter Academy and which was put at my disposal by Mr. Armstrong, the curator, when I visited the Academy in 1964. I also relied upon the recollections of Agee's teachers and schoolmates, and upon interviews or correspondence with such people as Freeman Lewis, Dr. and Mrs. Bryer, Helena Harap-Dodd, and others who took an interest in this study. Frequently Agee himself is the source of information to be found in his editorials or in his letters to Father Flye. I am especially thankful to Dwight Macdonald for the unpublished letters he allowed me to read.

(2) *Idem.*

(3) *E.M.,* XXX (Dec., 1925), 62. "Oh for the wide golden vodkas on which I grew to manhood . . ."

(4) ". . . permit your life to grow as it will," in "Largest Class in History," *E.M.,* XXXI (Nov., 1926), 49.

(5) Agee's scholastic record at Exeter:

Grades:	1925-26	1926-27	1927-28
Latin	2D	3C	4C
Math	1D	3D	4D
English	3A	4A	
French	1C	2D	3C
History	1C	2C	1D
Public speaking	1C	2C Music	2D
Residence:	Perham House	Abbot House	Hoyt House
Advisor:	Mr. Sweet	Mr. Hatch	Mr. Major

(6) The topic to be discussed was "To what extent do the ramifications of international trade affect the relations of the U.S. and the British Empire?"

(7) "Clumsy, no-howish, a tatterdemalion . . ." Darcy Curwen, one of his teachers, wrote of him ("Agee Collection"). The composition began with the sentence, "In the mountains, superstitions follow a man from the cradle to the grave and even beyond that."

(8) "Dedication," from *Permit Me Voyage* (*C.P.,* 9).

(9) *E.M.,* XXXI, 189-190.

(10) *E.M.,* XXX, 115-117.

(11) Letter to Dwight Macdonald, June 16, 1927.

(12) "Have you tried to write a play or story and got into a hell of a muddle about what the next line or even word was to be?" Letter to Dwight Macdonald, July 21, 1927.

(13) *E.M.,* XXX (Feb., 1926), 87-97.

(14) *E.M.,* XXX (March, 1926), 122-126.

(15) *E.M.,* XXXI (June, 1927), 107-109.

(16) *E.M.,* XXXII (May, 1928), 177-186; also in *C.P.,* 16-27.

(17) *E.M.,* XXX (Nov., 1925), 27.

(18) *E.M.,* XXXII (Jan., 1928), 86.

(19) *E.M.,* XXXII (March, 1928), 133-137. A young woman returns to her parents' home after the death of her husband. One can see Agee's constant search for variants on an initial situation: a bereavement or a departure.

(20) *E.M.,* XXXII (Nov., 1927), 25-40.

(21) "Jenkinsville," *E.M.,* XXXI (Dec., 1926), 71-72; "Minerva Farmer," *E.M.,* XXX (Nov., 1925), 30-42; "The Circle," *E.M.,* XXX (April, 1926), 143-151.

(22) "Between Trains," *E.M.,* XXXI (May, 1927), 171-173.

CHAPTER TWO

(1) A recommendation sent by one of his teachers, F. W. Cusha, to Harvard's Office of Admissions reads: "My first statement about Agee is that he was made for Harvard, and Harvard for him. He should thrive and grow there. He seems to all of us here a person of rare literary ability. His reading is very wide . . . He is an individual subject to moods, etc., but he is outgrowing any morbid tendencies."

In order to document this chapter, I consulted the archives of the Widener Library at Harvard for material dealing primarily with Agee's studies and university life, and his graduating class (1932). I also used material and recollections provided me by his friends, Robert Fitzgerald, Lincoln Kirstein and Robert Saudek, and letters that were entrusted to me by his first wife, Olivia Saunders, and his friend and teacher, Howard Doughty.

(2) An adaptation of Ode XXV, "To Lydia," appeared that year, 1929, in the *Harvard Advocate.*

(3) Editorial in the *Harvard Advocate* for Oct., 1931.

(4) "The Storm," *H.A.,* CXVI (Dec., 1929), 15.

(5) "A Walk Before Mass," (Christmas, 1929), 18-20.

(6) *H.A.,* CXVI (April, 1930), 27.

(7) Several years later Agee's revolt against this milieu, whose influence had long held him subject, was as violent and far-reaching as had been his infatuation with it.

(8) From Iowa, Agee sent two letters to Richard Wierhem, a friend from Tennessee, in which he described his work in the fields in terms that anticipate the descriptive passages of *Let Us Now Praise Famous Men.*

(9) *H.A.,* CXVII (Oct., 1930), 16-24.

(10) *H.A.,* CXVII (May, 1931), 9-23.

(11) "Let mirth be this and that," *H.A.,* CXVIII (Dec., 1931), 3.

(12) *H.A.,* CXVII (Christmas, 1930), 22. This sonnet appears in *Permit Me Voyage* (Sonnet IV), but the last two lines are changed to: "Whose backward length is broken in the dust/Frail through the dust and small as the dew's mesh."

(13) *H.A.,* CXVII (March, 1931), 18—*C.P.,* 134.

(14) *H.A.,* CXVII (May, 1931), 77—*C.P.,* 132.

(15) "Now my sick little trips at writing for beauty and if necessary conceding thoroughness of idea and strength to that such make me ready to roll over and writhe with shame." Undated, unpublished letter to Via Saunders.

(16) Among the members of the *Advocate,* Agee made some lasting friends: Arthur H. Sulzberger; James Laughlin, who later became editor of *New Directions;* John Slecum; and of course Robert Fitzgerald.

(17) See *Class Album,* 1932, 166-167.

(18) The whole group were specially published in the *Advocate* as "Agee's Winning Garrison Prize Poems," *H.A.,* CXIX (April, 1933), 5-9.

(19) "Class Ode," appeared in *Class Album,* 1932, 204.

(20) "Opening of a Long Poem (Maybe)," *H.A.,* CXVIII (June, 1932), 12-20.

(21) *Ibid.*

PART III

CHAPTER ONE

(1) On the evolution of *Fortune,* see Dwight Macdonald's article in *The Nation,* May 8, 1937, 527 ff.

The information on which this chapter and the following are based comes principally from Archibald MacLeish, Dwight Macdonald and Via Saunders; I also used Agee's still unpublished correspondence with Via Saunders and Howard Doughty.

(2) Letter to Via Saunders, Aug. 1, 1932.

(3) *Ibid.*

(4) The sonnets were later published in *Permit Me Voyage.* (See also *C.P.,* 37-49.)

(5) Agee returns to this experience in a passage in *Let Us Now Praise Famous Men, op. cit.,* 15.

(6) Letter to Via Saunders, Oct. 6, 1932.

(7) He saw *The Public Enemy, Karamazov, All Quiet on the Western Front* and *Monkey Business* again. Unpublished letter to Howard Doughty, late August, 1932.

(8) "Don Juan," Stanza 40, *H.A.,* CXVIII (June, 1932)—*C.P.,* 91. "We look at Russia and think we see light there. In spite of her pretensions to atheism, Russia has a faith. America could do worse than take a good, wholehearted fling at Communism," Agee wrote in "World War and We," *H.A.,* CXVIII (Feb., 1932).

CHAPTER TWO

(1) "The job is swell and by the way not nearly as Kapitalistic as I or you expected." Letter to H. Doughty, July, 1932.

(2) "A Project for a Poem in Byronics, 'John Carter'," Oct., 1932 (in *C.P.,* 79-81).

(3) "Baldness," *Fortune,* VIII (July, 1933), 52-55, 79-82.

(4) "Sheep and Shuttleworth," *Fortune,* VII (Jan., 1933), 43-81.

(5) *Fortune,* VII (June, 1933), 72-76.

(6) "T.V.A.," *Fortune,* VIII (Oct., 1933), 81-97.

(7) "Butler's Ball," *Fortune,* IX (March, 1934), 68-69.

(8) *Fortune,* IX (March, 1934), 90-146.

(9) "Arbitrage," *Fortune,* IX (June, 1934), 93-97, 150-160.

(10) *Fortune,* X (Sept., 1934), 53-63, 172-177.

(11) "Drought," *Fortune,* X (Oct., 1934), 76-83.

(12) Wilder Hobson told me of this incident.

CHAPTER THREE

(1) This is an unpublished letter inserted in a copy of *Permit Me Voyage* in the Houghton Library, Harvard University.

(2) In *Selected Letters of S. V. Benet,* ed. Charles B. Fenton, New Haven, 1960; 245.

(3) Foreword to *Permit Me Voyage,* Yale Series of Younger Poets, New Haven, Yale University Press, 1934; 6.

(4) References to this work will be to its reappearance in the *Collected Poems,* ed. by Robert Fitzgerald, Yale University Press, New Haven, 1969. The manuscripts have been preserved in the Yale Library and a comparison between early and final versions is possible.

(5) Reviews appeared in *The Spectator* and *The Times Literary Supplement* (London). In New York, Lincoln Kirstein in *The New Republic,* Horace Gregory in *Poetry,* Florence Goodman in *The Nation* discussed the faults and merits of Agee's poetry at length.

(6) See William Van O'Connor's Introduction to J. W. Beach's study, *Obsessive Images,* Minneapolis, University of Minnesota Press, 1960.

CHAPTER FOUR

(1) This and the succeeding poems are now included in Robert Fitzgerald's anthology, *The Collected Poems of James Agee,* Houghton Mifflin, 1968. I wish to express my thanks to Ms. Gladys Lea for allowing me to read (in 1964) some then unpublished poems by Agee.

(2) "Williamsburg Restored," *Fortune,* XII (July, 1935), 69-73.

(3) *Fortune,* XII (Dec., 1935), 68-75.

(4) "The Modern Interior," *Fortune,* XII (Nov., 1935), 97-103, 164.

(5) *Fortune,* XII (Nov., 1935), 97-103, 164.

(6) "T.V.A.," *Fortune,* XI (May, 1935), 93-153.

(7) "Saratoga," *Fortune,* XII (Aug., 1935), 100.

CHAPTER FIVE

(1) Agee described all the various stages of his research in different parts of his book. See especially the Introduction. References are to the second edition of *Let Us Now Praise Famous Men,* Boston, Houghton Mifflin, 1960, 471 pp. In this chapter I also make use of information I received from Walker Evans, who was kind enough to grant me several interviews.

(2) *F.M.,* 255 ff., in particular such images as "ditch full of hunched and convulsed muscles of clay."

(3) "James Agee in 1936," published in *F.M., op. cit.;* IX-XVI.

(4) *F.M., op. cit.,* XI.

(5) There were still other friends, Wilder Hobson, Joe Kastner and his wife, Daniel and Rosamond Sayre, who were talented musicians.

CHAPTER SIX

(1) *transition,* No. 24 (June, 1936), 7.

(2) The poetic experiment conducted by *transition* is described by Stuart Gilbert in the introduction to *Transition Workshop,* New York, Vanguard Press, 1949.

(3) "Temperance Note: and Weather Prophecy," "Red Sea," "In Heavy Mind," in *Modern American Poetry,* ed. Louis Untermeyer, New York, Harcourt Brace, 1936, 637-641. The page references are to the 1950 edition, since the 1936 edition was not available.

(4) *Forum,* XVII (Feb., 1937), 115-116.

(5) "Smoke," *Fortune,* XV (June, 1937), 100-102, 130.

(6) "In Memory of My Father, Campbell County, Tennessee," *transition,* No. 26 (Spring, 1937), 7.

(7) *New Masses,* XXIV (Sept. 14, 1937), 22. This poem is analyzed by Elizabeth Drew in *Poetry: A Modern Guide* (general editor, Richard Wilbur), 211-213.

(8) *Partisan Review,* IV (Dec., 1937), 40-43 (11 sections).

(9) The three poems were published respectively in *Common Sense,* VII (Jan., 1938), 27; *Harper's Magazine,* CLXXVI, 209; *Partisan Review,* IV (Feb., 1938), 8.

(10) *New Masses,* XXI (Dec. 15, 1936), 48. Initially the article is a review of Gertrude Stein's "Geographical History of America," recently published in *transition.*
(11) *New Letters in America,* Vol. I, No. I, New York, Norton, 1937, 37-55; also in *C.S.P.,* 169-198.

PART IV

CHAPTER ONE

(1) Information on the cruise was given to me by Walker Evans and Via Saunders.
(2) *Fortune,* XVI (Sept., 1937), 117-120, 210-220.
(3) This unpublished text was lent to me by Helen Levitt. The story is in dramatic form. Agee had hoped to make it into a script for a movie. He submitted it to his friend Helen Levitt, who was a professional photographer and was also involved in movie making.

CHAPTER TWO

(1) Undated, unpublished letter to Wilder Hobson, circa 1938.
(2) "I like titles when they are in place but very much dislike the obligation for any other reason to call a poem anything other than a 'Poem'." Undated letter to Dwight Macdonald.
(3) "Sharecroppers' Novels," *New Masses,* XXII (June 8, 1937), 23.

CHAPTER THREE

(1) The text, titled "Southeast of the Island: Travel Notes," is now available in *C.S.P.,* 197-228.
(2) Here I make use of Agee's unpublished correspondence with Selden Rodman, which the latter obligingly lent me.
(3) *Films,* I (1939), 51-60.

PART V

CHAPTER ONE

(1) According to T. S. Matthews in an article he wrote in *The Saturday Review,* April 16, 1966. Most of the information concerning Agee's work at *Time* was given to me by T. S. Matthews, who granted me several interviews.

(2) *Witness,* New York, Random House, 1952, 478-479, 493-494.

CHAPTER TWO

(1) Dwight Macdonald admits that he did not understand Agee's obstinacy until the publication, in 1965, of the Warren Report, which appeared in one of those government editions Agee had dreamed of fifteen years earlier for his own work. Agee had reasons for demanding this presentation and format, Macdonald says, which were more than simple caprice. (See *Esquire,* March, 1965, p. 59.)

(2) "Colon," *New Directions,* Norfolk, Conn., 1949, 181-192. Included in *F.M.,* 97-111.

(3) There is in *Famous Men* a very complete bestiary described in a most picturesque fashion with a humor not unlike Mark Twain's.

(4) Harvey Breit (*New Republic,* CV; Sept. 15, 1941; 115), Selden Rodman (*Saturday Review,* XXIV; Aug. 23, 1941; 6), and Lionel Trilling (*Kenyon Review,* IV; 1942; 99-102).

(5) Lionel Trilling briefly recalls the reception the book received and its success in the bookstores (in *Midcentury,* No. 16; Sept., 1960; 9). Its commercial failure was later the subject of a dispute: Houghton Mifflin was accused of having done little to encourage sales. In 1957 Dwight Macdonald even specifically blamed the editors (*The New Yorker;* Nov. 16, 1957; 224). L. Thompson, president of Houghton Mifflin, then announced that the publisher had waited until 1943 before stocking the book and had concerned itself with its sale until 1948. The title appeared on their list until 1953, that is, two years after the publication of *The Morning Watch.* (See *The New Yorker;* Feb. 15, 1958; 33).

(6) See Agee's article in *Time,* "Comment on '41," December 15, 1941.

CHAPTER THREE

(1) This piece, written by Agee in 1942, was later published in *Esquire* (Dec., 1963; 145).

CHAPTER FOUR

(1) *The Nation,* May 22, 1943. Most of Agee's articles for *Time*

or *The Nation* have now been collected in *Agee on Film,* Vol. I, New York, McDowell & Obolensky, 1958, 432 pp. See pp. 37-38.

(2) "So Proudly We Fail," *Film* I, 55.

(3) In the course of an interview I had with him.

CHAPTER FIVE

(1) "Pseudo-Folk," *Partisan Review,* XI (Spring, 1944), 219-223.

(2) "Mr. Agee and *The New Yorker,*" *Partisan Review,* XII (Winter, 1945), 112-119.

(3) *Time,* XLVI (Oct. 15, 1945), 24-25.

(4) *Politics,* III (April, 1946), 121-125. Now in *C.S.P., op. cit.,* 117-134.

(5) *Time,* May 5, 1947, in *Film* I, 370-372. *The Nation,* May 31, June 14 and 21, 1947.

CHAPTER SIX

(1) *Film* I, 296-297. See also an essay on the photographic art that Agee wrote at this time, which was published as a preface to Helen Levitt's collection, *A Way of Seeing,* Viking Press, New York, 1965.

(2) *Film* I, 191.

(3) *Film* I, 297.

(4) These genres are discussed in various reviews Agee wrote on specific films, *Film* I, 26, 45, 65, 161-162.

(5) *Film* I, 23.

(6) "Comedy's Greatest Era," published in *Life,* XXVII (Sept. 3, 1949), 70-88, and *Film* I, 2-19.

(7) A debate participated in, more or less directly, by Dwight Macdonald, E. Van den Haag, Manny Farber and Gilbert Seldes. See Manny Farber's article in the *New Leader,* XVI (Dec. 8, 1958), 104-113.

(8) *Film* I, 237 and 298.

CHAPTER SEVEN

(1) "Now As Awareness," *C.S.P.,* 142.

(2) "Religion and the Intellectuals," *Partisan Review,* XVII (Feb., 1950), 104-113.

PART VI

CHAPTER ONE

(1) "That fool of an unfortunate gambler came merely as a culmination, the apex of a human movement, and gets all the punishment," "The Blue Hotel," Stephen Crane, *An Omnibus,* New York, Knopf, 1961; 530.

(2) *Film* II, 487.

(3) "Undirectable Director," *Film* I, 320-331.

CHAPTER TWO

(1) References are to the *Botteghe Oscure* edition (VI, 1950, 339-409); the Houghton Mifflin edition (Boston, 1951) is no longer in print.

(2) To be compared, according to Father Flye, with the "mandatum," a new commandment associated with Holy Week and given to the Apostles. The name remains, although the observance is no longer practiced.

CHAPTER THREE

(1) *Film* I, 411-415.

(2) Frank Taylor was one of Agee's closest friends at this time.

(3) *Film* II, 356-390.

CHAPTER FOUR

(1) "Lincoln" has not yet been published. A copy of the script was lent to me by Omnibus Television Series. Most of the information compiled in this chapter was given to me by Richard de Rochemont, Helen Levitt and Howard Taubman.

(2) *Film* II; 3-147.

(3) Agee knew Tanglewood well. Over the years he had had many conversations about music there with Rozario Mazzeo, the director of Boston Symphony Hall.

(4) Mrs. Agee lent me Agee's manuscripts. The lyrics are now published in the *Collected Poems, op. cit.,* 164-179. None of the songs Agee wrote were kept in the final production as it was staged in December, 1956. Agee's project is discussed in his *Letters to Father Flye, F.F.,* 216

(5) The manuscript and notes for "Williamsburg" were put at my disposal by the Audio-Visual Center of Williamsburg. "Williamsburg" remained unfinished at the time of Agee's death; the script was sent by the Center to a number of writers and producers in the hope that they would complete it. But Agee had given his story too personal a direction for another writer to continue the work without betraying its spirit.

CHAPTER SIX

(1) *Thirteen Great Stories,* M. Talbot, ed., New York, Dell, 1955, 195-256; and *Criterion Book of American Verse,* W. H. Auden, ed., New Criterion Books, 1956, 256-257.

(2) From *Cambridge Review,* IX, 1956, 25, 41-61; *The New Yorker,* XXXIII (Oct. 5, 1957, 41-50; Nov. 2, 1957, 36-41).

(3) *Best American Short Stories,* Foley and Burnett, eds., Boston, Houghton Mifflin (1958), 1-20.

(4) This text is now published in *Collected Short Prose, op. cit.,* 142-144.

(5) The expression "All the way home" later served as title to the play adapted from the book.

(6) The scene testifies to Agee's gothic imagination and to his lasting curiosity about occultism and ancient superstition which (as he wrote in a paper when he was at Exeter) "in the mountain folk follow a war from the cradle to the grave."

(7) The quest for identity, an initiation reminiscent of young Nick Adams' in Hemingway's stories, relates the book to other contemporaneous works such as *Mountain Lion,* by Jean Stafford; *Other Voices, Other Rooms,* by Truman Capote; and *Member of the Wedding,* by Carson McCullers.

INDEX

INDEX